CONNECTED
Classrooms

A People-Centered Approach
for Online, Blended, and
In-Person Learning

KATHRYN FISHMAN-WEAVER **STEPHANIE WALTER**

Solution Tree | Press

Copyright © 2022 by Solution Tree Press

Materials appearing here are copyrighted. With one exception, all rights are reserved. Readers may reproduce only those pages marked "Reproducible." Otherwise, no part of this book may be reproduced or transmitted in any form or by any means (electronic, photocopying, recording, or otherwise) without prior written permission of the publisher.

555 North Morton Street
Bloomington, IN 47404
800.733.6786 (toll free) / 812.336.7700
FAX: 812.336.7790

email: info@SolutionTree.com
SolutionTree.com

Visit **go.SolutionTree.com/technology** to download the free reproducibles in this book.

Printed in the United States of America

Library of Congress Cataloging-in-Publication Data

Names: Fishman-Weaver, Kathryn, 1981- author. | Walter, Stephanie, author.
Title: Connected classrooms : a people-centered approach for online, blended, and in-person learning / Kathryn Fishman-Weaver, Stephanie Walter.
Description: Bloomington, IN : Solution Tree Press, 2022. | Includes bibliographical references and index.
Identifiers: LCCN 2021061309 (print) | LCCN 2021061310 (ebook) | ISBN 9781954631199 (paperback) | ISBN 9781954631205 (ebook)
Subjects: LCSH: Student-centered learning. | Effective teaching. | Web-based instruction. | Blended learning. | Classroom environment.
Classification: LCC LB1027.23 .F576 2022 (print) | LCC LB1027.23 (ebook) | DDC 371.39/4--dc23/eng/20220110
LC record available at https://lccn.loc.gov/2021061309
LC ebook record available at https://lccn.loc.gov/2021061310

Solution Tree
Jeffrey C. Jones, CEO
Edmund M. Ackerman, President

Solution Tree Press
President and Publisher: Douglas M. Rife
Associate Publisher: Sarah Payne-Mills
Managing Production Editor: Kendra Slayton
Editorial Director: Todd Brakke
Art Director: Rian Anderson
Copy Chief: Jessi Finn
Production Editor: Gabriella Jones-Monserrate
Content Development Specialist: Amy Rubenstein
Acquisitions Editor: Sarah Jubar
Copy Editor: Jessi Finn
Text and Cover Designer: Laura Cox
Associate Editor and Proofreader: Sarah Ludwig
Editorial Assistants: Charlotte Jones and Elijah Oates

*This book is dedicated to our new teachers.
These brave practitioners are stepping boldly into new
kinds of classrooms and instructional spaces. We look
forward to the hopes they bring, the connections they
make, and the important ways they continue to improve
and iterate this noble field of education.*

ACKNOWLEDGMENTS

As always, we are thankful to the young people in our lives. The elementary, middle, and high school scholars we work and learn with keep us grounded, give us hope, and are our reason for this work.

Much like our approach to school leadership, the process of bringing this book into the world was a community project. We are indebted to the practitioners who worked with us throughout our connected classroom research. Their wisdom and narratives are the gifts that bring this book to life. Because this text is about community in the classroom, it is important for us to acknowledge these professionals are members of our own professional learning community. Knowing and working with each of these educators has made us better educators and human beings.

We would especially like to thank Alicia Bixby, Thitinun (Ta) Boonseng, Adrian Clifton, Jill Clingan, Lisa DeCastro, Sherry Denney, Jeff Healy, Chris Holmes, Lou Jobst, Kimberly Kester, Jeff Kopolow, Anthony Plogger, Megan Lilien, Katie McClintic, Matt Miltenberg, David Prats Vidal, Roberta Mayumi da Silva, Greg Soden, Nina Sprouse, Nancy Stoker, Brian Stuhlman, Marilyn Toalson, Jason Williamson, Diane Johnson, and Karen Scales, who submitted narratives, shared stories, and participated in focus-group conversations that directly informed this book.

We are grateful to our school home, the University of Missouri's College of Education and Human Development in general and Mizzou Academy specifically. Both of us hold degrees from the University of Missouri and have continued to grow as scholars and practitioners in our professional work with the college.

We are also grateful for each other. Our journeys in education and educational leadership have led to countless late nights and early mornings planning conferences, reviewing student work, and supporting teachers. These journeys have also led to classroom visits across countries and oceans. We have created art and written poems with high school students in São Paulo and explored mathematics and science with middle school students in Hanoi. There was that stand-up paddleboard adventure gone wrong in Vitória and the kayaking adventure gone right in Hạ Long Bay. We're thankful for so many adventures we could never have imagined, and we're proud to count coauthoring this book among them.

We appreciate Sarah Jubar, Gabriella Jones-Monserrate, and the Solution Tree team for believing in this project and for helping us nurture it to publication. And finally, we are thankful for you, our readers. Thank you for choosing this book as your next read, for exploring the narratives and ideas within, and for applying them to your own practice as we strive together to cultivate people-centered approaches to education.

Solution Tree Press would like to thank the following reviewers:

Racquel Biem
High School Teacher
Saskatchewan Teachers Federation
Swift Current, Saskatchewan, Canada

Jay Clark
Middle School Principal/Assistant Superintendent
Van Buren Local School District
Van Buren, Ohio

Johanna Josaphat
Social Studies Teacher
The Urban Assembly Unison School
Brooklyn, New York

Benjamin Kitslaar
Principal
West Side Elementary
Elkhorn, Wisconsin

Elizabeth Love
Principal
Spradling Elementary
Fort Smith, Arkansas

Tara Reed
Fourth-Grade Teacher
Hawk Elementary School
Corinth, Texas

Britney Watson
Principal
Fort Smith Public Schools, Morrison Elementary School
Fort Smith, Arkansas

Visit **go.SolutionTree.com/technology** to download the free reproducibles in this book.

TABLE OF CONTENTS
Reproducibles are in italics.

About the Authors xi
Preface: Our Journeys to Blended Education xiii
    Stephanie's Background: Education Is a Journey Together xiii
    Kathryn's Background: Education Is a Public Health Profession xv
    A Note About Methodology xvii

Introduction: People-Centered Approaches to Teaching . . 1
    We Open With Heart 3
    Connection With Intention 4
    People-Centered Practices 5
    The Structure of This Book 6
    Classroom Habits of Reflective Practitioners *11*

PART I: REIMAGINING THE ONLINE CLASSROOM 13

1 Reimagining School as a Community Project 15
    Adaptation to Online Instruction 16
    Strategies for Establishing a Safe, Nurturing, and Trusting Virtual
        Classroom 19
    Strategies for Connecting Language and Community 23
    Strategies for Creating Community Through Extracurricular
        Opportunities 28
    Strategies for Building a Positive Classroom Culture in Blended
        and Online Settings 32
    Key Classroom Takeaway: The World Is Small and Deeply Connected . . 35
    Summary 36
    Chapter 1: Apply It to Your Practice *38*

2 Cultivating Strengths-Based Approaches for Inclusion, Support, and Counseling 43

Lived-Experience Case Studies. 46
Strategies for Building a Support System in Online and Blended Models . . 51
Strategies for Individual Planning 58
Strategies for Affirming Identities. 62
Strategies for Adult Learning 65
Strategies for Taking a People-Centered Approach to Student Support . . 68
Key Classroom Takeaway: Practice Radical Hope One Conversation
   at a Time 70
Summary 70
Chapter 2: Apply It to Your Practice *72*

3 Fostering Relationships Through Connection-Based Feedback 75

Feedback as a Conversation 76
Strategies for Connecting Daily With Students 79
Strategies for Connecting Through Feedback 81
Strategies for Cultivating Connection 86
Strategies for Using the Four-Step Feedback Process. 90
Key Classroom Takeaway: All Teaching Is a Conversation. 99
Summary 99
Chapter 3: Apply It to Your Practice *101*

PART II: ENSURING EQUITY AND INCLUSION IN THE ONLINE CLASSROOM 103

4 Centering Student Stories 105

Connection Built Through Stories 107
Strategies for Cultivating Empathy in Your Classroom 112
Strategies for Encouraging Connection Through Music and Poetry. . . . 116
Strategies for Supporting Gender Inclusivity in the Blended Classroom . . 118
Strategies for Making Global Connections 121
Key Classroom Takeaway: Story Sharing Makes Space for Empathy
   and Connection 122
Summary 123
Chapter 4: Apply It to Your Practice *124*

5 Honoring Multilingual and Multicultural Learners . . 127

Teaching in a Multilingual and Multicultural World 129
Strategies for Celebrating Home Language in Your Classroom 131
Strategies for Honoring Student Voice and Home Language in the
    Online Elementary Classroom 134
Strategies for Learning With Multilingual and Multicultural Students in
    Online Settings 141
Strategies for Building Culturally Responsive, Self-Paced E-Learning . . 144
Key Classroom Takeaway: Celebrate Linguistic Diversity 147
Summary 148
Chapter 5: Apply It to Your Practice *150*

6 Leveraging Opportunities for Gifted and Talented Students 153

Three Barriers to Learning for Gifted Students 154
Talent Development 156
Giftedness 157
Differentiation 158
Strategies for Bringing Coaching and Connection to the Online and
    Blended Classroom 161
Strategies for Engaging Learners Beyond Content Areas 166
Key Classroom Takeaway: Employ Wholehearted Teaching for
    Neurodiverse Classrooms 168
Summary 169
Chapter 6: Apply It to Your Practice *171*

Conclusion 173

Kathryn's Takeaways 173
Stephanie's Takeaways 176
We Close With Heart 179

Appendix: Focus Group Transcript 183

Glossary 193

References and Resources 201

Index 209

ABOUT THE AUTHORS

Kathryn Fishman-Weaver, PhD, began her teaching career as a special education teacher for a public K–8 school in Oakland, California. Since then, she has taught and led programs in special education, gifted education, English language arts, and teacher preparation. She currently serves as the executive director of Mizzou Academy. Kathryn supports the University of Missouri's teacher education program by coordinating required courses on culturally competent and community-engaged teaching practices. Prior to her appointment as executive director, she served for five years as the director of academic affairs and engagement for Mizzou Academy during a period of rapid international growth.

Kathryn has lectured and led professional development sessions around the world. She is the author of three additional books in education: *Wholehearted Teaching of Gifted Young Women*, *When Your Child Learns Differently*, and *Brain-Based Learning With Gifted Students*. Her work has appeared in numerous publications and been referenced by the U.S. Department of Education.

Kathryn holds a bachelor's degree in sociology from the University of Missouri, a master's degree in special education from San Francisco State University, and a doctorate in educational leadership and policy analysis from the University of Missouri.

To learn more about Kathryn's work, visit her website Wholehearted School Leadership (wholeheartedschoolleadership.com), or follow @KFishmanweaver on Twitter.

 **Stephanie Walter, MEd,** serves as the director of teaching and learning for Mizzou Academy. Throughout over twenty years of teaching, she has taught in public, private, and blended classrooms, meeting students from all over the world and encouraging them as they evolve as writers and learners.

During her tenure with Mizzou Academy, Stephanie has authored and coauthored over twenty-five online and blended courses and also led professional development and workshops around the world. Stephanie's current role affords her the opportunity to develop curriculum, support lead teachers, manage a large team of instructional specialists, and partner with classroom teachers. In these roles, she shares best practices in online and blended education and helps foster student success.

Stephanie holds a bachelor's degree in secondary language arts from the University of Missouri and completed her master's degree in creative arts in education through Lesley University.

To book Kathryn Fishman-Weaver or Stephanie Walter for professional development, contact pd@SolutionTree.com.

PREFACE
Our Journeys to Blended Education

It was August 2020, and the shadowy trepidation of that specific moment in education was palpable. More than one hundred elementary educators would join us for an orientation workshop on connecting and teaching online in just a few minutes. How do you orient teachers for an unknown and unprecedented school year? Stephanie and I (Kathryn) shared a quick nervous look. I noticed my coffee had turned cold and teachers were beginning to fill the digital waiting room. Stephanie dashed to her refrigerator to grab one more diet soda. It was time to draw on the lessons we had learned from our own experiences teaching and leading in online and blended contexts. As we worked with the elementary teachers in our session that day, we realized this global moment had already transformed education forever.

It was around this time we realized we had a story to share—a story about our experiences teaching and leading in online schools. This led us down a long path of research and reflection, and eventually to the book you are reading right now. However, our own story begins years earlier. It starts with two young women who didn't know each other yet and who were both still finding their ways. We did not start our careers as teachers, and when we did become teachers, we were both apprehensive about online education. Now, we both serve as administrators for a global blended school system. Origin stories matter. Journeys matter. Here is a little bit about ours.

Stephanie's Background: Education Is a Journey Together

I remember the exact place I sat on the day I decided I wanted to become a teacher. I was in a sturdy wooden chair surrounded by a loud, rowdy group of ninth-grade students in the classic U-shape—six girls and fifteen boys (most of whom were on the football team). We were reliving our favorite moments from *To Kill a Mockingbird*, sharing lively opinions about Scout's first-grade teacher, Miss Caroline, who smelled like peppermint and had questionable teaching methods. I was the teacher, and this was the very last day of my first year of teaching. I knew for certain I had found my happy place, my calling, and my passion—right in the middle of a rambunctious classroom filled with very opinionated fourteen- and fifteen-year-olds.

Right up to my first year of teaching, I was determinedly set against education as a general career path. As a fifteen-year-old high school student, I was in the middle of an algebra I class, tackling a set of particularly challenging questions, when my teacher overheard me explaining a problem to a friend in the dull roar of group work. Mr. G. said, in the way you might imagine an oracle proclaims the future to a wandering traveler, "You will make a great teacher someday."

Mr. G. balanced his passion for mathematics with corny jokes in his efforts to spur his young mathematicians to success. I often bothered him for his advice and respected his opinion. This time, though? I didn't hesitate.

"Oh, no! Being a teacher is the *last* thing I ever want to do. I can't even imagine it."

Years later, I met up with Mr. G. and told him I was teaching language arts to 137 ninth-grade students. The twinkle in his eye returned. "Of course you are," he said.

How I went from "I would never teach" to "I love to teach" was less a leap than a yearslong acceptance of something I realized exists in the fabric of who I am. I attended the University of Missouri as an eager journalism student with good grades, a love of stories, and high hopes. What I *didn't* have was a thirst for competition and the outgoing nature a journalist might need to get the scoop. This introvert quickly realized a career in journalism was not a good fit. Besides a vague dream of becoming a world-traveling author, I had really no direction for a career. So, my path to education began as a hasty declaration: "Well, I love to read, and I like kids. I guess I'll be an English teacher."

Three years later, I started work as a junior high language arts teacher in the midsize city of Columbia, Missouri. It was a far cry from my small-town roots, and I was both intimidated and awestruck I had made it this far. My concerns centered on things like, "Can I keep a class under control?" rather than on any excellent teaching strategies I might employ. A little excited and a lot shaky, I decided, if nothing else, I would enjoy traveling this journey with my students. I would do the best I could to share my love of literature and help them begin to express themselves through their own stories. I would fake it until I made it, even if I made it through only one year and then slipped away to pursue another career path.

All of this brings us back to that discussion of the peppermint-scented, well-meaning, misdirected Miss Caroline during the last hour with my first group of students. One feisty student who had both challenged me and given me great joy throughout the year said, "Well, you can't blame Miss Caroline. She's a first-year teacher.

They don't know *anything*." I laughed. "You know," I told her, "*I'm* a first-year teacher." The other students looked surprised. She said, "I had no idea! You seem like you've been doing this for years."

And that was the moment I embraced education. Not because I was a "good" teacher. Not because I had effective classroom management skills or could effortlessly lead students through studies of *To Kill a Mockingbird* or *Romeo and Juliet* (because that is not effortless). I knew I was in it for good simply because I came home at the end of every day utterly exhausted and ready for more. Something beautiful happens as a group of students and their teacher learn about one another, share the journey through the year, and evolve from one grade to the next. And there I was, living out what I loved most about education. Stories matter. Real life is tangled up with stories, and people connect and press forward through them.

In Mr. G.'s class, I thought I wanted to be a world-traveling author. Who knew becoming an educator would help me later realize that dream? I eventually took on a small role for an online school system, teaching creative writing and high school language arts to students online. That role evolved to lead teacher, to instructional coordinator, to assistant principal, and eventually to director of teaching and learning. In these roles, I've had the privilege of meeting with domestic and international students and educators to share the journey to learn together. I've written online interactive textbooks for middle school through high school, and now, I'm thrilled to be partnering with my fellow educator and leader of our school district, Kathryn, on the book you hold right now. I am excited to share a new journey with you as we consider the power of connection with our students and how to create magic in the online space.

Kathryn's Background: Education Is a Public Health Profession

I didn't plan on becoming an educator. After college, I moved two thousand miles to Berkeley, California, to work as a publicist for a social justice nonprofit. I told myself I would do this for a couple of years and then I'd start a master's degree in public health. I believed public health was how I would make a difference in the world. It turns out I was right.

One day taking the Bay Area Rapid Transit home from work, I saw an advertisement recruiting special education teachers to Oakland Public Schools. Something in my thinking aligned, and I realized education is a public health profession.

The CDC Foundation (n.d.) defines *public health* as:

> The science of protecting and improving the health of people and their communities. . . . Overall, public health is concerned with protecting the health

of entire populations. These populations can be as small as a local neighborhood, or as big as an entire country or region of the world.

This is what schoolteachers work toward every day. Educators strive to cultivate cognitive and affective wellness and development, to transform life trajectories, and to promote "equity, quality and accessibility" (CDC Foundation, n.d.). Viewing education as a public health profession is important to our book's emphasis on people-centered approaches to teaching. It was also important to how I approached my work as a first-grade teacher.

I've dedicated my career to working with neurodiverse learners (learners who experience a variation in the human brain regarding sociability, attention, learning, and other mental functions, such as students diagnosed with attention deficit hyperactivity disorder [ADHD]), fostering student leadership, and cultivating wholehearted approaches to school leadership. The first person I met when I started my career in public education was a parent leader who often helped families navigate our public systems, including health care. The second person I met was a school secretary who doubled as our school nurse and lead Spanish-English translator. My classrooms have welcomed refugees, immigrants, students with profound medical needs, and students experiencing food insecurity. I've worked with students whose parents were told by doctors that their children would likely never achieve functional literacy, and they experienced the miracle of watching those young people prove those claims wrong. My colleagues and I have had the gift and responsibility of being a safe person with whom young people could share their fears and challenges.

I feel at home in school buildings. I love the noise, the flurry of emotions, and the energy of young people surrounding me in the classroom. Therefore, when I received a recruiting call to join an online and blended school system, I wasn't all that interested. When the caller then shared that this online school system was welcoming thousands of international students, I agreed to a conversation.

Early in the conversation, I came right out and said, "I find online education . . . dehumanizing."

"Tell me more," the interviewer replied.

"Well, I am passionate about student leadership, differentiation, student support, service initiatives, and project-based learning. These are all missing from most of the online classes I've experienced."

"What if you could change that?" my interviewer asked.

That wasn't the response I expected. He continued, sounding genuinely interested in my answer, "Where would you start?"

This is one of the most important questions someone has asked me in an interview.

A few weeks later, I accepted a new position as the academic director for a large online and blended school system. I walked in on my first day of the job with a host of butterflies in my stomach and a sincere resolve to implement new practices in online and blended learning.

A Note About Methodology

Through our research, Stephanie and I (Kathryn) collected and analyzed many teaching stories. We spoke with educators whose narratives resonated with our own and educators whose stories were very different from either of ours. We spoke with educators who shared their strategies for connecting with students in face-to-face, online, or blended classrooms. These educators are part of a community of teachers who are passionate about relationships, growth, and cultivation of student leadership. We hope that when you read these stories, you feel like a part of this community. We encourage you to brainstorm strategies right along with us as you create connected classrooms that are authentic to your personality and narrative. Thank you for joining us for this moment, for living out your own story, and for sharing your good works with the young people in our communities.

Stephanie and I are both writers and former language arts educators. We believe deeply in the power of stories. As school administrators, we are often awed by the incredible stories told within our school and professional learning community. In our work in global and blended classrooms, we recognized that we were navigating a new narrative of education told through a multiplicity of stories.

We believed these stories were important to share, and we wanted to include them in a book that captures this heartfelt work and invites more conversation about the life-giving role of connection in the classroom. As we set out to accomplish this goal, we committed to intentional active listening, dialogue, and story sharing. Our backgrounds and values pointed us to narrative methods for data collection. We wanted to hear from educators in their own words about their experiences making connections and creating engagement in online, blended, and global classrooms.

Grounded theory is a research methodology that aims to develop hypotheses and theories through the collection and analysis of qualitative data, including stories and interviews. In our work, we used some concepts from grounded theory to guide our coding and analysis process (Charmaz, 2014). Through coding and dialogue about coding, we sought to create an "interactive analytic space" where we could better understand the processes, conditions, and strategies that make connection possible across many classroom spaces (Charmaz, 2014, p. 109). The written stories we solicited and received from educators across North and South America gave structure to our research on *connected classrooms*, a concept that continued to emerge as we coded and analyzed these stories.

In our research and planning for this book on connected classrooms, we interviewed nearly thirty educators who are actively teaching in face-to-face, blended, and online classrooms. We spoke with international teachers, instructional designers, counselors, and career educators. These professionals offered diverse experiences and perspectives. In addition to sharing stories through dialogues and unstructured interviews, each participant also wrote a personal narrative on their experiences in the classroom. The participants didn't hold back. In fact, it felt as though many had been waiting for an invitation to write these stories down. They sent in pages and pages of text, contributing to a large data set on the conditions and possibilities for people-centered practices in online, blended, and technology-mediated classrooms. Their narratives were story-rich and full of important takeaways for this new paradigm of teaching and learning. We have selected and excerpted several of these practitioner texts to illustrate each chapter of this book.

During our research, we spoke with educators who invited students' grandparents to join them in an online class, educators who orchestrated online research followed by community-based service projects, and educators who arranged for international guests to video in for in-person classroom meetings. These are just a few examples of the possibilities that open up when teachers can reimagine the classroom as a global community project, not a fixed room in a building. The practitioners interviewed for this project teach in a variety of school settings and live across North and South America. They are also part of our professional network, and most share a connection (as former or current colleagues, friends, and partners) to Mizzou Academy, the blended K–12 school system where we serve as administrators. Housed in the University of Missouri's College of Education and Human Development, Mizzou Academy serves a culturally, linguistically, and geographically diverse population of close to eight thousand students annually. While this is certainly not the only context we cite in this book, it does serve as a tethering space where many of the participants honed their own people-centered practices in blended education. As you read through the chapters, we hope you'll see these educator stories as points of connection to your own practice.

Please note in this book, we vigilantly protect personally identifiable student data. All stories and narratives that mention students by name use pseudonyms, create composite characters, and substitute analogous identifiers to further blur the identities of these students.

INTRODUCTION
People-Centered Approaches to Teaching

As a global community, we have a long way to go in ensuring that all children have access to learning. A 2019 UNICEF report states over 617 million children and adolescents around the world are unable to reach minimum proficiency levels in reading and mathematics. Further, one in five children is not in school at all (UNICEF, 2019). Many factors impact a child's ability to access a quality education, including poverty, geography, gender, disability, and health. In our own work in global education, we (Kathryn and Stephanie) have seen each of these factors disrupt and limit children's access to learning. We have also had the privilege and responsibility of venturing new solutions to help mitigate these challenges. These stories form the basis of this book.

UNICEF (2019) names access to learning as the greatest global challenge. This challenge does not refer to access to school buildings. With the right resources, strategies, and supports, children can access learning from many different spaces, including homes, community centers, and hospital rooms. With access to the right resources, educators can reimagine the traditional classroom setting. In fact, many educators are already building expertise in this area. For decades, educators have been testing flipped instructional methods, setting up journals and projects on Google Drive, using game-based learning platforms like Kahoot!

Essential Question

How can people-centered practices help educators teach beyond classroom walls?

for classwide competitions, using learning apps for homework and independent practice, and moving content to online learning management systems.

This increasing use of online and blended instruction is significantly shifting education. With it comes flexibility—chances for students to work at a self-directed pace, ways to access courses that may not be available in a physical building, solutions for medically fragile students, and different learning avenues for students who thrive in online environments. This shift also brings challenges for educators to solve together. A key challenge is how to create engagement and student ownership of learning when educators don't see their students face-to-face each day. Teachers tend to be a relational bunch of people who take a holistic interest in students' learning, personalities, hobbies, and social-emotional health. Building these relationships in online and blended spaces looks a little different than it does in a face-to-face context.

However, our research on connected classrooms repeatedly points to values that transfer across instructional spaces. These begin with practices that place student voices at the center of learning. Throughout this book, we make references to *people-centered practices* for teaching and learning in these spaces. People-centered practitioners recognize young people as the nucleus of learning and community in the classroom. The stories, lived experiences, and strengths each student brings to the classroom matter. People-centered practices include the following.

- Starting with story sharing and relationships to build a connected community
- Continuing to center these stories and relationships to further education
- Committing to strengths-based approaches by asking, "What can you (and we) do well, and how can we build from there?"
- Focusing on growth mindset to celebrate process, embrace challenges, and learn from experiences and successes (Growth mindset is further defined in chapter 2, page 43.)
- Supporting students with strategies and resources rooted in equity and a deep understanding of context and experiences
- Pushing past "the way we've always done it" to explore new possibilities for supporting this unique group of young people as they grow as scholars and community members

This book encourages educators to develop these practices in any teaching space. What does this look like specifically in online and blended contexts? In one situation, Kathryn introduced herself to a new group of online students with this norm: "We will start each class together with a social-emotional check-in." This check-in might look like a question in the chat such as, "What are you celebrating this week?" or "What's the last show you binged on Netflix?" And then later, when the students have established trust with one another, the teacher might start with the question, "What challenge are you facing right now?" or invite students to share their "roses and thorns" (in this conversation prompt game, the *rose* is something wonderful that is blossoming in a student's life, and the *thorn* is something difficult that may be holding a student back from reaching a goal). An educator we know asks students to display the emoji that best represents their mood at the moment (with fun screenshots to follow). A two-minute scavenger hunt to locate and share an artifact that connects to the lesson is also a popular way to get students up and moving and invite their voices into the online space.

How can people-centered practices help educators teach beyond classroom walls? Relationships are the heart of great teaching. This is a universal truth in classrooms across geographic areas, cultures, and contexts. Solving the grand challenges of learning access and equity requires new ideas, innovations, and the steady constant of relationships. Together, we will consider the global landscape of education and the potential of blended approaches to teaching and learning.

The narratives and strategies in this book point to a key takeaway that the world is small and deeply connected. Some strategies in this book, like people-centered practices, are essential whether in face-to-face classrooms, in blended classrooms, or in online classrooms. Others are most suited to particular spaces. Throughout each chapter, we've included intentional strategies for considering which learning activities should happen in person and which may be better suited online. Consider with us how to adapt and translate connected teaching strategies across many instructional spaces.

We Open With Heart

This book is the result of learning with approximately thirty educators from across multiple contexts, geographic areas, and specialties. The strategies and best practices included here call all teachers to center humanity in their work in the classroom. These practices rest on a belief in radical hope (Fishman-Weaver, 2017). They celebrate this noble profession, holding both students and educators to high expectations.

While we are proud to share these strategies and we believe in this framework for connected teaching, we also want to acknowledge that this is lofty and difficult work. It is heart heavy and head heavy.

As you build a connected classroom, you will assure your students that learning takes time and they all are works in progress. You will tell them that it is OK to make mistakes—that mistakes are part of the learning process. You'll encourage your students to take moments to reflect on what they do well and what their next goals are. You'll remind them that they are not alone and that they have a school community that roots for them and supports them.

All these messages apply to you as well. Teaching is a complex and beautiful effort. You, too, are a work in progress. Give yourself a break when you can't implement every strategy for connection every day; you'll have hundreds of casual conversations with your students and hundreds of intentional moments tied to lesson plans that strengthen connection over time. You will make mistakes, and that's OK. You will grow in confidence and expertise each day and each year. And, dear reader, you are not alone. You are part of a bigger school community that is rooting for you and can offer encouragement, camaraderie, and support as you follow this teaching journey.

We hope the following research, narratives, and strategies in this book will stir you to cultivate connected classrooms.

Connection With Intention

We live in an era of online communication. Means of communication with others are ubiquitous; email, social media websites, and Wi-Fi messaging apps are just some connecting tools. However, remotely connecting with others has its challenges, as it compresses multidimensional communication to very one-dimensional black-and-white text (perhaps sprinkled with emojis). These one-dimensional approaches to communication (as in one-way, short, direct, and closed) can lead to miscommunication or disconnection. The notorious, authoritative red pen marking mistakes across a paper is an example. So, too, is simply saying or writing, "Good job!" (which is a comment that sounds peppy but doesn't give the student anywhere to grow).

When people interact with others via online communication, they cannot read facial expressions or pick up on body language cues. People cannot hear tones of voice or vocal inflections that might indicate sarcasm, humor, or anger. Instead, they must rely on words as they are written and trust that they can decipher others' intent.

Miscommunication is detrimental in any sort of relationship, whether it happens between a parent and child, between partners, or between friends. Such miscommunication is particularly detrimental in a teacher-student relationship. An analysis of forty-six studies finds strong teacher-student relationships are associated with higher student academic engagement, better attendance, stronger grades, fewer disruptive behaviors and suspensions, and lower school dropout rates (Sparks, 2019). Those effects persist "even after controlling for differences in students' individual, family, and school backgrounds" (Sparks, 2019).

While in-person learning has its own challenges, it has the advantage of face-to-face interactions with students. Students can gather around the teacher's desk to chat. Teachers can observe students' body language and monitor their participation in class. In an online learning environment, even with the interactions provided by video interfaces such as Zoom and Google Classroom, these observations have limits. The strategies in this book encourage connection within a framework that requires more text-directed instruction.

People-Centered Practices

The concept of people-centered practice originated in health care, where practitioners put people, patients, and communities at the center of their care. This includes actively listening to patients when they report on their health and seeking additional community or family input as needed where people can participate in "trusted health systems that respond to their needs and preferences in humane and holistic ways" (World Health Organization, n.d.). This approach is also relevant to education, and particularly to this book on connected teaching. The strategies and stories shared herein point to humane and holistic possibilities where educators center students and their communities in the education process. An experience Kathryn had with the move to student-led individualized education program (IEP) meetings illuminates this practice. In these meetings, the students who are receiving special education services self-report on their strengths, challenges, goals, and frustrations. The voice of the young person being served becomes the lead voice in the meeting—a dramatic flip from an educator or administrator reporting on behalf of what they think a student is feeling or capable of.

Health care and education have many important parallels, including that both are fundamental human rights. According to the World Health Organization (n.d.), people-centered health is the practice of "putting people and communities, not diseases, at the center of health systems, and empowering people to take charge of their own health rather than being passive recipients of services." This book aligns with the approach of putting people right at the center of their own learning—aiming for engagement over passive reception. Health and educational practitioners can learn a lot from each other. In much the same way telehealth has transformed access to health care, online and blended pedagogies have the potential to transform access to education (American Hospital Association, 2019).

The Structure of This Book

We (Kathryn and Stephanie) believe that all learning happens through connection. We've divided this book into two parts, and each one explores a key question regarding creating connection in the classroom. Part I explores the question, *In what ways can educators reimagine online and blended classrooms as sites for greater connection?* Part II answers the question, *How can educators ensure equity and inclusion in online and blended classrooms?* The following sections detail how we have organized part I and part II of this book.

Part I: Reimagining the Online Classroom

In the increasing move to online and blended teaching, some educators have very quickly gone from one teaching model to the next, and others have had a little more time to consider the implications of teaching in online spaces. The following chapters will give you the tools to consider what effective teaching can look like based on your unique situation and community.

Chapter 1, "Reimagining School as a Community Project," addresses the question, *What shifts when educators think of school as a community project?* This chapter explores a primary guidepost of people-centered approaches to online teaching, namely that school is a community project. Other key concepts explored in this chapter include culturally responsive curriculum, culturally competent teaching, and global community.

Chapter 2, "Cultivating Strengths-Based Approaches for Inclusion, Support, and Counseling," focuses on the question, *How can strengths-based approaches transform student support?* This chapter draws on asset-based approaches to counseling and research in positive psychology and neuroplasticity. Pulling from counselors' experiences with struggling students, including neurodiverse learners, the narratives in this chapter highlight support approaches for the online and blended classroom. This chapter explores holistic support practices that affirm strength, inclusion, and well-being.

Chapter 3, "Fostering Relationships Through Connection-Based Feedback," focuses on the question, *How can educators foster great relationships through everyday teaching practices?* This curriculum- and instruction-based chapter offers specifics on giving feedback, honoring voice, practicing wellness, and supporting social-emotional learning. It also includes practitioner strategies on translating in-person teaching practices to online and vice versa.

Part II: Ensuring Equity and Inclusion in the Online Classroom

The three chapters in part II build toward intercultural sensitivity, global competencies, and culturally sustaining pedagogies in online, blended, and in-person classes (Bennett, 2017; Olson & Kroeger, 2001; Paris, 2012). Like everything good and important in education, this work begins in relationship and story. The strategies and narratives shared across these chapters challenge educators to consider how to cultivate inclusive and equitable classroom communities.

Chapter 4, "Centering Student Stories," explores the question, *How can educators cultivate connection through story sharing?* This chapter delves into what it means to make space for teachers and students to share stories together, and how this practice blends empathy and connection to create a positive classroom culture.

Chapter 5, "Honoring Multilingual and Multicultural Learners," explores the question, *How can educators honor the multilingual strengths and perspectives students bring to the classroom?* Across the globe, "business, employment and scholarship are increasingly global and multilingual, and citizens of the 21st century need a new range of skills and strategies" (Saville, 2018, p. 4). These include "code-switching and translanguaging" (Saville, 2018, p. 4), or the ability to transfer and translate quickly between one language and another. How is school cultural and linguistic diversity transforming classroom practice, and what might this mean for honoring voice, culture, and possibility? This chapter explores language learning for teachers and students, people-centered approaches to multilingualism, and strategies for the online classroom.

Chapter 6, "Leveraging Opportunities for Gifted and Talented Students," poses the question, *How can educators rethink space, place, and pace to help students soar in the classroom?* Honoring students' strengths, genius, and talent domains facilitates new learning possibilities. This chapter focuses on the potential online and blended classrooms have to support gifted and advanced students. Rethinking space, place, and pacing in education means the online classroom opens up the capacity for talent-based, passion-specific education that celebrates students' talent domains.

The book's conclusion addresses the question, *What are the most important lessons to learn next in education?* Educators must be flexible and prepared to meet students where they are in a variety of learning contexts, including face-to-face, blended, and online classrooms. The book closes with a forward-facing perspective on what strengths-based, community-focused, and global education could mean for the 21st century.

Key Terms

asynchronous learning. *Asynchronous* refers to components happening at different times. In the case of online learning, this refers to approaches that allow for students to work on their own time and at their own pace. For this reason, courses utilizing all asynchronous methods are sometimes referred to as *self-paced* courses.

blended learning. Used to refer to learning solutions in which educators use a combination of online and in-person methods for instruction. This digital approach is expanding globally (Hilliard, 2015). This method is also known as *hybrid learning*.

flipped classrooms. A blended approach where students learn content at home via online methods and then practice these concepts during in-person classes.

online learning. Used to refer to learning solutions in which all or nearly all the instruction and learning happen online in an either synchronous or asynchronous manner. Definitions of online learning are varied and have evolved over time alongside the expansion of technology and teaching approaches (Singh & Thurman, 2019). Online learning is also sometimes referred to as *e-learning*.

synchronous learning. *Synchronous* refers to things happening at the same time. In the case of online learning, this refers to approaches that require students to work at the same time as their peers. For this reason, courses utilizing mostly synchronous methods are therefore sometimes referred to as *scheduled* courses.

technology-mediated instruction. An umbrella term for a wide variety of methods that use digital technology for teaching and learning.

Finally, we include an appendix featuring an edited transcript from a focus group we held with five midcareer professionals who span the continuum of preschool through graduate school. This appendix provides a sample of the anecdotal data we gathered for this book and includes several more strategies for the classroom.

Key Terms for Online and Blended Learning Approaches

While the 2020 COVID-19 pandemic accelerated online methods, the global technological boom had long been building, and practitioners in online and blended settings were already influencing the way educators talk about classroom practices and possibilities. A 2018 article in the *Journal of Global Information Technology Management* predicted that "online education is on track to become mainstream by 2025" (Palvia et al., 2018, p. 233). Thus, educators must become familiar with terminology that reaches outside the boundaries of the traditional classroom. Each chapter highlights key terms integral to understanding the main points and narratives. The following are a few key terms related to digital approaches for curriculum and instruction.

Connected Teaching Commitments for Any Instructional Space

Whether educators are teaching in online, blended, or in-person contexts, certain commitments help support connected classroom communities. Compassion, patience, and a deep desire to connect with young people and their communities are strong themes that support our framework of connected classrooms. These values came up throughout our research with K–12 educators across content areas, cultures, and geographic borders. In the sections marked Connected Teaching Commitment in the following chapters, you'll hear from educators who share how they uphold these commitments in their classrooms. One English learner specialist we work with often shares that language learning takes time, compassion, and patience. Our research on connected classrooms reaffirmed our commitment to honor the humanity in our classes as we safeguard and celebrate the possibility and potential of the young people who bring those learning spaces to life. Each chapter presents teaching commitments that transcend instructional space and serve as helpful tenets for any classroom.

Space for Reflective Practice

Exercise coaches tell their teams to stretch their muscles after a workout. In the long run, it helps people exercise better and longer. Athletic trainers remind people it's essential for health. Yet many people forget, or simply skip, the post-exercise stretch. You've done the exercise already. What difference could a few toe touches or cat-cows make? Educators tend to treat reflective practice in a similar way; they know it's good for them, but they do not (or cannot) make the time.

Educators can find it hard to make space for a reflective practice. After teachers design a lesson, work with their students, and create and grade assignments, they have run out of energy. Doing those things daily is hard work. Educators' brains are full, and their bodies are weary. Still, we strive to create the space necessary to think about what went well (in a specific lesson plan, practice, or rhythm of the day) and what we might try differently next time. What difference can this type of metacognition or breathing room possibly make? For educators, the reflection step is essential before, during, and after doing the work. When teachers succumb to the whirlwind without reflection, the whirlwind takes over the narrative. Reflection is the *power of the pause*. In this space, take a deep breath, and think through what you are accomplishing and how it aligns with your set intentions and goals. That, in turn, allows educators to move forward thoughtfully, confidently, fully stretched, and ready for the next workout. As the paradox goes, making time for this practice will free up more time as you become more productive in the long run.

We hope you'll join us in committing to a reflective practice. Developing a reflective practice gives us a chance to ask what went well, what we need to improve, what we are learning, and what we appreciate. It also is restful in its own way, giving us a chance to pause and note the hard and good work we're doing. At the end of each chapter, we invite you to pause and commit to a reflective practice. You'll find a list of prompts tailored to the content of each chapter complete with writing space. These are all reproducibles you can find and print online for easier sharing. You can work through the following exercises independently or with your teaching teams.

- **React to the chapter:** What are your key takeaways from this chapter? What surprised you? What resonated with you? What ideas are you hoping to build on in your professional journey?

- **Define your purpose:** What is your *why*? Why do you teach? Why do you show up for students each day? Why do you pursue new information and strategies? (And what other whys are you curious about?) How does your why continue to inform your work in the classroom?

- **Set your starting point:** In the preface (page xiii), Kathryn shared how her journey into online education began by articulating how she would make a meaningful impact in this model. Where will *you* begin? What action steps will you commit to in order to make your teaching practice stronger and more effective, particularly in your classes that utilize online and blended approaches?

- **Share your origins:** Share your teaching origin story with your students; explain what led you to the class you share right now. Ask students to think of something they have committed to (like a sport, musical interest, job, or hobby) and discuss what steps led them to where they are now.

- **Question yourself:** Develop your own reflection questions suited to a particular focus of online or blended teaching, like student success, differentiation, or engagement; collaboration with teachers; family communication and relationships; or digital tools for teaching. Share your questions with your colleagues, and discuss ideas together.

Classroom Habits of Reflective Practitioners

This is your first reflective practice exercise. Use these prompts to think through what you envision you will accomplish and how it aligns with your set intentions and goals.

- Examine lesson plans for what's working well and what you want to change.
- Consider relationships with students.
- Note what engages your students and what they respond well to. (What topics and activities light them up?)
- Examine your instructional balance (lectures, interactives, teacher-directed work, student-directed work, independent and group work, and more).
- Look for patterns in student responses and understanding.
- Align the content you teach with students' core purposes.

PART I
Reimagining the Online Classroom

In my (Kathryn's) early ambivalence toward online education, I worried that online instruction was distant and dehumanizing. My prior experiences teaching and learning in online classes helped form this belief. While I saw the appeal for flexibility and acceleration, as a newer teacher, I viewed the online setting as more of a static textbook.

Through our experiences teaching and leading in online, blended, and global contexts, Stephanie and I have seen the possibilities that open up when teachers believe that magic and connection aren't bound to in-person places. We have also seen the ways intentional design can help us reimagine curriculum as a dynamic site for learning and connecting. In part I of this book, we invite you to reimagine the online classroom with us. In chapter 1, career educators will share how the vast technological shifts they have seen over the decades have expanded the ways they connect with students. In chapter 2, you will learn how to assess the unique strengths and setbacks of each student so you can tailor their learning to their needs. Building especially on Stephanie Walter's work around feedbacking, chapter 3 offers specific strategies for cultivating better communication and connection with students in online, blended, or in-person classrooms.

While sitting together in a shared space in real time absolutely has value, our experiences have taught us that connection is not place bound. Wherever you and your students are is the right place for magic, learning, and relationships. The following chapters offer examples, strategies, and stories that will expand educators' understanding of school from a static building to a global community project.

Reimagining School as a Community Project

1

Teachers might feel disconnected and alone in their individual classroom or online "room." Their tight-knit classroom is a focused space for learning and connection, but it does not exist in isolation; instead, their classroom community interconnects with other classrooms and the school community at large, and then connects out to their local and even global community. With intentionality and creativity, classrooms can become community-based constellations influenced by families, neighborhoods, partner educators, nonprofits serving youth, faith communities, sports, extracurricular activities, and more. This chapter encourages educators to zoom out from that single space and consider school as one part of a larger community.

As you read the educator stories in this chapter, you'll hear about the unique ways these teachers have found to create connection in any space through establishing norms, practicing active listening, connecting language and culture, and making room for every voice. Each narrative has opportunities for you to consider specific strategies that may apply to your own classroom (and school community) context, and then ends with a reflective place to imagine and plan for how you can build connection not only with your students but also with your community.

Essential Question

What shifts when educators think of school as a community project in online and blended settings?

Chapter Learning Objectives

- Recognize various communities within every school.
- Consider how an educator's view of lifelong learning and cultural responsiveness impacts the classroom.
- Generate creative ways to engage and welcome community voices in the larger school community.
- Use opportunities in the beginning, middle, and end of experiences with students to create community.

Key Terms

community-based learning. Intentionally connecting the classroom or content and the community in mutually beneficial ways that honor the inherent wisdom and richness of community-based spaces and organizations. (Service-learning or learning-through-service approaches sometimes fall under this umbrella.)

culturally responsive pedagogies. Teaching and learning practices that create opportunities for learners to (1) act with agency and leadership and (2) think beyond their own culture in competent and affirming ways. This framework comes from the seminal works of Gloria Ladson-Billings (1995) and Geneva Gay (2002), which continue to inform relevant teaching practices around equity, diversity, and high expectations.

culturally sustaining pedagogies. A belief that effective classroom practices must honor, affirm, and sustain the identities and cultural richness students bring to the classroom. This work comes from Django Paris (2012), who built on and affirmed the ideas buttressing culturally responsive pedagogies (Ladson-Billings, 1995) and extended them to specifically call out a commitment to asset-based approaches.

enrichment. Opportunities to extend or expand the content or curriculum.

learning management system. A software application to deliver, manage, and support student progress and curriculum.

school community. The social groups that directly affect students and schools through resources, cultures, and strengths. These include within-school groups such as classroom peers, faculty and staff, and the school population. They also include beyond-school groups such as families, neighborhoods, and cities. Throughout this book, we take a broad view that school is a community project with a myriad of influences and stakeholders.

Adaptation to Online Instruction

Powerful teaching and learning often result from developing the flexibility to see beyond the content and focus solidly on building relationships. Our (Kathryn and Stephanie's) team of educators saw this clearly in a professional development session with local middle school teachers who had quickly flipped their middle school curriculum from face-to-face to online instruction. As the digital meeting room filled up with over seventy teachers, two things became clear. First, the sense of community was palpable. Everyone appeared in tiny boxes on a screen, yet back-and-forth banter between colleagues, inside jokes, check-ins with each other, and warm greetings emanated across the grid. Our educator team reveled in the obvious care, dedication, and pure sense of fun these educators felt as they worked together on solving hard challenges even when they sat in isolated spaces, miles from each other.

Second, these educators were tired. The worry they felt over serving their students well and the hours they spent responding to technological challenges had worn on them.

Kathryn and I (Stephanie) often begin online professional development sessions with a quick check-in: "In two words, describe how you feel right now." On that day, the responses quickly filled up the chat box to the side of the digital meeting window and captured the push and pull between feeling excited and being overwhelmed.

- Tired, hopeful
- Busy, determined
- Excited, overwhelmed
- Hungry (There still isn't a known way to provide snacks and caffeine in an online gathering.)

When the middle school educators answered research questions about their fears and challenges surrounding the start of the year, their responses raised three main concerns.

1. "How do we navigate technology and facilitate access to it?"
2. "How do we build relationships with students?"
3. "How do we support students with different needs?"

These questions come up in every conversation that groups of educators have around online learning. The problems with technology are a given; technology doesn't always work as expected or needed. Relationships are the absolute heart of every dialogue. Educators instinctively know that they must build relationships and engagement before they can do anything else in the classroom. Pursuing relationship building leads to discovering the many types of learners there are. Modern classrooms are global and complex. Educators serve students from culturally and linguistically diverse (CLD) backgrounds (read more in chapter 5, page 127), students with disabilities and learning challenges (read more in chapter 2, page 43), students who are gifted or academically advanced (read more in chapter 6, page 153), and students who bring rich and varied lived experiences to school communities. Differentiating and connecting across so many identities is an exercise in problem solving and intentionality, to say the least.

With these realizations unfolds the most important realization of all: teaching in any space is difficult, worthy work. Teachers refuse to let the challenges of teaching in a brick-and-mortar building derail them from their passion and work. Working in virtual spaces won't thwart their ability to reach students either.

Change is hard, but it is not insurmountable. Just after our (Stephanie and Kathryn's team's) February 2020 visit to Brazil to launch a new elementary program, our partner teachers found themselves suddenly shifting all the curriculum they had planned to deliver in person to a new online space. The first month was jarring as they navigated new learning management systems and video conferencing.

None of us had planned for this, and we joined with teachers around the world who were working hard to figure out the best ways to support students quickly and well. The next months were frustrating. The learning curve was steep as we tried to tackle the questions around access, student support, and relationship building. Then, at some point, the excitement overtook the exhaustion, and the hope rose above the frustration. Our elementary, middle, and high school partner teachers found their rhythm. They began to embrace the online model and develop their own strategies for reaching students in this new space.

Teachers and administrators presented on best practices in mentoring new teachers, engaging students, building inclusivity, and practicing creativity in the online space, which was inspiring. In the following sections, you will read about how four different teachers approach building community. As educators live out their own narrative, the various communities in their respective schools become more identifiable. What communities do educators belong to in their classroom, across their content or grade level, with multilingual students, and in clubs and teams? What other communities might exist, and how can educators help draw them together within the larger school? The following practitioner stories share how educators have cultivated community-based learning from a culturally responsive or sustaining approach.

Marilyn Toalson: The Classrooms of Yesterday, Today, and Tomorrow

Marilyn Toalson was a teacher in public schools for over thirty-five years, including thirty years as a gifted educator and advocate. She has coached academics and athletics, and her students have been national winners in these fields. In 1989, Marilyn helped found College for Kids, a summer residential program for gifted learners, which she continues to codirect. She serves as an instructional specialist for Mizzou Academy. In this narrative, she shares about the importance of heart in the classroom.

I knew in first grade I wanted to be a teacher because my mom was a teacher. My next-door neighbor was my teacher. In my first teacher education class, a professor predicted that someday every classroom would have a computer and that technology would drastically change education. This was in 1975.

I grew up hearing family stories about my great-aunt Alpha who graduated from the University of Missouri in 1910, and then the next day took a horse and wagon to the East Coast to be a headmaster at a private girls' school. Similarly, my mother rode a horse to teach in a county school during World War II.

This legacy is still with us as teachers navigate new terrain today. Teaching is hard. But it has never been easy. I am pretty sure my mother had mornings she did not want to get on a horse before the sun came up as she traveled to "her school." Likewise, in 1978, the science book I was to use with my third-grade class started out with, "Someday man will visit the moon." The first moon landing was in 1969. Our book was a little behind science. So, what did I do then? What have teachers always done? What are teachers doing today? They are doing the best that they can to connect with their students and to engage them in meaningful learning.

Every child deserves to have someone who believes in them, like an adult who can help facilitate their success, demand that they do their best, and never give up on them. Can we do this in an online or blended classroom with the teacher in one building and the student far away in another building? Yes. How do we do that? It starts by managing your virtual classroom with the same heart you bring to your in-person classroom (M. Toalson, personal communication, January 3, 2021)

Strategies for Establishing a Safe, Nurturing, and Trusting Virtual Classroom

The following strategies come from Marilyn's experience as an educator. Each one helps you make connections with students so that they can actively engage in their own learning. Establishing a safe and nurturing environment means that every student who enters your classroom (whether virtually or in person) feels welcome and affirmed. There are three key aspects to consider when making sure students feel safe and welcome in your classroom: (1) physical safety, (2) intellectual safety, and (3) emotional safety (Novak, 2020).

Intellectual safety means letting students know that their voice is not only welcome but also necessary in your room. It also means teaching students to think for themselves, support ideas with facts, and build evidence to develop claims. This also means curriculum and content are accessible for your student community. In chapter 5 (page 144), you will read about Universal Design for Learning (UDL) as a tool to make curriculum more accessible for all learners. Physical safety looks different in different teaching spaces but has one goal in mind—that the physical space supports student inclusion and academic growth. Online classes use a variety of grouping structures, such as one-on-one chats (either with a chat tool or over video), breakout rooms for small-group collaboration, and whole-group sessions balanced with stretch breaks; periodic pauses for students to reflect and summarize what's been said before; and various discussion strategies to keep the conversation flowing in different ways. Finally, emotional safety is essential for both intellectual and physical safety. Make it clear from the beginning that you are *for* your students; being open to their questions, available to talk through problems, and happy to connect them to other caring adults are important practices in establishing emotional safety. As another practical support, make space in your lessons to teach social-emotional learning strategies (we share several in chapter 2, page 62) and model those for and with your students.

The following are several strategies and practices you can employ to establish intellectual, physical, and emotional safety in your classroom.

Set the Tone Before the First Day

In 2021, Marilyn talked to a fourth-grade teacher whose students would be learning virtually. Before school started, the teacher sent an email newsletter with a picture of herself and another of her family. She introduced herself to the students in student-friendly language on the first page, and on the second page, she addressed families. This connection was vital when remotely launching a new school year with elementary students during a pandemic. She followed that with individual online meetings with each family. This way, everyone could check that the digital meeting platform worked from their devices and families got to meet her right away. She then held an evening digital meeting with parents and guardians and demonstrated the various programs and activities that students would be engaging with. Before the school year even began, students and their families were looking forward to it.

You can employ a similar practice by sending out a classroom newsletter or welcome letter—one version to students and another to families—before the first day of school. Individual online meetings may be hard to arrange with all families, but you may extend the same open-door offer at the end of the newsletter or host a virtual open house, allowing parents to attend if they wish.

Listen to Students

What does it mean to actively listen to students, and why is active listening so important? Judy Willis (2018), neurologist and middle school teacher, writes, "Active listening encompasses being nonjudgmental, with an emphasis on listening and not immediately solving the issue or problem. Active listeners don't jump ahead to think about solutions while the speaker is still speaking. They also refrain from getting defensive." Active-listening strategies include the following.

- Looking at the speaker without distractions
- Using facial gestures that reflect what the speaker is saying (for example, a look of concern for something sad, or a smile or laugh for something exciting)
- Interjecting short comments to show that you are listening, like "Mm-hmm," "Exactly," or "Oh!"
- Asking follow-up questions or saying, "Tell me more about that."
- Asking for clarification if something is confusing
- Waiting for a natural break to share your comments
- Building your comments on what the other person has just said

Active listening is healthy for adults and students and builds community. Having your ideas, experiences, and opinions heard and validated sends the message that you are cared for by, seen by, and belong in the class. Teachers must explain the connection between respect and active listening, model it, and expect it from every learner. Creating this environment of trust is not one grand gesture. It often springs from having individual conversations, actively listening, and hearing and compassionately responding to the students in your class community. It is cumulative; a trusting environment forms over time with small, deliberate steps a teacher takes each day to make life and learning optimal for each student.

Build Relationships

Forming positive relationships is vital to the success of schools and organizations. It adds variety to your day, allows students and teachers to get to know each other in new kinds of conversations, provides a low-risk chance for collaboration, and can support social-emotional or academic skills you are already teaching.

Talk to other teachers, counselors, and club organizers in your community, and search online to develop a virtual backpack of appealing, reliable group games or activities to help the class members get to know each other. Many standard classroom games, such as *Two Truths and a Lie*, *Charades*, *Pictionary*, and *Would You Rather?*, can translate well to the online classroom. An educator we spoke with even organized an online escape room using video-conferencing software. The more voices and laughter you can introduce to the classroom, the better! Small moments each day can support this goal. Follow a routine with students so they each address the class in some way at the beginning and end of online group time.

Playful ideas for opening or closing your class include the following.

- Solve a riddle.
- Share the emoji that best represents your mood right now.
- Share a picture that represents a concept (such as your ideal vacation spot, your favorite chair in the house, a food you'd love to eat, or the best gift you've ever gotten).
- Answer a *Would You Rather?* question (such as, "Would you rather give up chocolate or potato chips for a year?" or "Would you rather only watch movies or only read books?").

Use these opening and closing moments as specific opportunities to connect to the lesson.

- "In two words, share the meaning of this quote from the author."
- "Take ninety seconds to find an image that captures the main point of our lesson today."
- "Share your top three takeaways from today's class discussion."
- "Give me a thumbs-up if you think you understand the directions and raise your hand if you have questions."

These types of activities are attention getting and attention focusing. Switch back and forth between more playful questions and more content-focused tasks to keep your students curious about what you might do next and to give them different ways to engage with the work.

Draw From Your School Community

All schools exist in the context of communities. When schools and communities work together, students can receive more robust and comprehensive support. This can look like partnering with community-based organizations for access to computers or Wi-Fi, asking a local leader to video in for a special presentation, identifying mentors from local businesses, or partnering with the public library for cultural events.

When teaching online, remember that not all students have access to the same support, space, or technology while at home. Some virtual learners may not sign in for live classes or upload their assignments on time. This affects all learners from early elementary through secondary. For example, Marilyn Toalson shared that two first-grade students were taking online classes in the house next door to her. Because she lives in an urban area, the students did not have a yard to play in, but she did. Therefore, Marilyn partnered with the family so that the students could take their breaks in her yard, which they referred to as "the playground."

While the students played, Marilyn also taught them about gardening, a personal passion of hers.

If they know their students' living situations, teachers can work through the challenges to help students become successful in the online or blended classroom. This may require leaning on community resources or using an approach that anti-racist educator and advocate Dena Simmons (2016) calls *asset mapping*. Asset mapping involves surveying the local community for strengths and supports that may make a difference in the social, academic, and emotional well-being of students. Example supports include mentorship, career planning, and internship opportunities. This work is:

> based on the belief that all residents in a community, regardless of their backgrounds or other characteristics, can play effective roles in addressing and solving important local matters.... Asset mapping allows [educators] to see community members as partners in enriching the lives of youth, which communicates to students that their families, their neighbors and they themselves matter. (Simmons, 2016)

Visualize Your Students

After retiring from public schools, Marilyn became an online high school teacher. She has now taught online for several years. In her opinion, working with students online makes building trust and support even more important.

Marilyn often receives notes from students in their assignment comments. She is dedicated to responding to every note or invitation for interaction. She uses these short conversations as a relationship builder, referencing them throughout the course. As she grades a student's assignment, Marilyn uses their name often and tries to "see" the student sitting next to her. She has found that visualizing the young person as she responds to their heartfelt work makes it easier to respond in a compassionate, helpful manner.

Strategies for Connecting Language and Community

The following strategies are three specific ways you can create community in your classroom through a celebration of language. Although David's experiences specifically come from working in multilingual classrooms, the lessons he shares are helpful to all teachers as they continue to celebrate student voice and culture in everyday practices and in specific teaching moments.

David Prats Vidal: Language-Learning Choices and Cultural Background in World Language Courses

David Prats Vidal is a world languages coordinator in an online school. He is fluent in five languages, loves to travel, and is passionate about encouraging students to learn about culture and community in the languages they study.

The reasons that drive high school students to choose to study one world language over another when registration time comes are diverse—academic requirements, job-market or career opportunities, or personal preference, to name only a few. Some students make this decision based on family origin. They have grown up speaking English and hope to learn how to communicate in the first language of a parent or their extended family.

My online school offers a variety of languages that are not always available to students in a traditional environment. Because of that, students who have family ties to, for example, Tagalog, Dutch, or Polish have the option to learn the language and explore the culture connected to the language. As students study the grammar and structure of the language, they also choose a small project of their interest to explore. We provide a list of options and some basic instructions, and we allow room for the students to follow their own interests. Students who are genuinely curious about culture and community will choose projects closely tied to cultural aspects.

One student who was born in Turkey and moved to the United States immediately after was excited to learn more about her Turkish culture. She perfected a dessert recipe and explained the significance that it had for her. Another student who had spoken English all his life learned Italian to connect with his family history. He watched Italian movies with his dad, reported the words and structures he learned, and reflected on the conversations he and his dad had about Italian culture and family memories.

The online context gives students time and autonomy to practice language skills. We can use this flexible format to encourage students to explore the meaningful connections between language and their family history. (David Prats Vidal, personal communication, June 10, 2021)

Create Context and Use Humor

Show students learning a language is much more than the spoken and written word. Language is deeply tied to its root culture. Formal versus informal language, the way people ask for what they need, terms connected to cultural activities and traditions, and the nuances of humor are complex. Ask students to consider these aspects in their home language, and then translate what they notice to their language exploration in other contexts.

Laughter and humor are powerful connectors. They are also often culturally specific. My (Kathryn's) grandmother's first language was Yiddish, and she always insisted on telling me jokes in Yiddish (a language I don't speak, but have started studying) because the jokes "simply don't translate to English."

Stephanie and I have seen this same perception across many cultural and linguistic contexts—for example, when we have traveled to Brazil or Vietnam to work with students in our blended program. Language learning and humor are always involved in how we connect with young people. I love to learn school-appropriate, short jokes or teenage slang in my students' home language and incorporate those into our lessons and interactions with students. Students also love to coach us on pronunciation, especially when the difference between two unrelated words is difficult for our English-speaking ears to discern. We've learned it's helpful to involve a native-speaking adult in these student-led lessons so that we don't end up saying something inappropriate!

A well-placed joke in any language, an invitation for levity, and a hearty laugh can change the temperature in the room after a challenging lesson or event. Encourage students to share jokes, riddles, and moments of delight throughout your classes.

Connect Choice, Language, and Community

Given the chance, students will find specific things about a language and its accompanying culture that excite them. They may be interested in recipes, family stories, art and music, or travel. Give them choices in how they explore this connection, and encourage them to come up with their own ideas too. David uses these ideas with his students. Here are some example exercises to explore the connection between a student's target language and its culture.

- Find a children's song from your target language. Record yourself singing it, and share!

- Play a game you are used to playing, but play it in your target language.

- Change the language on your electronics to your target language for a week.

- Find a recipe connected to the culture of your target language, make it, and share with others.

Explore World Language Learning

As students explore new languages, help them reflect on why they choose a specific one to learn. Here are some exploratory questions that educators can ask as they and students engage in world language learning.

- What is a language you are interested in learning? What draws you to that language?
- Is there a language (or more than one language) that you already have some prior knowledge of and want to build from?
- Is there a language (or more than one language) that is important to your family or cultural history?
- Do you have friends who speak another language that you would like to learn?
- Are you interested in a particular culture? If so, learning the language is an important step in cultural education.
- Are there languages connected to your career goals (such as business, medicine, international relations, or classics)?
- Do you have plans (or an interest) to travel to another country? If so, your travel goals and plans might point you to a language for further study.
- Are there ancient texts you would like to read in their original language?
- Is there a language spoken by many people in your school or local community that would be helpful for you to learn?

You can read more about how to support multilingual learners and world language learning in chapter 5 (page 131). Knowing why students are interested in a language is the first step to finding meaning as they explore it.

Thitinun Boonseng: Global Experiences, Online Spaces

Thitinun (Ta) Boonseng designs educational programs that create enrichment experiences for audiences of all ages from various international and intercultural backgrounds. As the world becomes more connected, his passion is to create a learning environment where more students get the opportunity to explore their interests while building international connections and fostering personal growth.

The best schools become a kind of home. Students spend at least eight or more hours each day with their friends, peers, teachers, and coaches in a traditional school building. In an online context, students can approach learning and opportunities unique to their preferences.

I coordinate the enrichment and extracurricular programs of a complex blended school system. Our aim is to provide students with the best learning experience they can find beyond their formal academic credits; we want to ensure students have a full, rich experience with opportunities to explore new interests and possibilities during their time with us. Often, our students are deeply involved in time-intensive commitments such as horse shows, dirt-bike racing, acting, and sports. Others blend online high school education with internships, college courses, or jobs.

Designing an extracurricular program for an online or blended school is tricky, but we've learned lessons from applying what we've done in the past in an in-person setting to the online context. We were happily surprised to find that online extracurricular opportunities aren't just a substitute for these opportunities in person or a way to make do. Instead, online resources let us cast a wider net to serve more students in more creative ways.

Every July, we recruit high school students from around the world for a two-week in-person experience in career exploration that encourages students to explore 21st century career possibilities and helps prepare them for the post–high school experience. We connect our students with university faculty members and industry professionals through simulating activities during site visits to academic departments, Fortune 500 companies, and nonprofit and government offices. The program is exceptionally well received by international students who explore new cultures and their potential future careers. The domestic students enjoy engaging with friends from other cultures; and for those two weeks, we form a diverse learning community.

In 2020, we needed to design a virtual enrichment program to provide a rich and fun experience for our students. The programmatic question became, How can we form a robust, tight-knit learning community in a short time without physical interactions? We began experimenting with these strategies, which we are translating into other extracurricular experiences with students. (Thitinun [Ta] Boonseng, personal communication, November 23, 2020)

> **CONNECTED TEACHING COMMITMENT**
> **Go Beyond the Classroom**
>
> Learn about every student's interests, passions, and strengths. Ask about hobbies and sports. Incorporate these into teaching examples, and celebrate them in class meetings. If possible, attend online or in-person events students take part in (such as band concerts, speeches, and recitals), or ask students to share or perform excerpts of these in class if they feel comfortable.

Strategies for Creating Community Through Extracurricular Opportunities

As you've read throughout this chapter, school is a community project. Extracurricular activities give students opportunities to pursue passions and try out options within a community they already are part of. Teachers, staff, coaches, and faculty who lead these opportunities have a great variety of resources to share. The structures and activities that work well for a student in one area often translate to another area. The following strategies are based on what Ta has learned throughout many years of organizing events and shepherding students through extracurricular activities. They are helpful to consider when structuring your classroom as well.

Intentionally Onboard Students, Faculty, Staff, and Guests

When starting a new student club, extracurricular activity, or educational program, it is imperative to build a positive culture and create a sense of belonging. That begins with a who's who and general program overview. Build a slideshow or handout with an overview of the program, its main objectives, and a list of all the people and their roles. Develop norms for expectations and behavior to establish the ground rules with the student group. Design a timeline for each meeting to see when students will join the session, who they will meet, what the conversation will be like, and how they can contact the adults if they have a technical difficulty. The clearer teachers can be regarding what the group is about and how it will function, the better.

Redefine Time

While there is definitely room for organic conversations online, meeting online requires a different pace to mediate screen fatigue and the sedentary nature of this kind of gathering. For a large, intensive program like the comprehensive virtual enrichment program that Ta runs, advanced scheduling and intentionality around how best to use synchronous time is paramount. In addition to what they do in their regular classroom, his students meet for two hours each day for ten consecutive weekdays. That's a total of twenty hours of engaging instruction and small-team activities, bolstered by self-directed projects with support, over a two-week period. Ta and his team have employed interactive experiences to help break up the time spent sitting and looking at a screen. Like Ta, you might try breaking up long video sessions with midclass movement activities, such as scavenger hunts or group stretches. The goal is that students have enough time to accomplish something without leaving the meeting group feeling drained or, worse yet, bored and demotivated. This requires a nice blend of interactive and movement-based activities, laughter, and virtual sessions that don't run too long. When planning for online sessions, look at your agenda. Have you built in health and movement breaks? Do you give students plenty of opportunities to interact and engage? Consider utilizing the games and humor suggestions from earlier in this chapter (page 21).

Invite Everyone to Participate

At the beginning of the meeting, encourage every member to share their voice in the room. Through conversation or in the chat, ask a question or implement a short activity so everyone has a chance to respond. Use short questions such as the following.

- Can you describe how you're feeling today in two words?
- When was the last time you laughed out loud?
- What book or show are you into right now?
- If you had a surprise free hour today, what would you do with it?
- What's one thing you plan to do this week that energizes you?

For activities, have students show off a favorite (or most ridiculous) dance move, do a facial impression of the emoji that best represents their particular mood, or run and grab the first thing they can find in a certain color or on a certain theme. Or ask students a series of questions with choices where they stand up if they agree with choice one and stay seated if they agree with choice two. These types of activities invite everyone to speak up, and teachers can build on the new energy to carry students through the rest of the meeting.

Encourage Playfulness During Class Time

In any mentoring group, there will be times of problem solving and hard work. Have fun together while working to accomplish tasks. Encourage sharing of memes and jokes of the day. Stephanie often gives students guidelines for school-appropriate humor and memes, including, "Keep it G-rated"; "If you wouldn't share something with your grandmother, don't share it in class"; and "Disrespectful or discriminatory jokes are not funny or welcome in our class." Create a team screen background to put up together in meetings (such as a common photo, a team collage, or a Canva design). Have wacky snack days, where everyone brings a food that reminds them of a celebration. Encourage theme days: hat day, days for certain colors ("Everyone wear red!" "Put on the most denim you can find!"), or pajama day. Ask everyone to show up in their best school spirit outfit. Get creative; bring fun and surprise to each meeting, and encourage students to contribute their ideas for variety too.

Mark a Strong Ending

Teachers will encounter several transitions and endings during their time with students. As each meeting ends, they should bring the group together with a question or focus. One question to consider together is, "What's one idea or action step you'll focus on between now and our next meeting?" It is vital that you send a reminder message to recap with students what they learned that day, what they need to work on before the next session, and what they should do when they have questions.

As each project or task ends, take some time to celebrate. Ask students to reflect on what they did well and what they would do differently next time. Share any teacher observations and encouragement for the team and for each individual. Encourage students to treat themselves after a job well done.

Finally, as the group ends for the semester or year, celebrate big. Consider inviting students to a final online meeting, and ask that they bring their own snacks on a certain theme, make a group collage of words or images to reflect their experience (Jamboard and Canva are great for this), or come ready to share highlights from previous class time together. Taking these moments throughout class time together to say, "We did it!" helps build a strong community and create excitement for the group.

Jeff Kopolow:
Classrooms Do Not Exist in a Vacuum

Jeff Kopolow is a veteran social studies teacher of over fifty years who currently teaches in an online school. He refers to himself as adventurous, a sixties kid, and a little bit of a rebel. He often comments that nothing can surprise him anymore, which makes him a go-to for both experienced and new educators seeking wisdom (which Jeff provides with his trademark dry humor).

One of the most common questions I hear is this: How have students changed from the time you started teaching? This is a simple question. But the answer may not be quite so simple, as it requires educators to think about more than just students in the context of their classroom culture. Teachers must consider how that culture interacts with a school culture, a family culture, a religion culture, and many more. Educators know their classrooms do not exist in a vacuum, and no matter what they do to create a culture in them, teachers must be aware of all these other factors.

What is classroom culture? It is best explained as follows:

> Classroom culture involves creating an environment where students feel safe and free to be involved. It's a space where everyone should feel accepted and included in everything. Students should be comfortable with sharing how they feel, and teachers should be willing to take it in to help improve learning. (Point to Point Education, 2018)

The operative words here are "creating an environment." Let's explore this.

For many, not being able to stand a few feet from live students and establish a culture within a physical classroom is uncomfortable or intimidating. However, if teachers show confidence that the virtual classrooms are viable and will work, students will believe in them. If teachers continue to accept their students for who they are and let them know teachers value each of them as unique individuals, students will relate to them. If teachers demand academic and behavioral performance consistent with their students' abilities and do so in a clearly fair and equitable manner, students will measure up. Whatever their concept of good teaching is, or how they believe students learn, teachers must have a classroom culture supportive of these concepts.

I think of Tom, a junior in my in-person U.S. history class. He grumbled that he absolutely hated history. I asked if he wanted to graduate from high school, which he did. I pointed out that he was in a required course that he had to pass. I said that if he would just do enough work to give me a reason to pass him, I would. "For real?" he said. "For real!" I answered. As it turned out, Tom did more than the bare minimum. Once he realized I was with and not against him, he felt less pressure and became engaged and willing to try different tasks. He ended the year with a strong B, and I wrote his college recommendation. Teachers can make classroom culture work, one student at a time. (Jeff Kopolow, personal communication, September 14, 2020)

Strategies for Building a Positive Classroom Culture in Blended and Online Settings

Recognizing the unique attitudes and needs in your particular classroom is an important step in impacting a positive classroom culture. A positive classroom culture is complex; at its center are opportunities for students to engage and participate safely, and encouragement for them to think more deeply and develop toward goals—all facilitated by a caring, invested teacher. In short, if students feel seen and heard, and if they must communicate thoughtfully and respectfully, then the culture of a classroom thrives. The following strategies come from Jeff Kopolow's over fifty years of experience as this kind of caring, invested educator. The breadth of Jeff's career is unique, and here, you have the opportunity to learn from an influential educator with a strong voice as you consider how these strategies can apply to your classroom.

Create a Community Code of Conduct

To learn and take risks, students need to be and feel safe. The blended and online classroom requires that teachers become sensitive to disparities in the health and technological access facing households. Teachers also need to focus on emotional safety. They must establish a learning code of conduct. Also sometimes called the *class norms*, a *learning code of conduct* sets expectations for how a class behaves, builds relationships, and functions on a daily basis (see the example in figure 1.1). What are the ground rules for participation? What are the expectations for using the chat feature or taking screenshots of virtual meetings (Brackett, Levy, & Hoffmann, 2020)?

The best learning codes of conduct are those the class designs together. Teachers can do this over several days at the beginning of the semester or year, and then periodically revisit the list. This list will serve as an important reference point when beginning new projects, tackling something challenging, or recalibrating things that are a little out of balance. To begin brainstorming a learning code of conduct, you can ask students to envision their ideal class. Have some fun thinking together about the year ahead.

> **Our class agrees to follow this learning code of conduct.**
>
> 1. Keep the focus on learning.
> 2. Show respect in your words and actions.
> 3. Make space for all voices.
> 4. Ask for help when you need it.
> 5. Keep technology focused on classwork.

Figure 1.1: Example learning code of conduct.

Define

What is the class code of conduct? Once the main ideas are in place, the class is ready to create a code of conduct together. Here are some things to keep in mind.

- Use positive language that articulates what the class wants to see. "Use kind and respectful words and actions" is better than "Don't talk over each other."
- Create general-enough guidelines that specific rules can fall under them. An example guideline is, "We all have important ideas to share with the class." A rule might be, "Each person in your group must participate."
- Shorter is better. A strong code of conduct is short enough that students can easily remember it or at least take it in at a glance. Five to seven guidelines are plenty.
- Some teachers ask students to read the code aloud and verbally agree to follow it. Others ask students to sign a copy. Create focus and buy-in in a way that feels authentic to the class community.

Support

After establishing a learning code of conduct together, display it where students can see it. If feasible, begin each online meeting with a slide that presents the code of conduct in a creative, colorful way. Or create a class chant capturing the essence of each guideline, and repeat it with students each time the class meets, or once a week or as often as seems best for the class. When introducing a new rule, explain which guideline it fits under. When a student strays in behavior or focus, refer to the guidelines. The point is, keep the code of conduct present in everyone's mind to focus on class welfare and productivity.

Review

It might also be helpful to review the code of conduct periodically. As the students grow together, and through the ebb and flow of the semester, their needs might change. Is there anything to change or replace? The code of conduct must serve the students in meeting their goals, and it can be a living code that grows with the class. Reviewing this code of conduct before major projects, during times of stress, and at the start of each new quarter can be grounding and beneficial.

Maintain High Expectations

Holding students to high expectations is an act of care and affirmation (Fishman-Weaver, 2019). Communicate to students that you believe they are capable of achieving at elevated levels and you support them in doing so. Set individualized learning goals for students, allowing students to self-select the level of challenge they need and can manage right now.

CONNECTED TEACHING COMMITMENT
Honor Student Voices

> Listening deeply to students and saying yes to their ideas is a transformative teaching practice. When teachers listen deeply and are open to taking lessons in new and student-led directions, they can launch projects, initiatives, and dialogues they could have never imagined on their own. As the technical tools available to teachers continue to expand, they have new opportunities to honor student voices and make room for youth stories. Through podcasts, visual essays, collaborative journals on Google Docs, and mini-documentaries, educators can harness digital tools to support students in sharing their stories and amplifying their voices through new mediums and in new spaces. These practices send an affirming message that students matter.

Brainstorm Learning Goals and Values

As the class brainstorms, allow students to say what they really want. Expect some answers like, "No homework!" or "Lots of free time!" All students will have a chance to narrow down the list as the class works together; plus, their funny or extra-hopeful answers about playing video games and avoiding homework will give teachers insights into activities individual students enjoy doing.

Use the following questions to begin this activity.

- What three words describe a class you enjoy?
- When you are learning something new, what is most helpful to you?
- What distracts or prevents you from learning?
- What does respect mean to you? How about safety?
- What role does technology have in learning?
- What is one thing you wish teachers knew about you?

After having a rousing and eye-opening discussion about what they value and find most helpful in school, the class is ready to start narrowing down ideas into categories. The goal is for students to think through and articulate what it takes for a class to move smoothly. In other words, how can the teacher and students together create an environment where all can learn, grow, and even have some fun? You might find it helpful to start by thinking in four broad categories, or create ones that best fit your classroom. How should the teacher and students treat the following?

1. **Learning:** "What does it take to create a space where different personalities can learn?"
2. **Each other:** "How can we show respect, be kind, and offer help to those around us?"
3. **Materials and technology:** "What are we responsible for? How can we use technology as a benefit and not a distraction?"
4. **Themselves:** "What do we bring to the classroom? What part do we play in contributing to conversation and projects and helping others?"

By this point, you will have a lengthy list of hopes and ideas for a safe, productive classroom. Ask students to begin sorting through this list in small groups or with partners to identify common ideas. Which parts of this list are similar, and which can they combine? Create another, shorter list of the ideas that stand out as essential and those that have been repeated several times in different ways.

Key Classroom Takeaway: The World Is Small and Deeply Connected

Marilyn's narrative spanned across time and place. David considered the multiplicity of world languages. Ta demonstrated how he brings students together from around the globe. Jeff shared how he has built positive classroom cultures across many different contexts. All these stories point to a fundamental truth: the world is small and deeply connected. Drawing on the wisdom and resources of your school community opens up new possibilities for learning, connection, and support. This community includes within-school groups (such as classroom peers, faculty and staff, and the school population) and beyond-school groups (such as families, neighborhoods, and cities). Casting school as a community project asks educators to build bridges beyond their classroom walls. This includes inviting and affirming the cultures, identities, and wisdom that their students' families bring to the learning space.

Educators are at an intersection between traditional learning models and an emerging online space. Many believe that emerging space is overdue. For decades, teachers have grouped students by age—or, as Ken Robinson (2009, p. 230) puts it, "date of manufacture"—and geography. Teachers have taught students in models rigidly bound by place and space. Online and blended solutions are opening up new possibilities, each with expansive potential to rethink what it means to teach and learn well beyond the four walls of the traditional classroom. In conducting research for this book, it became clear to us that talented educators around the world are teaching in spite of challenges and because of a belief in connecting with students.

Online and blended models cause educators and school leaders to think differently about space, place, and community. As learning shifts to living rooms and kitchen tables, new school conversations are happening at different times and between different family members. Further, students learn classrooms are flexible constructions, and learning can happen anywhere. Equitable classroom practices begin with relationships and community. When teachers know their students well, not only as learners but also as young people with families, they are better able to respond to needs and challenges. Educators are also more likely to respond from a place of care and compassion.

As classes transition to more online learning options, educators must advocate for equitable access, ask hard questions, implement new solutions, and vigilantly continue to put students first. As you strive to do this, take a moment to reflect on ways to apply all that you've learned in this chapter to your educational practice.

Summary

Building relationships is vital to a successful global community project. As educators reimagine student support in online and blended contexts, they often find rich and surprising resources available within their schools and larger communities. This chapter laid the groundwork for building the foundation of this community project, beginning with identifying what communities exist within your broader educational community. Situating your classroom within the broader context of school and student communities puts you more in touch with your students and deepens the intentionality of your educational practice.

We learned from Marilyn Toalson that the work of building connection often begins even before students log on for their first class. Taking steps to meet students and begin conversations before class starts will help ensure your online course feels warm and inviting to students and their families. From David Prats Vidal, we learned how to creatively engage community voices and welcome them into the larger school community through language learning and a celebration of culture. Thitinun Boonseng wisely advised to bring structure to the online experience by marking strong beginnings and endings. When students do not physically enter or leave a space, teachers must recreate the sensation of entering and exiting learning time. Jeff Kopolow taught us the importance of working with students to set clear expectations and class values by honoring their voices, opinions, and individuality as teachers create their class structure. He emphasizes the transformation in student achievement and engagement that can occur when students know a teacher is really listening to what they say.

All these strategies share the common goal of achieving a more intentional and encouraging sense of connectedness between educators and students. In chapter 2, we will build on the work of inclusion and community building by identifying the unique advantages of online learning, and we will consider how educators can build on strengths and implement school counseling and student supports in the online and blended classroom. Please find your space for reflective practice for chapter 1 on the following page.

Chapter 1: Apply It to Your Practice

Working individually or in learning teams, reflect on these questions, and implement the commitments to your practice (for more information on engaging with these questions, please see the section titled Space for Reflective Practice on page 9 in the introduction). As always, strive to move your reflection to action.

React to the Chapter

What are your key takeaways from this chapter? What was surprising to read? What did you connect with?

Analyze School Community

Each school community is composed of many related and intersecting communities. Brainstorm a list of the various communities in your school. Start big, with the entire school as one type of community. Work down from there. What large communities do you notice? For example, do most families come to you from a specific neighborhood? Which smaller ones are present? Are there youth programs or faith communities that many of your students participate in? What identities are represented in your school demographics, including race, ethnicity, and country of origin? Which are best served? Which might be underserved? Use this information to guide your action steps as you help build community in your space.

Identify Community Strengths

Marilyn Toalson shared that it takes teachers, family, friends, and peers to support students in all the ways they need. Who is in your community? What community organizations might you connect with? What peers, faculty, staff, family, and friends do you know who would join you in speaking into students' lives? Who has special talents or skills to share? You may have a friend with a special talent who can be a guest speaker to interested small groups. You and another teacher might be talented in teaching different kinds of topics or skills; perhaps you could periodically trade classes to teach in your passion area and build community between classes. Remember your community extends beyond the school's faculty and staff. Seek ways to invite families and communities into the classroom not only as guests but also as experts (readers, lecturers, coaches, and demonstrators).

Build in Purposeful Individual, Small-Group, and Whole-Group Activities

As teachers develop online or blended classrooms, students need a combination of synchronous (online or real-time instruction) and asynchronous (offline or anytime practice and instruction) strategies. Use different combinations of whole-group, small-group, and independent sessions to help students master concepts, learn skills, and practice new strategies (Abadzi, 1985). Use synchronous moments to build community, talk through class material, and directly teach new concepts. Brian Stuhlman, a middle school educator featured in chapter 6 (page 163), offers guidance in the following chart on how teachers might organize their independent, small-group, and whole-group time around connection and learning.

Online Planning: Ways and Means		
Independent Time	Small-Group Time	Whole-Group Time
Individual students can: - Read - Watch videos - Take surveys - Interview people (family or neighbors) - Design and conduct projects - Make real-world connections - Experiment - Use the writing process	Small groups of students can experience: - Comprehension checks - Topic discussions - Peer review - Differentiation supports - Time management and organizational support - Feedback	Whole groups of students can experience: - Focusing moments - Lecture - Discussion - Preview of reading - Socratic seminars - Demonstrations of strategies and specific skills - Mathematics modeling

Learn With and From Your Community

In her seminal essay "Mirrors, Windows, and Sliding Glass Doors," Rudine Sims Bishop (1990) uses the analogy of windows and mirrors as a call to diversify the books and resources teachers ask students to read. Windows transport people outside their experience into new realms. Mirrors reflect who they are. Sliding glass doors invite people to step into new realities. Use this language with students as you explore books and resources and honor the wealth of backgrounds and insights students bring to your classroom. What is a mirror to one student will be a window to another. Organize language celebration days and play games to learn about words, customs, and cultures; invite students and families to be the teachers at these celebrations. Make time to discuss what feels like home to different students, and think about how you might reflect this in your class space.

Sources: Abadzi, H. (1985). Ability grouping effects on academic achievement and self-esteem: Who performs in the long run as expected. Journal of Educational Research, 79(1), 36–40.

Bishop, R. S. (1990). Mirrors, windows, and sliding glass doors. Perspectives, 6(3), ix–xi.

Cultivating Strengths-Based Approaches for Inclusion, Support, and Counseling

2

Our (Kathryn and Stephanie's) school context is blended and asynchronous, meaning some students work individually at their own pace through a course, while others spend some time working in a classroom with a teacher and some time working at their own pace. In blended classes, teachers schedule chats across multiple time zones and thousands of miles. For example, our students log in from an island off the coast of Honduras; a learning center in Hanoi, Vietnam; and a bedroom in Lawrence, Kansas—all to chat together about advanced statistics. In our asynchronous classes, students use messaging and video chats to meet with instructors and our student-support team. The connections between people and communities are getting easier to form over distance, thanks to technological advancements allowing digital connection.

Proximity is often central to how educators think about school counseling. For example, when you imagine a school counseling session, do you set the scene in a cozy office? Are fidget toys on a nearby bookshelf and tissues on the desk as students explore big feelings, challenges, and graduation plans? If the family joins, do you have to pull in a few more chairs and crowd them together in this small, warm space? In blended learning models, we find other meaningful ways to connect when physical proximity isn't possible.

Essential Question

How can strengths-based approaches transform student support in online and blended contexts?

Chapter Learning Objectives

- Consider the unique physical, emotional, and intellectual advantages of self-paced, online, or blended learning.

- Identify the *village*: community members who support students in a variety of ways.

- Design a multitiered system of supports for students.

- Honor story and individual context in student-support plans.

Key Terms

504 plan. Section 504 of the Rehabilitation Act of 1973 is a disability civil rights law in the United States. Students may qualify for services under section 504 if they "have a physical or mental impairment that substantially limits one or more major life activities" (Office for Civil Rights, 2020). If a student qualifies for services, schools may write a 504 plan, which is an articulated plan for accommodations or supports to ensure the student can access the full range of school activities. Some examples of these supports include extended time on tests, health breaks with the school nurse, audio resources, larger print, and a quiet place to take exams.

comprehensive school counseling. A systematic and holistic approach to student support including guidance curriculum, individual planning, responsive services, and system support (Gysbers & Henderson, 2012).

growth mindset. Carol Dweck's (2006) theory that talent development is malleable (as opposed to fixed). Educators who work to cultivate growth mindset in their classrooms emphasize process over product and teach that hard work and persistence are teachable and important skills in achieving goals. Dweck's research asserts that "it is our [educators'] responsibility to create a context in which a growth mindset can flourish" (Gross-Loh, 2016).

individualized education program (IEP). In special education, a legally binding document outlining a qualifying student's goals, services, accommodations, and needs. The public school a student attends must carry out this plan. Qualifying for an IEP requires an identification and evaluation of a student's disability. Note: Some educators have transferred the idea of individualized education programs to other student populations beyond special education.

Individuals With Disabilities Education Act (IDEA). A federal law in the United States that guarantees every student access to a free and appropriate public education in the least restrictive environment possible.

multitiered system of supports (MTSS). Models that are often illustrated by a pyramid with a broad Tier 1 layer as the foundation (supports all students receive) and a smaller pointed Tier 3 layer at the top (intensified supports needed only by a small percentage of the school population).

radical hope. The practice of embracing possibility in the face of challenges. Radical hope asks people to assume positive intent from others and to be open to new and unfamiliar solutions.

I (Stephanie) often have the chance to meet with students who need some extra support one-on-one. Students determine the setting—some prefer messaging, some like to meet online with the camera off, and others like to meet over video face-to-face. One of my students is neurodiverse and experiences other health issues that make it difficult for her to attend school every day. For Emily, our self-paced online option is a solution that allows her to both work at her own pace and attend to her health needs. She and I meet upon Emily's request to check in, talk over her progress in her classes, and set pacing plans to help her finish all her classes so that she can meet her graduation goal of 2023. At first, these meetings felt a bit awkward; there were long pauses as we got to know each other and strange transitions as we tried to move from chit-chat to more focused conversations on academic progress. Emily's collection of *squishies* (stress balls in various shapes and sizes) helped us break the ice. I noticed her rather large collection on the shelf behind her, and she lit up as she grabbed several and described their different textures and functions. Now, each time we meet, she shows me her newest acquisition, and she models it and how it works as we turn our attention to her courses. We meet online, but her willingness to show me an important coping skill she uses helps connect us and gives us an avenue to explore other topics. (I'm considering building my own collection of squishies.)

In chapter 1 (page 15), you learned about the importance of connection and community. Chapter 2 draws from conversations with school counselors, student-support professionals, and administrators who are wrestling with questions about individualized learning in the context of international, online, and blended schools. We explore how to implement comprehensive guidance models and an MTSS, how to take expansive spaces and make them small, how to bridge distance, and how to individualize learning plans across cultures and contexts.

MTSS models are often illustrated by a pyramid with a broad Tier 1 layer as the foundation and a smaller pointed Tier 3 layer at the top (Buffum, Mattos, & Malone, 2018). Figure 2.1 is an inverted MTSS triangle that illustrates how educators can move from universal supports to targeted interventions based on student needs.

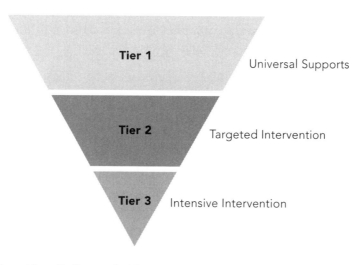

Source: Adapted from Buffum et al., 2018.

Figure 2.1: Multitiered system of supports model.

It is important to note that this graphic may not represent all school realities or contexts. For example, some schools may have a higher percentage of students needing more targeted interventions. The three tiers of a multitiered system of supports are as follows (Swenson, Horner, Bradley, & Calkins, 2017).

- **Tier 1 (universal supports):** All students in the system receive these foundational and universal supports. Tier 1 consists of rigorous curriculum and varied instructional strategies joining with social-emotional learning, development, and relationship building. These pieces effectively meet the needs of a vast majority of students.
- **Tier 2 (targeted intervention):** This tier consists of brief targeted interventions designed to meet the needs of students struggling academically or socially and emotionally. Traditionally, this may mean tutoring or reteaching or a few visits with a school counselor until the student is able to thrive on the Tier 1 supports.
- **Tier 3 (intensive intervention):** This tier provides intense and ongoing support for the small percentage of students with acute or chronic needs.

You'll see the narratives in this section iterate all, parts, or adapted versions of these support tiers. Please take inspiration from their practical application to create a multitiered support system that suits your educational community's needs.

Lived-Experience Case Studies

The narratives in this section are offered by counselors and support service staff. They represent lived experiences young people bring to online and blended classrooms and underscore the need for compassionate, asset-based individual planning.

In a connected world, stories are the shortest distance between people. Students everywhere are living diverse and important stories. Serving students well and meeting them right where they are require knowing and honoring these lived experiences. We'll begin with Matt Miltenberg's experience building a multitiered system of supports.

Matt Miltenberg: Building a Multitiered System of Supports for Online and Blended Schools

Matt Miltenberg's experience as a counselor, teacher, and coach spans a variety of settings and grade levels ranging from his global online and blended experience with Mizzou Academy to work in brick-and-mortar comprehensive high schools and elementary schools. Currently, he serves as a counselor and student-support specialist at Poudre High School in Fort Collins, Colorado.

The following (paraphrased) widely referenced parable is familiar to educators, coaches, and counselors. It is often attributed to Irving Zola (Heath, 2020).

> "Help!"
>
> On the banks of a river, two men are fishing when they hear thrashing and shouting. One of them makes out the head of a child in the rapids, dives in, and manages to safely bring the child to shore. After a few moments, the child heads off into the woods and the men resume fishing.
>
> A few minutes later, another child splashes by, and the second fisherman jumps in to save her. Before he is ashore, the first fisherman spots a third child and finds himself back in the water. Not long after, two children float by together. Then three. As the first man prepares to jump to the rescue again, he sees the second fisherman takes off into the woods.
>
> "Hey! Where are you going? These kids will drown!"
>
> "I'm going to the village upstream to find out why all these kids are falling in the river!"

The themes in this parable are foundational to the way educators structure their schools and work with students. As the story unfolds, educators can recognize how their own context is much like the setting of the parable. There are caring adults in villages and along the riverbank. There are children who face challenges. There is a river that represents the dangers those challenges can bring. However, when educators translate this work to the hybrid or online space, they must ask themselves several questions as they consider the challenges they see and work to discover these challenges' sources and how they can help overcome them: "What does the river look like? Can we still see it? Can we hear the shouts for help? If we hear them, can we wade into the river ourselves? Is there one village upstream or three villages? Five villages? A hundred?" In short, educators' takeaway about this parable is that support for students is complicated. At times, educators must act immediately to address problems for a short-term solution and safety. They also need to be proactive by analyzing system processes and address challenges in a way that sustains their school community over time.

These questions underscore the unique challenges facing professionals working in student support and intervention in an online, hybrid, or co-taught model. In these spaces, educators must be more intentional and creative about going upstream, designing an infrastructure supporting social-emotional learning and academic skill development. Educators must build relationships allowing them to effectively identify and access students when they struggle.

For several years, I worked with an international blended school system that served thousands of students across the globe. These students learned in a variety of settings, ranging from the individual student taking one online course on their own to students learning in co-teaching classrooms with classroom teachers in Brazil, Honduras, China, and elsewhere. Our rivers were vast, varied, and branching, with hundreds of upstream villages in each tributary. To support this vast array of student backgrounds and needs, we focused on adapting an MTSS model; the following details outline how educators can use this model to support each student in their school community.

Build the Foundation (Tier 1)

As our school rapidly grew, faculty and staff quickly got to work building a support structure to help students succeed in a blended model. Through conversations with partner teachers and intentional learning about our student population, we identified the key foundational skills to put in place quickly. This included creating an avenue so that every student was connected to an adult, and creating opportunities for relationship building, professional development on social-emotional learning in a blended environment, and clear systems for when instructors noticed safety concerns in student submissions and communication.

We collaborated with educators and counselors to develop support plans and resources. The plan initially turned to academic skills in reading, writing, research, and test preparation, and that was only a start. Beyond those skills, the goal was to give students strategies they needed to navigate adolescence more broadly. Being a child is hard, and some strategies adults take for granted require a learning curve and a lot of practice for young students. Our aim was to teach strategies for neuroplasticity and growth-mindset development; mindfulness and stress management; sleep, exercise, and healthy-habit development; basic listening skills and antibullying or upstander behavior; goal setting; and mental contrasting. These evolving resources remain available in online, blended, and in-person formats.

This type of learning and development couldn't happen in a silo; it needed to infuse our broader curriculum. As we considered this, we discussed Shane J. Lopez's (2013) psychological construct of hope and dived into Angela Duckworth, Katherine L. Milkman, David Laibson, David Scott Yeager, and James J. Gross's research focusing on developing skills that help students thrive, such as grit, curiosity, growth mindset, gratitude, zest, and more (Duckworth & Gross, 2014; Duckworth, Milkman, & Laibson, 2019; Duckworth & Yeager, 2015). We built these concepts and opportunities across interdisciplinary courses, and realized knowing these concepts and practicing these skills were only part of what would keep students safe as they navigated new and uncertain waters. Student resilience depends on relationships; each student needed to connect with an adult in their village.

Again, because our villages—our communities—looked so varied, this required multiple layers and approaches. One constant was the use of feedback to build relationships. Our instructional team went through orientations, trained on sample papers, and continued to work together to provide consistent and warm rubric-centered feedback. Every single submitted assignment received copious feedback focused on building a connection with the student by ensuring they felt what they wrote was seen and important.

For online students, we looked for opportunities to foster connections for students locally, restructuring our personal development course so students would connect weekly with a local mentor of their choosing for guided discussions and reflections. Reading the reports from these conversations was affirming; there were ripples spreading into communities worldwide.

For students in blended contexts, we required an advisory period to provide unstructured time for one-to-one support, as well as relationship- and team-building activities. The team-building activities could be as simple as a fun game or as involved as a group service project, as long as they built a trusting human connection. Students felt cared for and knew they were part of a thoughtful learning community. This meant that when students struggled, they were more willing to stretch and take academic risks, knowing they could reach out to their academic community for help when needed.

Respond to Higher Needs (Tiers 2 and 3)

Universal supports built a strong foundation; however, extenuating circumstances and special needs sometimes required additional interventions and supports. A primary strategy I sought to establish in the large online school system where I worked was capacity building. Although my school served thousands of students, the student-support team was quite small: two trained counselors and two thoughtful administrators working with students all over the globe. By fostering relationships with key learning partners, their team created a vast and connected network where students were never too far from a caring adult. That adult might be able to quickly lend a hand, reteach a skill, or coach a student through a personal challenge. They could also trigger a higher-level support response for more intensive Tier 2 or Tier 3 student situations.

To consistently identify higher-tier needs, we trained our instructional team and co-teachers to look for signs indicating struggling students. We invited students to be more personal in their writing, and it wasn't uncommon for concerns around self-harm, anxiety, or abuse at home to show up in their work. We created an efficient system to centralize and monitor student concerns through an instructor's recognition of a red flag coupled with a quick referral to counselors and administrators who then reviewed student submissions and developed intervention plans. In some cases, we made direct calls to parents, advising families how to monitor the concern at home or seek services locally, and coached our co-teaching partners on how to best enact an effective local school or community response.

When student needs (such as medical treatment, learning disabilities, or trauma responses) required ongoing intervention, we developed student success plans similar to 504 plans internally or with our teaching partners. In some parts of the world, this formal process for support planning around inclusion and disability is a new concept. One of our Brazilian partners, Roberta Mayumi da Silva, became a maven at crafting support structures and interventions that would work with our co-teaching model and the student's home school. With ongoing support structures in place, many students thrived. I am proud of the way we helped students succeed in an online learning environment despite the mental health challenges that would have prevented success in traditional schools.

As the adage goes, no one cares how much you know until they know how much you care. We consistently found this to be true in our work. During my first trip to Brazil, our team walked into South American schools to smiling students who felt like they already knew us. I can still feel the hug in a hotel lobby just off Avenida Paulista in São Paulo from a teacher in tears because we had identified a student's suicidal ideation in an essay and helped intervene before it was too late.

Educational structures will continuously evolve in new and innovative ways, whether by intentional design or due to unforeseen circumstances like a global pandemic. My work in online and blended education taught me no matter what your learning community or village looks like, you can connect with your students and teach them to learn and play safely at the river's edge. (Matt Miltenberg, personal communication, December 29, 2020)

Strategies for Building a Support System in Online and Blended Models

Matt Miltenberg has served as a school counselor across a variety of in-person, online, blended, and international settings at the elementary and high school levels. He brings to this work a deep commitment to the idea that students are well known by adults in their communities and well connected to peers and resources. I (Kathryn) have been fortunate to work with Matt across these different school contexts and work closely with him on student support. In the following sections, Stephanie and I share some key strategies we have learned from working with Matt to expand access to compassionate student support in our own global blended school system.

Survey Your Context

When considering how to provide student support, you must first learn *where* students need support. Sometimes, these issues are clear and obvious, like a student who is failing a class or has withdrawn from groups. Other times, they are subtle and require educators to intentionally notice them, like a student who stops eating lunch or shares dark metaphors in a writing assignment.

With your school community, take some time to analyze both the concerning issues and the supports around you. Talk with teachers and staff to learn their perspectives. Gather information from conversations with families. Listen to what students say or demonstrate when they struggle to succeed emotionally, behaviorally, or academically. Consider distributing more formal surveys to gather information about where students tend to face challenges. Look for repeated instances, alarming issues, and patterns to help discern where to first focus on student support. At the end of the chapter, you'll find a reproducible with starter questions written for collaborative dialogue with school community groups (page 72).

Connect With Your Village

Students' school communities are made up of peers, families, teachers, administrators, counselors, and other learning partners. These groups may be small and tight-knit or expansive and varied. Identify those who can offer a meaningful perspective on a student's learning strengths, challenges, or needs. Consider these connection ideas while developing a student-support action plan.

- **How can we connect as a community?** Student support takes time and focus. What does this look like on an organic level through day-to-day conversations? Think in terms of beginning, middle, and end. A morning check-in between teachers on mood and expectations for the day, a coffee or lunch together to brainstorm a specific strategy, or an end-of-the-day (or end-of-the-week) connection to reflect and make plans goes a long way in building space for support. Formalize these student-support conversations through work in your professional learning community's (PLC) collaborative teams or other collaborative groups. Finally, while some of these conversations are school based, the local community is also a valuable resource. Book studies, TED Talks, podcasts, guest speakers, and local experts can all deepen your understanding of what social-emotional support means.

- **What are our team strengths?** Each learning partner in a local school community has something to offer when it comes to student support. Some may have specific training in addressing mental health issues. Some may be experts in tutoring in certain content areas. Others are born encouragers who come alongside students with an uplifting word. Others still are connectors who can help students find activities and groups to broaden their boundaries. Notice the compassionate and expert efforts of surrounding faculty and staff while preparing to build out success plans and supports for students.

- **What kinds of resources can we offer?** Matt Miltenberg talked about blending an online resource with tips and tools for growth, one-on-one interactions with caring educators, and multitiered approaches to student support. What accessible resources are already in place to help students learn and grow? IEPs, 504 plans, report cards, student assignments and projects, and teacher and coach feedback begin to identify student strengths and areas of growth. What resources might you like to develop? Consider developing resources centered on student voices, such as student advisory boards, book clubs, and leadership opportunities. Student support is a community project. Leverage the strengths of families, educators, support staff, administrators, counselors, coaches, and club leaders to develop holistic support strategies.

Promote Asset-Based Approaches

A teacher may see a student struggling and want to rush in to share the answers or alleviate the discomfort. After all, teachers have successfully made it through school, and therefore have a lot of good advice to share! Certainly, when a student is in immediate danger or experiencing an acute mental health issue, you must intervene for their safety. In most instances, though, there is no immediate physical or mental danger. Instead, teachers witness concerning patterns. Students may seem stuck, dejected, or unmotivated, and their discomfort may show up in low grades and behavior concerns. Choosing an asset- or strengths-based approach over deficit thinking will cultivate support for the long term. An asset-based approach pauses to recognize where students are in a certain moment and how they are doing well. It then sends the message, "I see you and believe in you." Walk alongside the student, intervening with empathy and an unwavering belief in their agency and ability to navigate difficulties. Table 2.1 (page 54) provides more information on the important differences between deficit-based approaches and asset-based approaches.

Asset-based classrooms are sites for celebration, possibility, and radical hope. Classrooms are rich spaces for reasons to celebrate. These reasons to celebrate can include accomplishing big goals and smaller goals. Did a student make an A on a project they worked hard on? Celebrate! Did an introverted student speak up in class? Wow! Did someone offer a helpful peer review in the middle of a long project or ask a thoughtful question in a class discussion? Wonderful. Those times when students move out of their comfort zones, show perseverance, and take part in the class community are noteworthy. Celebrating them authentically and regularly, even through quick encouraging comments, can help build a more positive classroom community. Highlighting strengths and celebrating together can also send the message that an educator sees and believes in their students not only for what they can do right now, but also for all the skills they are developing. For instance, Carol Dweck's (2006) work highlights the importance of the word *yet* (as in, "I just can't solve this tough mathematics problem *yet*"). In asset-based classrooms, educators find opportunities to build on strengths and to believe that great things are possible.

Table 2.1: Deficit-Based Versus Asset-Based Approaches

	Deficit-Based Approach (Avoid this.)	**Asset-Based Approach (Practice this.)**
What it is	Deficit-based approaches focus on limitations, challenges, and growth areas (both real and perceived).	Asset-based approaches focus on strengths, opportunities, and skills (both present and in development).
What it looks like	A deficit-based approach can be covert or overt and includes generalizations; low expectations; an absence of relationships; tracking of and an overemphasis on prerequisites; comments about "these kids" or "their families"; gossip; and lengthy conversations about communities, families, or young people being broken, dysfunctional, or less than.	An asset-based approach can be bold or subtle and includes specific praise; high expectations; a focus on relationships; counseling; support to take stretch classes that ask students to learn outside their comfort zones; visible learning displays celebrating student work, leadership, and projects; and inclusion of communities, families, and young people in curriculum and classroom events.
What it says about youth and communities	Deficit-based approaches, including the savior complex, suggest students and their communities are lacking or broken and need a teacher to swoop in and save them (Brown, 2013). This is often racialized and more pronounced in marginalized communities.	Asset-based approaches acknowledge students have the skills and wisdom to persevere from within. These approaches recognize students and their communities bring essential strengths to school communities. Asset-based approaches also acknowledge systems may be unjust and resources may be distributed inequitably. These are the broken things, not people. Teacher leaders, administrators, and community advocates can intervene in powerful ways.
What young people learn from this approach	In deficit-based classrooms, students learn challenges and breakdowns are indicative of their worth as human beings. More troubling, they may experience hopelessness and a sense there is little they can impact or solve on their own.	With compassion and high expectations, students discover there is as much (or more) to learn in how to address challenges and breakdowns as there is in how to work hard and see successful results right away. More importantly, students learn they have agency to problem solve and make a difference in a variety of ways.

CONNECTED TEACHING COMMITMENT
Focus on Strengths First

Oftentimes, educators race into problems and challenges wanting to solve or fix them. Reframe this approach to challenges by focusing on strengths: "What is going well, and how can we build on that? What strengths does this student bring to class?" First, how can educators mark and celebrate those strengths, and second, how can they leverage those strengths to address challenges? This approach changes relationships, solutions, and culture. Teachers can use it in hallway conversations when they need to speak with a student about a discipline issue. They can use it in IEP and support conversations when considering goals and accommodations. Teachers can use it in instructional moments such as in feedback given on quizzes and assignments. For more on this strategy, see chapter 3 (page 75).

Practice Radical Hope

In this chapter on inclusive and supportive classrooms, you are meeting educators who discuss affective development, social-emotional learning, and skills such as grit and growth mindset (Duckworth & Gross, 2014; Dweck, 2006; Fishman-Weaver, 2018a; Simmons, 2017). Stephanie and I (Kathryn) want to spend a few moments early in this discussion unpacking important justice work around these concepts. In particular, we want to acknowledge that social-emotional learning, while valuable, is not a magical, one-size-fits-all solution for establishing safe and inclusive classrooms. Educators can develop and deliver social-emotional learning in culturally responsive and sustaining ways or in limited and even damaging ways (Gay, 2002; Love, 2019; Paris, 2012; Simmons, 2017).

Dena Simmons (2017), whose work explores the intersection of social-emotional learning, racial justice, and healing, reports that nearly half the United States' public school students are youths of color; yet teachers of color compose only 18 percent of the teaching force. Simmons (2017) goes on to say:

> Though rarely discussed, most of the social-emotional learning curricula—like much of the education curricula in the United States—is based on dominant white, Western, and individualistic culture. This exclusion likely contributes to a student-teacher disconnect, imposing on students of color a particular set of values and beliefs about behavior, conflict resolution, relationship building, and decision making.

Cultivating inclusive and affirming classroom spaces requires educators to think critically about how and for what ends such curriculum is being developed, and who is included and represented within that curriculum (and whose voices are missing). Social-emotional learning will not on its own disrupt systems of injustice, and further, failing to acknowledge these systems puts unfair pressure particularly on the most marginalized students, who find they can't just *persist* or *growth mindset* their way out of institutional racism, homophobia, or generational trauma (Love, 2019). "Without also changing the teaching behaviors, curricula, and school policies that can be assaultive to our students, particularly students of color, incorporating social-emotional learning into teaching will not be enough" (Simmons, 2017).

In a connected classroom, students must see themselves and their lived experiences reflected and affirmed across the curricula and teaching practices. For example, how are Black history and the stories of anti-racist work in your community situated and celebrated within your social-emotional learning curriculum? In talking about goals and grit, it would be difficult to find more powerful examples than those whose goals continue to be the rights to live, to matter, and to end racism. Bettina Love (2019), abolitionist educator and professor, asks the following:

> Is 400 years long enough? You cannot measure this type of grit, nor should you ignore it. African Americans are resilient and gritty because we have to be to survive, but it is misleading, naive, and dangerous to remove our history on both sides of the water from the conversation about grit. We have rebelled, fought, confronted, pleaded with the courts, marched, protested, and boycotted all just to survive the United States of America. Grit is in our DNA… But grit alone will not overthrow oppressive systems of power. We need teachers, school leaders, and policymakers who have grit for justice.

What would it look like for educators to have what Love (2019) calls "grit for justice"? In our research, Stephanie and I (Kathryn) used a related tethering concept called *radical hope*. Radical hope is about facing situations with eyes wide open for challenges and injustices, committing to problem solve through a values-based framework, and believing that schools and communities can be more just and humane places. The original values I (Kathryn) highlighted in my first iteration of the radical hope framework were learning, communication, care, and equity (Fishman-Weaver, 2017). However, as a PLC or school community, you will want to determine which values are your moral compass and how you can best use them to continue moving forward.

The students in classroom communities arrive with diverse lived experiences, identities, and needs. How can educators meet these diverse needs and approach students as the unique individuals they are, even when they are joining the classroom from eight thousand miles away? How can educators safeguard people-centered approaches as physical space becomes more flexible? For us, this work begins in honest and courageous relationships that honor the challenges our students navigate while celebrating their specific strengths, talents, and assets. In the following sections, we share strategies for developing personalized support plans; leveraging the connections, resources, and assets from students' local communities; and celebrating strengths and resilience (Simmons, 2017).

Alicia Bixby: Individual-Planning Case Studies

Alicia Bixby has over twenty-five years of school counseling experience. She has extensive expertise in student support, graduating planning, and mentoring student leaders.

Whether students are located on an island in the middle of the Pacific Ocean, newly living in Vietnam, receiving treatment at a hospital, or training in a hockey rink, taking a people-centered approach to meet students right where they are has introduced me to some amazing young people. I've been able to journey with students living unique narratives and keep up with their studies through online approaches. The following are three stories that stand out for me.

Amelia was born in Mongolia and attended school there for first through eleventh grades. Her family moved to Vietnam for her senior year, and she needed a plan to complete high school while living in Vietnam (with plans to apply for college in the United States). She was proficient in English and Mongolian but not Vietnamese, so attending a local school was not an option. Her family came to my online school to map out a plan for her to graduate. We were able to transfer in her three years of Mongolian high school, and she could then take her senior-year courses online with us. Amelia was a high achiever with a strong work ethic. She and her dad had lots of questions about navigating the U.S. college admissions process, and they called from Vietnam quite often. I truly enjoyed talking with them and answering their questions. Amelia graduated on time and was accepted into a prestigious university in the United States.

Jack and James were in one of more than a half-dozen families I've worked with who planned to sail around the world over a period of years. When they started out, Jack was beginning his senior year and James his sophomore year. Together, we worked out a plan so they could go on their adventure, graduate on time, and be accepted into the colleges of their choice. They were diligent in their studies. They completed their self-paced courses by sailing for a few weeks and then spending a few weeks at a time anchored at a port or island. It was fantastic hearing about their experiences, which they described in detail in their assignments. Both young men graduated on time and were accepted into excellent colleges.

Clarissa was born with multiple physical challenges and had not been expected to live more than a few days. When I met her, she was a teenager with the biggest smile I have ever seen. She wanted a plan that would culminate in graduating from high school and attending a four-year university. She was hardworking, enthusiastic, cheerful, and a talented actress who performed in theater. While she had complex medical needs, our online structure addressed many of the academic accommodations she might have needed at a traditional school. All Clarissa required to soar were flexible pacing for her medical treatment, which our online and asynchronous school provided, and the ability to use digital devices to submit work instead of a pen or pencil and paper. Rather than a detailed support plan, she found that the online environment coupled with our encouraging team gave her all the support and flexibility she needed.

Clarissa excelled in our online classes and served as a leader in our scholarly and service organization. One winter, she organized a service project caring for multiple retirement centers and nursing homes through food drives and visits. She graduated on time and was accepted to her first-choice college, where she continues to excel.

These are just three examples of individual planning with students. These students' journeys inspire me, and I am thrilled to have been a part of the solution allowing them to pursue goals and solve challenges through self-paced learning. (Alicia Bixby, personal communication, December 11, 2020)

Strategies for Individual Planning

Individual planning requires carefully and thoughtfully attending to the unique needs of specific learners in your school community. The resulting plans include formal individualized plans, such as IEPs and 504 plans, and more informal individualized plans, such as success plans and learning contracts. All individualized plans should begin with informed knowledge of the student's goals, strengths, and challenges. These three areas, coupled with the available resources at your school, help point you to the appropriate accommodations. While individual planning focuses on an individual student, it should not occur in isolation. The best support plans are developed by teams of people in your school community who know the student and care for their well-being and success. These teams should always include the student and their family. They may also include a general education teacher, special education teacher, administrator, counselor, and coach. The following sections share strategies informed by our (Kathryn and Stephanie's) work in student support, as well as our conversations with Alicia about the preceding case studies and her career as a school counselor.

Accommodate a Recent Move

Families face moves of different kinds. Some move from home to home across states and countries, others transfer from school to school, and others move from online or blended spaces to in-person classrooms, and vice versa. Like Amelia, each of these students will need extra support to feel welcome in their new environment. Your classroom can function as a home base for them as they acclimate to changes in many areas of their lives.

Keep these tips in mind when welcoming a new student to your class.

- Focus on social-emotional aspects from the start. Make time to chat casually with a student and get to know them holistically. The same techniques you use with any student to build connection are especially important with someone who is entering at a different time than the rest of the group.

- Arrange a one-on-one conference with the student to find out more about their past school experiences, their strengths and interests, and what questions they have. Revisit this conversation periodically, and build on what you learn.

- Conduct frequent check-ins across a variety of platforms—hallway chats, in-class connections, online messaging, and video class. Check in to see how the student is doing, follow up on questions, and be available for more questions. Also, check in with other faculty and staff; students often form strong bonds with one or two community members, who might offer helpful insight for support.

- Quickly and intentionally connect each new student to others in your school community. Look for opportunities to pair a new student with strong, friendly groups of peers.

- Look for other opportunities to connect students within the entire school community. Consider sports, clubs, community events, and organizations. These options create connection across the school community and increase a sense of belonging and purpose.

Create Stability During Periods of Instability

In our careers as educators, Stephanie and I (Kathryn) have supported many students as they navigate periods of instability, including housing insecurity, foster care, and family illness. Alicia's case studies echo the role school can fill as a stable constant during an otherwise unstable time. She shared stories of a student with complex medical needs and a family who lived on a boat. The online and blended classroom can provide increased access for some of these areas of need; however, technology on its own is not a support strategy.

- **Begin in relationship:** Great teaching rests in great relationships. These relationships are particularly critical during periods of instability. Before going over academic expectations, check in on well-being by building in time for connection. The more teachers can learn about the young people in their classrooms, their unique strengths, their needs, and their context, the more they have to build on.

- **Utilize wraparound resources:** If you know a student is between housing situations, safety and access to basic resources come before academics and technology. There are often school and community resources available to help youth in difficult situations, including food pantries and community health centers. However, not all students and families know how to access these. Work with your school community and particularly your school counselor to help connect students to appropriate wraparound services. Devices, hot spots, and access to computer labs are important resources for student success if your class requires technology and a strong Wi-Fi connection.

- **Embrace flexibility when possible:** Navigating instability can be a full-time job, all the more so when the person navigating it is a student who is also trying to keep up on schoolwork. Be patient and flexible, and act with empathy. Teachers teach students first and content second. These situations require creative and flexible thinking around deadlines and support. Couple your high expectations with grace and humanity.

Anthony Plogger: Virtual Program Case Studies

Anthony Plogger has worked in support services for a program offering various education options to students who are homeschooled, enrolled in a public school district or charter school, or medically unable to attend school in an in-person setting.

Sam enrolled in my virtual program for an alternative option to high school. This student had previously been enrolled in a small school district where they experienced bullying due to their gender identity. Prior to the student's gender confirmation surgery, they were an A student. After their transition, they were receiving Cs, Ds, and even Fs. Sam's parents decided to try a new approach and enrolled their child in our online, self-paced program. Upon enrolling, Sam quickly acclimatized to the virtual learning environment and enjoyed the autonomy of a self-paced classroom. Together, Sam and I navigated teacher-student interactions, course time-management skills, and technical troubleshooting. Sam was elated to regain control of their life and their education. At the end of their time with me, they sent me a kind email thanking me for my time and guidance. I was so happy to be a small part of Sam's story as they found a path to success.

The flexibility of being able to log in at various times has been a solution for many students. Bia wanted to take Advanced Placement courses but had medical conditions preventing her from attending morning classes in her home district. With the flexibility of our online courses and the ability to work on her own time, she was able to complete her Advanced Placement courses.

Clara has been with us since the ninth grade. She attends a small school district with minimal course offerings. Since Clara enrolled with us, she has completed physical education, three years of French, and various other electives. Clara loves her French courses and is starting our most advanced level (French IV). Clara was one of the first students I worked with, and seeing her growth reminds me access to high-quality online education opens different doors for different students. For students like Clara, our virtual program gives them access to courses and subjects previously unavailable in their rural districts.

The virtual program has built an important bridge for students seeking education options to mitigate district offerings, medical conditions, travel realities, and ill-fit environments. As an educator, I am grateful to build relationships with young people, families, and school districts to expand access to educational programming across the state. Each year I have served in this position, I have seen our enrollments grow, and I am hopeful for what the future might hold in terms of reimagining space, place, and access in education. (Anthony Plogger, personal communication, December 15, 2020)

Strategies for Affirming Identities

We (Kathryn and Stephanie) visited with Anthony shortly after he had created a tutorial on establishing safe space in the online classroom. "The values of inclusion, safe space, and acceptance can be reflected in our virtual and in-person classrooms," he shared, adding that the "middle and high school years are a formative time. One teacher's actions can cause a series of reactions that continue well into adulthood. Our job as educators is to support and nurture students to be successful members of our diverse society." Anthony offered us three specific tips for establishing safe space in the online classroom. These tips centered on supporting LGBTQIA+ students, but these principles extend to cultivating inclusive and affirming classrooms for students from many different backgrounds.

Make Your Commitments to Safe Space Visible

As soon as a student enters your classroom, they should know that they are welcome there. While teachers' relationships with students are critical indicators of acceptance, students also notice the examples, posters, and ways in which different identities are represented in the classroom space and curriculum. Can your LGBTQIA+ students see themselves and their identities affirmed in your classroom space?

Engage in Professional Learning Focused on Diversity, Inclusion, and Equity

Seek out opportunities to grow as an educator and human being. Attend trainings and engage in book clubs on culturally responsive and culturally competent teaching to expand and give legs to the diversity, equity, and inclusion (DEI) initiatives at your school. Possible focus topics for professional learning in your PLC include providing anti-racist teaching, establishing safe space for LGBTQIA+ youth, and welcoming refugee and immigrant students to your class.

Include Your Pronouns

Many of the educators we worked with for this book include their pronouns with their Zoom name or email signature. For example, I use *Kathryn Fishman-Weaver (she/her)* in these and other spaces. Pronouns such as *she*, *he*, and *they* are how people identify themselves beyond their name. When referencing a person in conversation, you typically use a pronoun—for example, "She just made a great point!" Personal pronouns are not always obvious when you first meet someone. This is why educators need to create a safe space and normalize sharing pronouns.

The University of California San Francisco's LGBT Resource Center (n.d.) sums it up nicely: "Using someone's correct gender pronouns is one of the most basic ways to show your respect for their identity." While including pronouns is an important step in cultivating a safe space for students of all genders, it is also useful in the global online context, where not all cultural norms, names, and identities may be familiar to the educator (GLSEN, n.d.).

Stephanie and I (Kathryn) have experienced this with many of our Vietnamese students, as neither of us has as much experience with these names as we do with the names of students from European or Latin American backgrounds. For this reason, our enrollment process includes a space for students to list their preferred name and personal pronouns, and our team refers to this information before responding to student and teacher communications.

As discussed in our introduction (page 1), people-centered approaches originated from health care. Throughout our work in education, we have seen many important crossovers between health care and education. For example, cultivating an inclusive and affirming classroom environment has been directly linked to health outcomes. The Trevor Project's 2020 National Survey on LGBTQ Youth Mental Health found that trans and nonbinary youth who reported having their correct pronouns used by most or all of the people in their lives attempted suicide at half the rate of those who did not have their pronouns respected. Committing to getting these few letters right may seem like a small thing, but it has a significant impact on the lives and well-being of young people in your classroom. If you do not yet have a lot of experience using personal pronouns such as *they*, *them*, *ze*, or *zir*, find an accountability partner and practice together until using them becomes more natural for you.

This commitment to gender-inclusive language (like the singular *they*) and nongendered language (like "friends" instead of "boys and girls") also extends to work in online curriculum and communication with families. By cultivating intentionality around names, pronouns, and language, educators can take important steps in respecting and affirming every student and building relationships in any classroom space.

Sherry Denney:
Adult Learning Case Study

Sherry Denney has over twenty-five years of school counseling experience. She moved from in-person buildings to an online and blended school system later in her career.

When I met her, Aliyah was in her midthirties and had children of her own. She had left high school after having her first baby. That baby was now a teenager and encouraged her mother to go back to school. Aliyah was excited to experience coursework and broaden her knowledge. Online classes let her choose the courses that would help her reach her goal of earning her high school diploma.

It was then our journey together began in earnest. Our weekly phone calls centered on helping her acclimate once again to the culture of school. Although she struggled with spelling and written expression, her thoughts were passionate and powerful. She was an assistant manager at the store where she worked and had extensive experience collaborating with her work team. She was trying hard to connect what she was reading in the course about character with the business she conducted every day in her work life. The words *behavior*, *values*, *responsibility*, *goals*, *self-esteem*, *motivation*, and *determination* had authentic meaning to her. She wasn't just learning content; she was developing a cognitive network for application and real-life problem solving.

Throughout the course of her education with me, Aliyah developed aspirations to go to college and expressed wanting to major in business. Her dream was to open her own restaurant, and she wanted to know how to make her dream come true. In addition to getting regular feedback from me about the course, she often talked with me about her favorite recipes and what she was cooking that day. While on the phone, she was often mixing, chopping, and checking what was on the stove or in the oven. She prided herself on always having baked goods waiting for her children to welcome them home from school. When we finished our discussion about the weekly assignment, the conversation inevitably turned to her future restaurant. We had fun thinking of different names for her business and ways she could distinguish herself from a marketing angle.

Although we were obviously connected academically as a teacher and student, we also connected as people and became friends. I am honored I could share a part in her journey. She finished both of my courses and added two more credits to her transcript.

I still miss our weekly phone calls, which always began with, "What are you baking?" I wonder what Aliyah is doing now, and I hope she is continuing to check off goals to make her dreams come true. (Sherry Denney, personal communication, November 22, 2020)

Strategies for Adult Learning

Throughout our (Kathryn and Stephanie's) research on connected classrooms, we encountered powerful stories of adult learners. We heard of refugee moms who took English classes; a grandmother who returned to high school to graduate with her grandson; a married woman in her thirties who, for the first time, had the stability to finish school; and a custodian who had always wanted to go back and get his high school diploma. Returning to secondary school as an adult takes courage. Honor that bravery and commitment in your interactions, feedback, and curriculum. The following strategies highlight two important considerations with working alongside adult learners.

Teach From a Place of Respect

Teaching from a place of respect means that while you may have a different educational narrative than the adult learners in your classes, you recognize the value and rich experiences every student brings to your class community. Guard against a savior (or knight) mentality, where you believe that the person you are working with (or in this case, teaching) needs to be saved and that the best person to come to their rescue is you. This can look like an overemphasis on vulnerability, trauma, or tragedy. It can also look like a performative or patronizing way of talking about success. It feels like you single-handedly changed someone's life or are responsible for setting them on a new trajectory. Practice humility. The adult learners in your classes are the protagonists of their story. Intentionally engage in reciprocal knowledge by relating to your adult students in a way that honors their lived experiences. The following strategy elaborates on how to do this.

Value Lived Experiences

Adult learners come to the classroom with a robust set of lived experiences. While younger students are taking in concepts and learning to apply them to new situations, adult learners have experienced many of these situations already. Throughout this book, we have celebrated diversity as one of the greatest strengths of the school community. Intergenerational classes and adult learners bring important strengths and diverse experiences to schools. The following are a few tips for practicing strengths-based approaches when working with adults.

- As always, take time to get to know each learner. The details students feel comfortable sharing about past educational experience, work experience, and family life will help you build relationships and inform connections you might make between their experiences and the curriculum you teach. These relationships take time and vulnerability; be patient as you get to know each other.

- If you are teaching an intergenerational class of younger and older learners, design activities that encourage story sharing. Encourage everyone to share their perspectives on past experiences that relate to content, strategies they use to study, ways to apply past learning to current assignments, and reflections on how they learn best. These types of discussions promote active learning and create a welcoming and respectful classroom environment.

- Invite feedback. Adult learners come to your class with a wealth of experiences in other arenas. They will have authentic feedback to share about the way they receive the content and curriculum. These connections can inform your instruction, highlight blind spots, and improve instruction for the whole class. Encourage adult learners to reflect on their experiences as students and share what's working well and what would help them be even more successful.

Roberta Mayumi da Silva: Increasing Inclusion at a Brazilian Bilingual School

Roberta Mayumi da Silva is one of the school leaders mentioned in Matt Miltenberg's case study earlier in this chapter (page 46). She leads the bilingual blended high school program at a private school in Brazil. This program gives students the opportunity to earn a second high school diploma in English, a non-native language to them. The following is an adapted transcript of a talk Roberta gave on her experiences expanding inclusion for students with disabilities in this program.

Cultivating a growth mindset and challenging students to overcome their difficulties are what make my school community special. Our team differentiates instruction, personalizes goals, and implements interventions. Differentiation is an essential component to how we prepare learners to think, collaborate, and create. Our students are motivated to develop their potential and to know their challenges and strengths to reach their goals.

When I started working at my school in Baru, São Paulo, as the U.S. high school coordinator, I wanted to follow the same approach of inclusion and bring it to the blended model. I wanted to learn more about autism, dyslexia, ADHD, and other medical needs to be able to give support to the students considering the English-immersion high school program. I had concerns about how best to support these students and whether we could implement adaptive strategies. Earning two high school diplomas (both a Brazilian and a U.S. one) is a significant challenge for everyone.

We have five hundred students in our school, and close to seventy are enrolled in the dual-diploma program. Out of the seventy, seven students have a special accommodation plan. Our usual procedure when students with disabilities or learning differences reach the age and grade to enroll in the program is to meet with students and their families to see whether they are interested in the program. If they are, we gather background information from previous teachers and ask questions to learn about each student's needs and strengths. We research the strategies our core teachers and psychologists are using to help the student in their in-person home language program.

Once we know what kinds of accommodations will work best at our local school, we take this information to our online partner school to see if we can create an accommodation or success plan based on what we are doing in our Brazilian setting. We model some of our approaches on U.S. legislation such as the Individuals With Disabilities Education Act (IDEA) and section 504 of the Rehabilitation Act of 1973 (IDEA, n.d.). Together, we analyze all the information and needs, including medical or psychological documentation and action plans used by our Brazilian teachers. Then we come up with an individualized plan for every student who wants to enroll in the program.

We have high expectations, so we start with as few accommodations as possible. Through our believing in our students' ability to succeed from right where they are and incentivizing their success, many of them manage to focus on their strengths and strategies to overcome their difficulties. It is always rewarding to watch them grow and to create this net of emotional and educational support with teachers, parents, and professionals. We know we can always increase support, but by starting with few accommodations, respecting their self-pace, and having continuous feedback, we can serve their unique needs.

Some common accommodations we use include extending time and having a reader for exams, allowing breaks during exams, increasing the font size for written assignments, and centering relationships with a critical person. This last accommodation often looks like consistent coaching, grading, and feedback by a trusted teacher.

> It is important we keep ongoing communication about what is working and what needs to be adjusted. It is a challenge, but everything we do has a purpose. For instance, we had a ninth-grade student with a language-learning disability who worked relentlessly. Using the strategies I just explained, this same student was accepted to the National Honor Society in eleventh grade. This is just one of the success stories proving how important it is to continue this work.
>
> You must be present, believe in young people, develop ways to motivate them, and listen fully with all your senses. For every need, there is an applicable accommodation. These are important life learning options for students because later in life, they will have to negotiate and articulate their own strategies in college and in the workplace.
>
> By negotiating and learning their strategies, students can be protagonists and autonomous learners. They can be autonomous when they are after their own strategies, even if they sometimes need to ask for help. Having an environment to foster overcoming these challenges and celebrate every achievement is what motivates us and creates these great stories. (Roberta Mayumi da Silva, personal communication, June 2, 2021)

Strategies for Taking a People-Centered Approach to Student Support

As Roberta reminds educators in her narrative, "Listen fully with all your senses." Each conversation and interaction is an investment of time that says, "I care for you. You are important." The following strategies highlight three steps you can take to build an inclusive and people-centered classroom.

Learn About Specific Needs of Students With Disabilities

Regardless of your professional training with special education services, you will welcome students with learning differences and disabilities to your classroom. Just as Roberta demonstrates in her narrative, take the time to learn about specific disabilities. The Individuals With Disabilities Education Act recognizes thirteen disabilities that may impact learning: (1) autism, (2) blindness, (3) deafness, (4) emotional disturbance, (5) hearing impairment, (6) intellectual disability, (7) multiple disabilities, (8) orthopedic impairment, (9) other health impairment, (10) specific learning disability, (11) speech or language impairment, (12) traumatic brain injury, and (13) visual impairment (IDEA, 2017). This may be a good starting place for expanding your knowledge of the nuances and specific needs of students with disabilities.

Learning specialists, school counselors, and psychologists may also be able to point you to continued-learning resources beyond reading materials. Understanding different disability categories, common accommodations and modifications, and the unique strengths of these disabilities can equip you with some helpful background knowledge on supporting students who learn differently. How a disability presents is unique for each learner. For example, taking a soccer break when tensions are rising may work wonders for a student in your second-period class, but it may fall flat for a student in fourth period even if they have the same disability. As always, getting to know the students' unique strengths, challenges, goals, and personalities is central to effective support planning.

Learn From Past Teachers

Each year is a fresh start, filled with possibilities. Still, students and teachers do not exist in a vacuum. Previous teachers have important information to offer about your incoming students' needs and strengths. Work with your administrators and counselors to organize a method for success sharing about previous students. This focus on strengths is important. This strategy should emphasize building on celebrations. Framing categories include:

- Specific strengths
- Key interests
- Important relationships
- Something the teacher wishes they had known
- A favorite memory the teacher has of this student

If done with an emphasis on strengths, this exercise can provide a powerful springboard for support strategies as students come into your classroom.

Keep Expectations High

In one of my (Kathryn's) teacher education classes, I ask future teachers how many of them believe that with the right supports, all students can achieve at high levels. Inevitably, every hand goes up. As teachers continue in their careers, we want to continue nurturing this belief in the power and possibility of high expectations.

High expectations and support plans should always work in concert. Accommodations do not change learning expectations; they simply adjust how teachers present work to a student or how a student demonstrates what they have learned. Roberta shares that her school starts "with as few accommodations as possible." She adds, "Through our believing in our students' ability to succeed from right where they are and incentivizing their success, many of them manage to focus on their strengths and strategies to overcome their difficulties." When considering accommodations for students, start small. Extending time on tests, allowing breaks during exams, and pairing a student with a mentor are all common accommodations that offer students the initial support they need to thrive. Continually send the message that you believe in and are rooting for your students.

Key Classroom Takeaway: Practice Radical Hope One Conversation at a Time

This chapter's first narrative began on a proverbial riverbank running through an increasingly connected world. As the education landscape shifts to more global, online, and blended contexts, how can educators identify the conditions upstream and help students thrive? The case studies explored in this chapter offer more information about the lived experiences of students living and learning on this new riverbank. These stories prove noticing and listening matter. Every classroom is marked and strengthened by racial, ethnic, gender, linguistic, cultural, and neurological diversity. As educators consider system supports and new counseling models for this new frontier in education, the temptation is to think big. Across these stories, though, is a reminder to also think small, to pay attention to nuance and connecting moments, and to honor the ways relationships are built one conversation or interaction at a time.

"Hope is a universal form of resistant imagination. To hope is to believe situations, circumstances, and practices can be better" (Fishman-Weaver, 2017, p. 10). For most educators, the world they are teaching in is not the same world they were educated in. This world presents a multifaceted array of challenges and possibilities. Committing to the possibilities is an act of radical hope. As we close this chapter, we invite you to consider how to employ radical hope in your own teaching practice, particularly in the ways you connect with students through inclusion, support, and counseling strategies.

Summary

In-person, blended, and online school options give families a choice about how learning best works for them. For students who travel, like athletes, dirt-bike racers, or equestrians, online education gives them the flexibility to pursue a passion or career and stay on track to graduate. For students who have taken a break from a formal school experience and want to graduate on a different timeline, including adult learners, online education gives them a pathway to earn credit while balancing other life responsibilities. Online classrooms can also be welcoming spaces for students who learn differently, or who have medical needs or social challenges that make in-person learning more complicated or less safe. The online environment also gives students a chance to pursue their educational goals without worrying about missing school due to illness or access issues, or to recover from a traumatic event while still making academic progress.

In this chapter, you heard from educators who have worked with students across these lived experiences and more. Matt Miltenberg shared specific ways to translate the multitiered system of supports to the online and blended context. Alicia Bixby and Anthony Plogger gave examples of how students navigating geographic, physical, emotional, and social challenges, including trauma, found support in online schools. They explained how a blend of one-on-one time and specific expectations and goals allowed these students to work toward solutions, and Sherry Denney showed how to adapt these same strategies to adult learners. Finally, Roberta Mayumi da Silva detailed the specific steps her school takes to foster inclusive practices in a blended classroom.

Student support is complex and essential. Teaching requires knowing the whole student and evaluating how they can best reach their goals. Developing a support plan relies on strong relationships, community partnership, and specific academic and social support systems. In chapter 3, you'll see how the daily interactions teachers have with students (including grading their work, developing a warm and positive tone, and finding small moments of connection) also help them build relationships and support students. Please find your space for reflective practice for chapter 2 on the following page, as well as a handy guide to starting a collaborative dialogue with your school community group.

Chapter 2: Apply It to Your Practice

Working individually or in learning teams, reflect on these questions, and implement the commitments to your practice (for more information on engaging with these questions, please see the section titled Space for Reflective Practice on page 9 in the introduction). As always, strive to move your reflection to action.

React to the Chapter

What are your key takeaways from this chapter? What was surprising to read? What did you connect with?

Celebrate Small Goals

In Sherry Denney's case study (page 63), you read about Aliyah, the connection she shared with her counselor and teacher, and some important progress she made toward her goals. After Aliyah finished the two classes in this story, she needed to take another break from pursuing her high school diploma. In pursuit of a big goal, people check off little goals, reach obstacles, pivot, and (with hope) persist. How can you celebrate persistence and progress toward small goals in your classroom?

Honor Lived Experiences

Educational pathways are often nonlinear. Consider the lived experiences Amelia, Jack and James, Clarissa, Sam, Bia, Clara, and Aliyah brought to their studies. How are you honoring the diverse lived experiences of your school community?

Enter Collaborative Dialogue

The following are some starter questions written for collaborative dialogue with school community groups (Fishman-Weaver, 2017).

- **Learning:** What is our school community (classroom, school, and district) learning through this process? What are our individual stakeholders (student, teacher, support staff member, and administrator) learning through this process? Are we safeguarding learning at high levels? How is this lesson pushing our school or district forward?

- **Care:** Who needs support in this situation? How can a class, school, or district give support? What support would I want if I were on the other end of this decision?

- **Communication:** How are we honoring our commitment to active listening? How will this decision and rationale be communicated to all stakeholders? What opportunities are there for teachers or students to have agency in the communication and implementation of this decision?

- **Equity:** Are we fully considering the needs of this particular community (classroom, school, or district) or community member (student, teacher, support staff member, or administrator)? Have we explored ways to ensure equity and access? Have we considered the roles different lived experiences might play inpthis situation? Are we valuing diversity?

- **Radical hope:** How will I practice radical hope in my classroom? (In your planning and decision making, create space for new possibilities and solutions. When people, including young people, are challenging, commit to assuming positive intent and giving community members the benefit of the doubt.)

Fishman-Weaver, K. (2017). A call to praxis: Using gendered organizational theory to center radical hope in schools. Journal of Organizational Theory in Education, *2(1), 1–14.*

Fostering Relationships Through Connection-Based Feedback

3

As educators and administrators, Kathryn and I (Stephanie) have had hundreds of conversations with teachers in which we learn why they chose to go into the field of education. We often hear these two replies again and again: (1) they love young children, middle schoolers, or teens and want to spend their days inspiring them and learning with them, and (2) they are passionate about a particular content area and want to teach others all about it. Similarly, when we talk about their least favorite teaching tasks, we often hear one answer: "Grading. All that grading!"

It's true. Teaching requires assessment, and assessment requires time and feedback. Often, assessment feedback is formative, a quick check-in or short review, such as an exit slip or a holistic comment. Other times, it's much fuller and longer, like rubric comments for an essay or specific feedback on a multistep project. Not all assessment feedback is written. It can also come in the form of a conversation. You might be the one giving feedback, or you might utilize peer feedback, and students might receive this feedback well and use it, or disregard it. Whatever the form, assessment and feedback are essential to student learning. The hope is that teachers can deliver feedback in such a way that learning happens—that students identify specific skills and goals and apply them to the next assignment.

Essential Question

How can educators foster great relationships through everyday teaching practices in online and blended classrooms?

Chapter Learning Objectives

- Consider what it means to be there for students and look for points of connection.

- Reframe the focus of grading (giving feedback) as an opportunity to build relationships with students.

- Practice the four-step feedback process on key assessments in your classroom.

- Develop a feedback tone that encourages students and points them forward.

Key Terms

feedbacking. The complete process of assessing a student's work through considering the goals of the assignment, designing rubric- or goal-centered comments, and balancing individual points scoring with a holistic assessment.

the four-step feedback process. A step-by-step process designed to offer warm, full, rubric-centered feedback to students.

holistic comments. General comments that give an assessment of the overall assignment. They are written in a clear space on the assignment and use the sandwich technique to give advice.

holistic grading. An assessment style that takes into consideration whether students are in or out of control on a prompt, their general work on an overall piece, and their growth over time.

point comments. Constructive and positive comments that directly relate to certain parts of student work and tie to the goals of the assignment. They are written to the side of student work and are brief, friendly, and specific.

rubric-centered grading. An assessment style that connects teacher comments on student work to specific rubric strands (or goals and objectives).

rubric comments. Comments that give general advice for what is especially well done and what could be improved in an assignment. They are written in the rubric strands with an encouraging tone.

the sandwich technique. A set of comments that emphasize what is well done while also pointing forward to growth. This is structured as a positive comment followed by a suggestion for improvement, and ending with another positive comment.

In this chapter, you'll consider how shifting your approach to assessment can transform your classroom and positively impact your relationships with students. Assessment is not an add-on. It's not the thing teachers do after the assignment is turned in that lets them record a score and move on to something else. Assessment *is* relationship. Educators talk to their students through their comments, and this gives them a powerful opportunity to build rapport and support student learning using a common daily or weekly routine.

As you read the educator narratives and strategies in this chapter, think about your own goals for assessment. What do you want students to get out of each assignment? Or, to put it more directly, why does what you are teaching matter? You'll learn some helpful strategies for getting clear on why and what you are assessing, how you can grade more efficiently, and how you can make feedback one more way to have a conversation with students.

Feedback as a Conversation

It can be tempting to view grading and assignment feedback in a box—necessary, but certainly not the most exciting or joyful part of teaching. By choosing to view teaching through the lens of passion about the content, the hope that students will build critical-thinking and creative skills, and anticipation for all the rich class discussions and activities students and teachers will explore and experience together, grading assignments becomes just one way to assess student work. For most educators, if they're honest, grading assignments is not the highlight of the day! However, it is possible to fine-tune the perspective a bit so the everyday practice of grading can become a more meaningful way to communicate and build relationships with students.

Assessing student work is not just a necessity; it can be a conversation that helps students focus on growth and possibilities. Use the strategies in this chapter to turn the act of grading into a relationship builder—whether in the same room with students or separated by miles and a computer screen. Read on for stories of how fellow educators have used these tips to help in-person, online, and blended communities thrive.

Connection doesn't happen by accident. It requires an intentional commitment to check in at every desk every day, to start online learning sessions with celebrations or temperature checks, to remember birthdays and special moments, to celebrate accomplishments, and to schedule family events. Being intentional about connected teaching shifts how teachers lesson plan, because instead of planning only for standards and learning targets, they also start planning for the individual students in their classrooms. What are their strengths and passions? It changes how a teacher prioritizes time because it means students matter before the content or, said differently, the content matters because students matter. Some of the educators we worked with during our research track contacts to make sure they never miss anyone. They put a check mark by every student they speak with on a given day, schedule their calls home ahead of time so that they leave no one out, and write icebreakers into their daily agendas. The following teacher narrative reflects on empathy through the lens of being there. Read Chris Holmes's poetic reflection about showing up in online spaces with intention and connection.

Chris Holmes:
Being a Human Presence Online

Chris Holmes has over twenty years of classroom experience, during which he has worked across many different educational settings. He's an innovator, researcher, and believer in the power of hope. Chris created a dropout prevention program, helped found a school for students who learn differently, and currently serves as a gifted education specialist for the Clayton School District of Missouri. In 2015, he was named the Missouri Teacher of the Year.

Many teachers taught right through the COVID-19 pandemic. During this crisis, my students and I also experienced a social-emotional unearthing. We asked big questions about our identity, our experiences, our worth. How could we not? For me, this season of reflective practice led to an existential epiphany of sorts. As I navigated teaching at a distance, I learned important lessons about proximity and connection. I learned (or relearned) the important truth that we matter—even from afar.

I love the interplay of *matter* with both meaning and weight. Our matter has inertia. When in motion, we often stay in motion; when at rest, we often stay at rest. However, a body at rest is not the same as a mind at rest. Sometimes, it is in the quietest moments that we find great meaning.

As a high school teacher and motivation researcher, I keep finding meaning in talking with young people, in hearing their stories, and most importantly in continuing to be there.

Here is an example of a small yet transformative interaction I had with two students in my online class. A seventh-grade student and an eleventh-grade student were both attending school virtually and both failing several classes for lack of production. They wanted help (sort of).

What they really wanted, though they didn't realize it, was human presence. I met with them via a web conference one evening. I provided very little content instruction or even motivation or inspiration. I was just there, watching them complete work they had avoided for the past several weeks. It took very little effort on my part, and even less expertise. They needed attention, potential access to help if necessary. It was rarely necessary; the attention was enough.

To believe someone can be, will be, and wants to be there for you is a powerful thing. To feel the presence of help. Someone there. And all I did was watch them work.

Whether you're a teacher, parent, or neighbor, never underestimate the positive power of your presence in a student's life. Be there. Keep showing up and reminding students that they matter. When the days (or years) are long, remind yourself that you matter too. (Chris Holmes, personal communication, November 5, 2020)

Strategies for Connecting Daily With Students

Because Chris started with empathy, he made relationships a priority. He made space for students to do what they needed to do, both honoring their capacity to succeed and providing a steady, friendly presence to bolster them. Empathy means, as Chris puts it, "to be there." The following are strategies for intentionally using daily interactions to foster trusting, open relationships between teachers and students so teachers can *be there*.

Use Intentional Icebreakers

"If you had twenty minutes free right now, and the only rule was that you had to use the time to move around, what would you do? Would you stay inside or go outside? Call a friend for a walk? Lift some weights? Have a dance party in your kitchen?" These types of questions, which seem purely playful, serve the higher purpose of sparking relationships with students. This is a helpful strategy to use as students enter the class space, as well as throughout each lesson and throughout the semester.

Set a Daily Greeting Ritual

To start, call students by name as they enter your classroom. Ask how their day is going. Ask what new or interesting things they have seen or done lately. Get to know their hobbies and interests. Also, invite students to ask questions and share personal stories. Note the details students share (and write them down), and then ask follow-up questions later in the week.

Use Digital Chat Rooms

Manipulating the digital space the class shares can provide visual variety, which is good for the mind and eye. Collaborative spaces like Jamboard, Google Docs, and breakout rooms engage students. The chat feature and reactions of computer-mediated communication elicit different kinds of responses (Nadler, 2020). Physical props like a whiteboard, puppets, posters, and anchor charts also add dynamic elements to the digital classroom.

Model Emotional Literacy

Devoting time to creating connection does not delay learning; it creates a path to learning. This lets students know that the teacher is there for them and everyone is in this class together. Focus on wellness and the importance of articulating feelings to students to build emotional literacy. Weave breathing and physical movement, art, music, creativity, and meaningful pauses into the class's daily rhythms (Fishman-Weaver & Walter, 2021). Make time outside of the class to meet with students individually or in small groups. Model emotional literacy by talking through your reflections. Share when you are stressed or challenged by something, and encourage students to do the same. Keep making space until the space is comfortable and open.

This work matters. In fact, this work is what helps students absorb the content they are working on at the time. This work creates community. It brings meaning to the course. Without empathy, teachers are all about facts and words and test scores. With empathy, teachers are about using those facts and words to make a difference in the world.

Nancy Stoker: Your Presence Matters

Nancy Stoker is an instructional specialist in an online program who offers feedback to thousands of students all over the world. Nancy's ability to share warmth and good advice with students solely through text is remarkable. Partner educators share with her team that Nancy is an excellent communicator who makes their students feel heard and supported. In the following narrative, Nancy shares her top tips for having real conversations with students in a solely online context.

As an educator, I believe it is my responsibility to be a positive external force to help students experience their own positive internal forces.

I am an instructional specialist who gives feedback to students on their paragraphs, essays, presentations, projects, and reflections. I give all my feedbacking online. Students never meet me in person; we have only our names on the page and our words to connect with. I approach every submission with a choice: Will I come across as an expert imparting instruction for what students should and should not do, or will I help students reach their own level of success? It's that decision that shifts grading assignments online from marking what is right and wrong to "seeing" the student behind the assignment and wrapping them in feedback that conveys, "I see what you invested in this assignment. I see you."

This philosophy came alive the first time I went live grading an assignment online. I put my name on the assignment as the grader, and it really hit me that this student and I were about to connect even if just through this exchange of his submission and my feedback. I remember visualizing the student as he received notification that his assignment was graded. I pictured him wearing a powder-blue short-sleeved shirt. I have no idea why this was the particular visual, but it was important because it made the name in the upper-right corner of my screen a person. I needed this student to trust me, which meant investing in his assignment and working to learn something about him through his writing. I imagine I am sitting next to each student, pointing to certain passages of their work. *See this part? You explained your opinion with an example that really made me see your point! Over here? That's a spot where you could use more descriptive language to help us picture what you experienced.* When I imagine a student, the student is typically looking at the paper until I ask them to look right at me, in the eye, so I can "tell" them what I'm, in reality, writing in the comment box. The eye contact matters, so I create it even if just in my mind. It keeps me both accountable and connected.

Part of my goal is to look holistically at the student's overall progress and design my feedback from that viewpoint. Does this student need celebration of a job hard fought and well done? Do they need some gentle urging to always push past their first effort into their best effort?

I once provided feedback to a student whose speech was about her aspiration to be a journalist. In my comments, I noted that I am a graduate of the school she desired to attend. To my surprise, I received a response from her that included the statement of how excited she was to have had a "real live graduate" of the school review and be impressed by her work. This moment showed me students online crave to be seen for who they are the same as those in person do.

Building the trust to have this belief and a connection is certainly a process. There is no greater effort to make for online students than to take every opportunity to close the physical space between them and you. (Nancy Stoker, personal communication, December 26, 2020)

Strategies for Connecting Through Feedback

Using feedback as a vehicle to carry educators toward connection takes time and practice. Nancy Stoker approaches written feedback as a conversation with her students, and she sets clear targets for what she wants to accomplish with students in a grading session. The following strategies draw from Nancy's work with students; approaching written feedback with these targets in mind can help focus your energy and even create a little joy as you tackle groups of papers to grade. These strategies build on Nancy Stoker's work on presence and feedback.

Pause and Picture Each Student

Before beginning a big stack of grading, Nancy sets an intention. She often uses this intention: "No matter the score on the paper, I will find a few spots to write feedback that says, *I see what you're trying here. I see how far you've come. I am rooting you on.*" Another practice that can help with this intention is pausing to consider the scholarly body of work that each student is building. Grading each set of assignments not only assesses student progress and growth but also gives teachers a way to encourage students to grow and to make connections with them. When possible, pause for a moment between papers or submissions to reflect on how each student has progressed from the first assignment, or the previous assignment, to the assignment you see before you.

Draw on Your Own Experiences

When I (Kathryn) was in first grade, I brought my teacher, Ms. Crawford, a new story every day. I worked on these stories the evening before, set them on her desk first thing in the morning, and knew that after morning recess, she would return my story with encouraging comments and stickers! Ms. Crawford's positive and consistent feedback kept me writing all year long. Many have similar stories of a teacher whose feedback encouraged them. When giving feedback to others, Nancy recommends drawing on those positive experiences. Here are some reflective questions to consider as you grade and leave feedback.

- "Is my feedback encouraging? Does it say, *I believe in you*?"
- "Is my feedback friendly? Does it sound conversational?"
- "Is my feedback personalized? Do I call the student by name and look for specific opportunities to connect?"
- "Is my feedback specific? Do I point out several strengths in the assignment and one or two specific areas for learning and growth?"

As you hone your feedback process, spend some time thinking about feedback styles and examples. Meet with colleagues to share examples of feedback notes and talk about what works best. Share these questions with your students; this kind of openness to how they best learn can be empowering. Then, experiment with your tone and your comments to give constructive advice *and* build up students at the same time.

Most important, be authentic in your feedback. Stickers and bright-colored comments worked for Ms. Crawford, but they might not be your style. Teachers often tell their students to use their authentic voice in writing. That goes for teachers too. Are you funny? Thoughtful? Witty? Caring? Let your students get to know you through the grading comments. At the end of this chapter (page 101), you'll find handy prompts in the space for reflective practice to help you identify your authentic teacher voice and identity.

Consider Your Goal

Nancy's main goal in giving feedback is to encourage growth mindset in students. Through connecting with them relationally and helping them recognize their strengths, she hopes they'll take what they learn from each assignment and grow toward the next. Beyond scoring an assignment to contribute to a student's class grade, what is your feedback goal? What do you hope students will learn about the work or about themselves through your comments to them?

Sometimes, you have broad feedback goals in which you're assessing many skills—content knowledge, structure, development, support and evidence, and grammar (depending on the content area). Other times, you want to focus on a specific skill for some targeted work. Remember, sometimes too many comments can be detrimental. They can be overwhelming on the page, and you risk losing student interest. The more intentional you can be about what you are assessing, the more you can target your feedback so that students can absorb it. As a general approach to each assignment, start with asking yourself, "What do I hope students will learn about the work or about themselves through my comments to them?" The following are some questions to help you determine a feedback goal for specific assignments.

For Tone

- How can you be succinct so that students can digest your comments?
- How do you want a student to feel after reading your comments?
- What specific words and phrases can you intentionally use to encourage and equip students?
- How can you recall something a student did well and apply it to a growth area?

For Content Assessment

- Do you want to reinforce one particular skill or a variety of skills on this piece?
- Is this a quick review with holistic comments as you grade the piece as a whole?
- Is this a more in-depth review with specific comments that target various skills?
- Are you most interested in assessing content knowledge, writing style or structure, or both on this piece?
- How important is grammar in this assignment?
- What have you recently taught that you want to see reflected in the assignment?

Amplify Your Tone

Since students can't read the facial expression or hear the voice of the person grading their paper, educators can take extra care to let their voice translate to the written word. Often, this requires precise word choice and some cheerleading. The following comments are some examples of intentionally amplified tone.

- "I love your voice in this piece. Your personality really comes through in this writing."
- "You made a fresh insight here! Great observation."
- "Way to go on using that semicolon correctly!"
- "You made some terrific revision choices from your rough draft."
- "I like how you did _____ because _____."
- "I noticed you _____; that works really well because _____."
- "The connection you made between _____ and _____ stood out to me because _____."

Use Care in Critique

In cultivating a positive and encouraging tone, make sure constructive criticisms are, in fact, constructive. Avoid harsh criticism that may deflate or defeat student confidence. Grading should coach students to recognize areas they can develop and encourage them to stretch as learners. Pointing out errors is just one small part of a teacher's job; bolstering students' confidence to learn from those errors is the better part of the job. Give them resources and opportunities to improve. Here are some examples of comments to use in critiquing and supporting student work.

- "What other examples could you use here to show what you mean?"
- "Check out this resource on proofreading to help you edit your paper next time."
- "I see your point here! You can make it even more powerful by _____."
- "Reorganizing your structure with a strong beginning-middle-end would help me follow the thoughtful points you are making."

Be Authentic

Finding your teacher voice is worth some self-examination. If you feel comfortable in your classroom, if you have a sense of creativity and feel energized, and if your students respond well to your teaching style, you have likely found your voice. Or, you might find yourself struggling to communicate, perhaps often second-guessing conversations or students' reactions to you. You may not be completely comfortable in your classroom yet, and that's OK—it takes time! The following are some actions to take and questions to ask in considering what your teacher voice is and how you can develop it.

- Consider the difference between the way you speak to friends and family and the way you speak to your students. Certainly, teachers are more professional and intentional with the words and topics they share while in their classrooms. That said, your general tone should be similar.

- Do others comment that you have a great sense of humor? If so, do you share that humor in class when appropriate? Look for ways to share jokes, make humorous (but not sarcastic, as that tone can be extra hurtful coming from an educator) comments, and show your appreciation for student humor too.

- Are you a quiet person who is trying to be louder in the classroom? That may not be a comfortable fit for you. You can be soft spoken and still be impactful. Tom Hierck's (2017) *Seven Keys to a Positive Learning Environment in Your Classroom* provides some excellent advice on classroom management that has nothing to do with how loud your voice is.

- Ask a friend or colleague to visit your class, or record part of a teaching session. Afterward, reflect with the friend or colleague on how you present yourself in this group setting. What differences and similarities do they notice between the way you are one-on-one and the way you are in a group? Decide what qualities you want to bring into the classroom.

- Give yourself permission to be you. Teachers are diverse and complex, just like their students. The best thing you can do for your students is to encourage them to be their fantastic, original selves, and that goes for you too. Authenticity is freeing and sends a message for students to be confident in their own skins as well.

Jeff Healy: From Marketer to Maestro

Jeff Healy brings a unique perspective to online, international education, having spent several years as a classroom teacher in Southern Brazil before transitioning to an instructional specialist in an online school. Jeff's ability to build relationships with multilingual learners has been instrumental in his success in the classroom and in virtual learning spaces.

> I once had a quote pinned to the wall of my cubicle: "Stop selling and start helping." Before beginning my career in education, I held various sales and marketing positions and had become an expert at building relationships with clients. However, this success wasn't fulfilling. I wanted to have a more meaningful impact on people's lives. It wasn't until I took a leap of faith toward a career in education that I discovered my place in the world.
>
> A sales manager once told me, "People buy from those they like." I found this holds true in education, where students learn from those they like. I was good at developing relationships with my clients on a level that made our business relationships seem more personal. So how could I transfer this skill to a new career in education? I couldn't just jump right into content without knowing my students first. As an untrained classroom teacher, I found my experience in sales helped me not only survive but also thrive in the classroom. I have been able to adapt several sales techniques with teaching strategies that work to build relationships with students in a culturally diverse environment both in person and online. (Jeff Healy, personal communication, June 15, 2021)

Strategies for Cultivating Connection

The following strategies come from Jeff Healy's experiences applying what he learned in one professional space to his teaching practice. The general attitudes and approaches he developed are good tips for all educators as they teach in various spaces.

Relate to Challenges

To relate to your multilingual students, become a language learner with them. For Jeff, learning Portuguese while working with English learners in Brazil allowed him to connect with his students and understand some challenges of language acquisition. Use conversations with your students to practice learning in their first language. This will help you appreciate the challenges they face as they work in a second language, and it will affirm in a big way that you are interested in learning about your students. Ask students to teach you how to count and label everyday objects in their home language. Beyond that, practice asking and answering questions in casual conversations; this creates a language-learning culture in your class that applies to both students and teachers. If you want to go further with your own language learning, you can take a language class or use an online learning tool like Duolingo, Babbel, or Rosetta Stone.

Connect on a Personal Level

Jeff Healy set out to develop strong relationships by talking about sports and other favorite activities, as well as comparing foods, habits, and traditions between home countries. He found that once he built a strong connection on these comfortable topics, it became easier to move on to more challenging topics. As you set out to establish this kind of rapport, be authentic. Explore your students' interests with a genuine curiosity, and show them that you are comfortable answering questions they may have about your experiences too. Seek out opportunities to discuss life outside of the context of the coursework. Interactive and engaging warm-up activities provide a great means to do this.

Have Fun

School can be stressful. Look for opportunities to have fun while building relationships. We (Stephanie and Kathryn) have organized dance parties, game days, talent showcases, joke days, and poem-in-your-pocket celebrations to have fun with students. Having fun builds community. Further, all these examples ask students to practice language learning, collaboration, and creativity and to take healthy risks. These are exactly the kinds of affective, or social-emotional, skills teachers want to build in their school communities.

Change the Environment

Some say more business is done on a golf course than in a meeting room. This may be because people are more comfortable on the course, away from the pressure that comes with a formal environment. Jeff shared a story with us about how he filmed and produced a series of music videos, clip by clip, over several weeks with his students' help. Once he had the footage for an entire video, he edited it together. Jeff lights up when he talks about this: "The students loved making and watching them! Having fun together outside the classroom allows students to become more comfortable inside the classroom."

For in-person settings, look for ways to venture outside the classroom sometimes. The outdoors offers a great opportunity to read literature, compose a poem, or look for natural symbolism. Students can also explore real shapes, angles, measurements, biology, and ecology. They can draw from different perspectives, listen for natural rhythms, or gather a collection of sensory objects.

For online spaces, accessing the outdoors is just as important. These outdoor activities just might take a little more planning and require extra-clear guidelines. One online teacher we talked with during our research surveyed all families in her before-school conferences to see what kinds of safe access students had to outdoor spaces. She then used this information to create accessible activities for her diverse learners who lived in different kinds of environments. The following list offers a few more suggestions for changing the environment.

- Set clear boundaries for when students will leave their computer and return. You can tell students something like, "When I say *go*, I want you to walk outside your front door, stand still, and notice as much as you can with your five senses. I'm setting a timer, and I want to see everyone back on my screen in five minutes and three seconds. On your mark, get set, go!"
- Give students time to share what they accomplished and how it related to the task you assigned. You can say something like, "Everyone, put in the chat one thing you noticed with the sense of hearing." Or, "Hold up your fingers to show how many senses you used when you were outside."
- Make plans for students who need support. Depending on age or ability, they may join an older sibling or caregiver for these explorations.

This structure works best with a specific task in mind—something students can go accomplish and then come back and share. Ways you can make movement and fresh air part of your lesson include having students design a scavenger hunt to find an object that represents something connected to the lesson, compare the measurements of two objects found outside, do a quick sketch of an object, or take a photograph.

CONNECTED TEACHING COMMITMENT
Use Your Teacher Voice

I (Kathryn) host early morning teas and lead late-afternoon dance parties (even on Zoom). I love to organize huge events (both virtually and in person) with my students. Stephanie has the perfect GIF for every occasion, can go right to the heart of what a stressed-out student (or colleague) is saying and respond with clarity and warmth, and often finds herself in heart-to-hearts with teachers amid huge conferences. If I sent a GIF, it would likely fall flat. If Stephanie hosted a dance party, it might feel forced. Just as all students are unique individuals with specific strengths, preferences, and personalities, so are educators. While cultivating class culture and connecting with students, be authentic and true. Are you a jokester? Are you an introvert? Do you love basketball? Are you an artist? Yes, you can borrow ideas from colleagues, but you have to use who you are to connect with students. Authenticity always rings true. When teachers practice authenticity and honor their own strengths, they give their students permission and encouragement to do the same.

Stephanie Walter: Four-Step Feedback Process

Throughout over twenty years of teaching, Stephanie Walter has taught in public, private, and blended classrooms, meeting students from all over the world and encouraging them as they evolve as writers and learners. Her current role affords her the opportunity to develop curriculum, support lead teachers, manage a large team of instructional specialists, and partner with classroom teachers. As one of the authors of this book, Stephanie has spent significant time developing an effective feedback process that meets the needs of online students.

In our school context, we (Kathryn and I) work with thousands of students in over forty countries. We serve on close-knit instructional teams of lead teachers and specialists for content areas, who give feedback to students through our learning management system. We often work with partner teachers who present our curriculum and support students through the creative process to turn in their final drafts. This exciting chance to participate in a global educational model provides some unique challenges. First, how do you show students you care about them in such an expanded space? Next, how do you even grade that many papers and get them back to students in a timely manner? Finally, how do you make sure teams are grading fairly and giving consistent feedback to these groups of students?

As our team members thought together about how to approach grading using a team model and serving so many students at one time, we started by articulating our most important goals. Eventually, we agreed on the following top three commitments.

1. We aim to use a warm and supportive tone so our students know we respect and care for them.
2. We are committed to giving full, constructive feedback.
3. We are dedicated to scoring fairly and consistently through rubric-centered feedback.

Once we set those goals, our next step was to design a feedback model that would help each instructor on our team use a warm tone, give full and developed comments, and tie these comments to each assignment's rubric. Our team, probably like yours, has centuries of grading experience combined. We broke down our grading process to see what really works in terms of giving students feedback that they can digest and that instructors don't need an hour per paper to deliver! Eventually, we set in place our four-step feedback process and began to test it on the papers

> we graded. We quickly (and with relief!) found that it worked to align our team members' diverse grading styles and helped us stay true to our student-centered values.

Strategies for Using the Four-Step Feedback Process

Using feedback as a vehicle for instruction and relationship building is at the heart of how the instructional team at my (Stephanie's) school approaches teaching. We practice the four-step feedback process to create a positive tone through feedback comments that relate to clear objectives. This conversational feedback points students forward and makes an important difference in how students receive and digest encouragement. The following strategies describe this four-step feedback process with examples to help you implement a strong grading structure in your classroom.

Step 1: Focus on the Positive First

Quickly read the student's assignment once to get a general sense of it. While reading, stop to make several positive comments that celebrate enjoyable or well-done parts of the work. This easy, quick step switches your focus from the red-pen mentality (as in, "Let's find what's wrong in this submission") to a strengths-based approach (as in, "Let's start with what's going well in this submission"). Making sure you share several encouraging comments gives students a strong "I'm rooting for you!" feeling when they read feedback comments all the way through.

Point comments are an effective way to leave positive commentary. These short comments tie directly to specific parts of the assignment (see figure 3.1).

Step 2: Tie Feedback to the Rubric

Have you ever sat down to grade a paper and felt overwhelmed by the sheer number of issues you want to correct or give advice about? It can be difficult to find just the right balance in feedbacking. Too few comments, and the student doesn't know how to improve and prepare for next time. Too many comments, and the feedback overloads the student with too much information to absorb (and probably discourages them as well). Plus, all this feedback takes time!

Rubric-centered feedback helps students focus on the rubric to analyze their work and see why they earned a certain score. Focusing on the rubric also helps teachers streamline their feedback to be powerful and focused, rather than spending too much time commenting on the multitude of things they could mention. Go down the list of rubric criteria, and use that list to guide the comment-

> **Positive Point Comments**
>
> What a sharp insight!
>
> Way to go on supporting that idea with textual evidence.
>
> This is a fantastic example of an open, curiosity-based question.
>
> You show a lot of growth in this area since last time.
>
> Nice use of specific steps to solve this problem.
>
> I love the way you incorporated [insert relevant information here].
>
> I can follow your reasoning very well here.
>
> This part really made me think!
>
> My imagination went wild when I read this part—nice sensory language!
>
> Interesting, creative solution to this problem!
>
> This part made me laugh out loud, literally.
>
> Wow! These steps are specific and actionable.

Figure 3.1: Sample positive point comments.

making process. Focus on specific moments in the assignment to emphasize something well done or to give support. Also, give more general feedback about the criterion to help students see patterns and areas to focus on.

With rubric-centered grading, keep in mind that it is a gift to stay focused. The single graded paper is not an educator's only chance to share feedback with any one student. Students will hear from the teacher often throughout the year, and they have many other teachers giving them feedback as well. The more targeted a teacher stays with each paper, the more easily students can digest the most important areas they can focus on. It's best that students, and teachers, tackle a skill or two at a time. Note that if your school does not use a formal rubric, you can apply this strategy to the guidelines or objectives for each assignment.

Teachers can leave their rubric-related notes in the form of point comments and rubric comments. Rubric comments are the happy medium between point comments and holistic comments. The rubric is a good place to point out areas that are especially good and to give general feedback, tips, and resources for areas that need more work. As with all feedback, the best rubric comments are uplifting and helpfully point to ways to learn and improve.

Figure 3.2 (page 92) lists examples of constructive comments that tie to rubric criteria, objectives, and goals.

> **Rubric Comments**
>
> This would be a great place to add a specific example or an anecdote.
>
> What additional ways might you reach this solution?
>
> Using chronological structure would make this section even stronger.
>
> What might happen if you reorder this by starting the piece with your last sentence?
>
> Tell me more about how you came to that conclusion.
>
> What specific evidence can you add to support this claim?
>
> Check out the text for more specific examples to add to your opinion.
>
> To make this even more specific, add what types of exercises build strength.
>
> What challenges do you need to overcome to meet this goal?
>
> Reviewing your work before you submit will help you see both what you're doing well and where you can improve.

Figure 3.2: Sample rubric comments.

Figure 3.3 is a sample rubric from an upper-level English course. Notice that the rubric comments are more general than specific point comments while also giving advice on overall skills to focus on next time.

Step 3: Award a Holistic Score

The rubric is a powerful guide to grading. It helps educators thoughtfully assess specific areas of each assignment. It provides a focused and succinct way to break down aspects of the assignment and make sure the student hears from their teacher on each important objective and guideline. However, consider this scenario: You read through a student's paper and think to yourself, "Hey! That was pretty good. I really enjoyed their voice, and they made some good points." Then, you score the paper according to the objectives or rubric, and the student ends up with a low C or D. Your gut said, "That was pretty good!" but the scores don't match your original assessment. What happened?

In some types of assignments, especially those of a subjective nature, the individual scores on each rubric strand don't always tell the whole story. As the gestalt principle reminds us, "The whole is greater than the sum of its parts." This is where a teacher's holistic assessment of student work comes in. Because the teacher has already scanned the paper, looked for positive and encouraging parts to point out, and made notes that tie to the rubric, they have a solid grasp of the paper as a whole by this point. As the teacher wraps up consideration of the paper, they need to give it one more look to be sure the final score is fair.

Essay Rubric	
Criterion	Example Comment
Focus	You remained tightly focused on the prompt throughout the entire essay.
Introduction: Hook	An anecdote is one great strategy to catch your readers' attention!
Introduction: Preview of Main Points	You alluded to your main points; be more specific next time so that your intro serves as a clear map to readers about where we are going in this essay.
Introduction: Thesis Statement	Excellent. This thesis is concise and defendable.
Supporting Paragraph 1	Clear topic sentence that relates to the main points in your introduction. Add in more specific details from the text to support your main idea.
Supporting Paragraph 2	Excellent details and examples in this paragraph!
Supporting Paragraph 3	Again, your details are strong and support the main idea! A concluding sentence that emphasizes your stance would make this paragraph even stronger.
Conclusion	Your conclusion is fitting; work more to make it a sibling to your introduction rather than a twin.
Transitions	Beautiful job of transitioning between paragraphs!
Mechanics	Overall, your essay is easy to read and follow. Next time, proofread to correct run-on sentences.
Writing Process and Reflection	You show thoughtful change from your first to your final draft. I like how you incorporated some of your peer reviewers' ideas but stayed true to your own style in this essay.

Figure 3.3: Sample rubric.

While grading, consider whether a student is "in control" or "out of control" of the prompt or objective for the assignment. These terms are defined as follows.

- **In control:** Students who are in control of the prompt earn an A or B. Their writing shows that they understand the prompt, demonstrate some critical or creative thinking about it, can support their ideas, and can develop a piece from beginning to end.
- **Out of control:** Students who are out of control of the prompt earn a D or F. Their writing may approach or circle around the prompt, but there

is little evidence that the student fully understands what the prompt asks. The writing is mostly summary or, if it shows development, off prompt. There is little critical or creative thinking, minimal support of ideas, and weak structure.

When you finish the paper review, enter the individual rubric scores, and determine the total score by dividing the points earned by the total possible to see whether the grade matches your original judgment. If the points match the original holistic assessment, then the final score is likely fair. If the points and the holistic score don't match, look over the paper one more time to be sure the final score is fair, given the work shown in the overall paper.

Step 4: End on a Positive Note

Now, you have fully reviewed the paper, and any feedback comments you have left on it are uplifting and constructive all the way through. To finish, quickly look at the comments through the eyes of the student who wrote the paper. Ask yourself, "If I received these comments, would I: (1) feel supported in my work, (2) know what I did well, and (3) have a clear idea of how to improve for next time?" Take time to add more positive comments if needed. Then, one quick step remains. A holistic comment on the paper sums up the main assessment and gives a final verbal high five to the student. On short or check-in assignments, this holistic comment may be the only comment on the paper. On longer or summative assignments, the holistic comment serves as the capstone of all the feedback.

Use the sandwich technique to end student review time with encouragement: include (1) a specific compliment about something they did well on this assignment, (2) your best tip to help them focus on one big thing to improve for next time, and (3) a general compliment or encouragement for next time.

Figure 3.4 includes examples of holistic feedback from several different types of courses.

After using the four-step feedback process for five years, our team adjusted it to best fit different types of assignments. Holistic grading is most helpful on longer or more complex assignments, subjective assignments, assignments that act as scaffolds to another assignment, and key assessments that have a major impact on students' grades. For instance, mathematics classes don't rely on holistic scoring as much as social studies courses do. However, all our teaching team's members have found the value in using rubric-centered grading and considering the whole body of work our students submit. Some students have sent replies to feedback to give teachers thanks for noticing what they're doing or to continue conversations teachers started through the comments. Many on our team have also found success applying this process in face-to-face classrooms. One instructor said, "I

	Holistic Comments
Course	**Example Comment**
Algebra I	James, you demonstrated good mastery of the processes we're studying in this lesson. I have attached some extra problems for more practice to solve by factoring. Overall, you show strong reasoning as you work through these problems!
Chemistry	Sandra, you thoroughly described the process and outcomes of your lab experiment. I wrote specific notes in places you could describe specific processes; please see those and let me know if you have questions. Overall, you are asking effective questions to guide your investigations!
Composition and Literature	Giulia, you specifically introduced your compare-contrast topic. Next time, use more specific examples from the story to show the differences between the characters. Keep up the great work in maintaining a consistent focus on the prompt all the way through!
Debate	¡Buenos días, León! Thank you for presenting on plastic waste! Your hook really captured my attention, and you did a great job of supporting each of your main points with evidence. As you prepare for your next speech, practice making eye contact with your audience. Your confidence is growing, and your writing is developing! I look forward to seeing your next speech. ¡Buen trabajo!
Economics	Anne, you have a strong consideration of how you spent your time this week. I love your idea to try the time analysis one more time to see what changes. Be sure to see my comments about some other tools to help you chart the data. You clearly present how you spend your time, and you analyze it quite well. Nice work!
Health	David, your presentation is well researched and eye appealing! On your next assignment, follow our outline for help strengthening your presentation or message structure. Your creative ideas for promoting a healthy lifestyle came through strongly in this assignment.
Photography	Ruth, the angles and balance in these photographs really captured my imagination… One thing to consider for the next assignment is when to focus on the background or environment and when to focus on the foreground or single subject. Your last shot was astounding—the clouds floating behind the bare trees created an otherworldly effect.
Physical Science	Brett, your observations are clear and well explained. Next time, remember to write a full, succinct summary of the results. Overall, you have done a great job of supporting your statements with qualitative and quantitative data.

Figure 3.4: Sample holistic comments.

continued ▶

	Holistic Comments
Course	Example Comment
Precalculus	Ginny, your work shows strong reasoning and organized thought. There were a few problems where you needed to show your work, so check carefully for that next time. Overall, you show great mastery of this problem set. Good work!
U.S. History	Henry, your analysis is full and well reasoned. On your next essay, spend more time relating to these primary sources. Overall, this is a strong analysis. Keep up the good work!
World Religions	Emery, thank you for your hard work on this submission. Your interview questions were very insightful and really captured the goals of this course well with your emphasis on internal diversity! I would have loved to hear the voice of your interview participant, though. You could have recorded the interview with him and included the audio in your podcast. Your editing with the music, the transitions, and the flow of the episode is wonderful.

wish I had learned a process like this years ago!" Rubric-centered grading has introduced a steady and efficient pace to the feedback process and refocused the teaching team on each assignment's main goals by reminding them to stay positive during conversations with students.

Sometimes, it is not necessary to implement the entire four-step feedback process. This process is best for major and summative assignments where teachers will want to provide comprehensive feedback. Teachers can mix and match point comments (and similarly, rubric-centered comments) and holistic comments (general comments that apply to the work as a whole) for formative assignments like drafts, practice papers, and quick checks. Teachers can use point comments to comment on specific parts of the work and use holistic comments to give an overall assessment of the work.

Try the steps out on the next major graded assignment. At the end of this chapter (page 101), you'll find a handy reproducible with prompts to help practice implementing the four-step feedback process. Students will warm up to this kind of feedback, and with a little practice, grading time will become more efficient and more enjoyable. The following strategies deepen the four-step feedback process.

Think Like a Student

Teacher feedback will not help students if they can't take it in. Think carefully about sharing comments with students, especially when you're not in the same physical space as them. Think about what kind of tone helps put students in the right state of mind to digest feedback comments.

Plan From the Beginning

Make sure each prompt or objective is clear and directions are straightforward. Also, your method for grading an assignment must match the experiences students have had time to practice and the clearly stated guidelines. What may seem obvious or clear to you may be lost on students. As you consider your feedback style, also consider your assignment presentation style. How can teachers make all assignments' goals clear for students? What scoring guides, rubrics, objectives, and outlines can teachers share to help students understand their goals in completing the assignments? Consider the following.

- Before each assignment, go over the assignment prompt and rubric with students. Let them know that you will grade their work according to these guidelines, and they should refer to them often as they work to make sure they are on the right track.

- Ask students to share any questions they have about the assignment or the rubric.

- Before students turn in an assignment, ask them to self-grade their work using the rubric. This helps them focus on the guidelines and begin to look at the assignment through an instructor's eyes. It will set the tone for when you return the assignment later.

- Use peer review on some assignments. Again, encourage use of the rubric to emphasize its importance to the reviewer and the reviewee.

Note That Points Can Be Tricky

Grading holistically is especially important on assignments that are worth only a few points. A ten-point scale makes it easy to assign reasonable point values that align to grades A, B, C, D, and F. But a five-point scale has no point value for a C. Grading gets even trickier on a three-point scale, where a two out of three is a D. Consider the grading scale as a tool to help make grading fairer, and use the in-control versus out-of-control guidelines earlier in this chapter (page 93) as a helpful tool to balance the total points and a holistic score.

Hone Your Grading Style Through Peer Review and Self-Review

When you grade, are you a Santa who tends to give a lot of grace, a Grinch who tends to be exacting, or something in between? Meet with a partner teacher or team to grade similar assignments together. Use the four-step feedback process to grade a few sample papers and analyze each other's feedback and scoring style.

Reflect on this experience to further develop your feedback skills and consistency, and regroup every month or quarter to compare grading styles and continue your discussion about scoring consistency.

Next, practice using the four-step feedback process on several assignments—checking that your tone is encouraging, you comment on each assessed objective, your holistic comments give students something to work on *and* point out what they did well, and the final score lines up with your overall assessment of the piece. With time, this process won't take as much concentration as it may at first. It will start to feel natural. Taking time periodically to hone your grading style through self-reflection, your colleagues' feedback, and your students' responses will help you develop feedback in a way that works well in your particular context.

Make Feedback Meaningful by Inviting Student Responses

You might be the kind of educator who instills a lot of heart and energy into your student feedback. But all that feedback will get lost in the daily shuffle if you don't create the expectation that students will read and apply this feedback. Tell students often that your feedback is meant to support them, and give them the time to apply it. You spend time grading their work so they know how they did on an assignment and so they can learn how to grow as communicators.

The following tasks can give students the necessary space to digest feedback during class.

- Turn to a partner or use the chat to share one compliment you received in feedback on your work.
- Your exit slip today is to write down one thing you learned from this assignment that you will try to do next time.
- Everyone, share the biggest challenge you had with this assignment. Let's look for patterns in this class and see what we can learn from each other.
- Copy down one sentence with a grammar error. Rewrite the sentence correctly, and resubmit it. Ask for help if you need it!

If you don't have time during class, students can asynchronously do similar tasks and message you their answers or turn them in next class period. Be open to questions, and encourage students to make sure they understand your feedback. If you see several questions of the same type, a short skill lesson or even a class discussion that acknowledges a common trouble spot can help students understand they are not alone and they can learn a certain skill. By inviting students into this conversation, you can show them that you expect them to use your feedback in future work and that you respect their learning process.

Key Classroom Takeaway: All Teaching Is a Conversation

Classrooms are busy, complex spaces, but within the complexities are many practices educators can use to build relationships. Sometimes, relationships come through casual conversations. Other times, relationships form through specific classroom activities or discussions. The varied strategies teachers can call on to keep the connections strong and growing are always present somewhere in the background.

Earlier in this chapter, Chris Holmes celebrated the simplicity and power in being present for two students. They had fallen behind. Assignments had piled up, and they both felt paralyzed with uncertainty at how to get started again. Chris was a friendly face on the other side of the screen. A few encouraging words and the gift of time with him were all it took to break the ice, and these two students started working and found their rhythm again.

This experience came when Chris's school was just transitioning to an online context. Chris was facing his own challenges as a teacher who was used to being super engaged in a face-to-face classroom space and had to learn to connect with students across a screen.

Our (Kathryn and Stephanie's) team spoke with Chris again when he had a year of experience connecting with students online. The lesson of being present remained. Chris said, "I virtually tutored a half-dozen kids from California to Massachusetts this year. Almost all of them respond the same way as the students from the story you are sharing; just the presence of someone (who may or may not be asked to help) makes all the difference. Just knowing someone is there matters." This experience taught Chris (and us) that being there for students doesn't always require huge, grand gestures. Being there is in the daily grind; teachers do it moment by moment with students, no matter the classroom context.

Summary

Fostering student voice and engagement in any classroom requires time, wisdom, honesty, vulnerability, and patience. People might miss some everyday cues in technology-mediated spaces. For example, students might not catch a teacher's lopsided smile that indicates they are joking. Students might not see the twinkle in a teacher's eye when they offer a suggestion. Students can't feel a reassuring pat on the back or even a high five. The relationship that might form within days or weeks in a face-to-face classroom may take more time to solidify in an online space.

Additionally, students sit in one place for far too long, layering a physical challenge onto learning that might be new to them. Videos and interactives, which used to provide a break from lectures and reading, have now become the repetitive norm. *Zoom fatigue*, exhaustion from concentrating on a screen for hours at a time and knowing that you are being watched, is real (Nadler, 2020). Expressing oneself through only words, with little reliance on body language or facial reactions, can certainly cause disconnect. Students may miss the camaraderie of their classmates, inside jokes, the easy rhythm of conversation, and even the art of goofing off just enough to create a break before getting back to work. These things all look different in the online space. This space can be uncomfortable for most people and downright dejecting for some.

And yet, research and emerging practices show there is an alternative. Educators can facilitate connection, camaraderie, wellness, and humor in blended classrooms through everyday cues. In this chapter, you learned how seeing students as individuals is the first step in approaching teaching and giving feedback. Chris Holmes reminded educators that small, simple moments with students have a big impact on their attitudes and success. Nancy Stoker detailed how she prepares herself for grading an assignment, including imagining the student sitting right beside her. Jeff Healy discussed using his passion for marketing to experiment with ways to get students excited about learning and improving their work. Finally, you read about the four-step feedback process, designed to help you grade efficiently, maintain a positive and warm tone, and develop comments that are both meaningful and relational.

These experienced educators' strategies will help you give feedback in a way that matters. They also encourage you to approach each student as an individual with strengths, identities, and lived experiences that matter, and to always look out for ways to encourage and call students to great success. In chapter 4, you'll continue to think about why conversations matter as you consider the power of story sharing in your classroom. By avoiding the ever-present pressure to rush right into the content, educators can hold firm to the belief that relationship building is the most important part of what they do. The delightful result is that students become even more engaged as they interact with the class content with critical thinking and personal connection.

Chapter 3: Apply It to Your Practice

Working individually or in learning teams, reflect on these questions, and implement the commitments to your practice (for more information on engaging with these questions, please see the section titled Space for Reflective Practice on page 9 in the introduction). As always, strive to move your reflection to action.

React to the Chapter

What are your key takeaways from this chapter? What was surprising to read? What did you connect with?

Evaluate Your Assignments for Clarity

Before feedbacking, make sure your assignment directions are clear and students know exactly what each one will assess. Answer the following questions to help you evaluate assignments, projects, presentations, and exams in your practice.

- Does the assignment tie closely to a meaningful objective?

- Is the prompt, or goal, clear to students?

- Do the instructions help students map out what they need to accomplish?

- Does the rubric clearly assess the intentions of the assignment?

Starting with just an assignment or two, experiment with the assignment prompt, directions, and rubric. Implement some tweaks or major revisions to make each one clearer and more usable for students.

Analyze Your Feedback for Compassion

Choose a group of student work that you have given feedback on. Read that feedback as if you were a student or a nonexpert in the class. Overall, does the tone of your comments present as positive and encouraging? Do the comments give specific advice for how to improve? Do you end on an upbeat note? Consider your feedback overall, and decide where you would like to tweak it for a more positive tone or more rubric-centered comments.

Practice the Four-Step Feedback Process

Instructors who use the four-step feedback process share that their grading has purpose, it goes quickly, and students receive it well. Like any good thing, this process takes practice. Choose an assignment, and experiment with using this process. What feels awkward as you try a new approach? What goes smoothly? Notice where you would like to tweak and practice using the process as it becomes a tool for connection and efficiency in your grading.

Be There

Being there for students includes an array of possibilities: simply being present, making space for important conversations, and building relationships through daily practices like feedbacking. Describe a time when you were there for a student and what it meant to both of you. What skills from that experience apply to other work in the classroom? What other opportunities do you have to be there for students in online and blended contexts?

PART II
Ensuring Equity and Inclusion in the Online Classroom

In part I, you read about how focusing on students as individuals with unique voices, strengths, and experiences can guide your approach to student support, feedback, and relationship building. In this next part, we build on this work and extend it to explore intercultural sensitivity, global competencies, and culturally sustaining pedagogies (Bennett, 2017; Olson & Kroeger, 2001; Paris, 2012). We share stories from educators who are engaged in humanizing practices in online and blended classrooms and are committed to expanding equity, representation, and access across all spaces where they work with youth.

As you read through part II's chapters, consider how diversity, equity, and inclusion commitments are situated in your school or district community. In chapter 2 (page 56), we introduced Bettina Love's (2019) work, which calls on educators to "have grit for justice." We return to that concept here. Does your class, school, or district view DEI as isolated—one more thing to report on, not connected to other work of school? Or does it view DEI as integral—the work that drives its academic commitments? What specific targets for representation, belonging, safety, and equity do you want to set within your immediate sphere of influence (often your classroom) and within larger communities (such as your school and district)? You are doing transformative work. We have no doubt that you are building meaningful relationships, saving lives even, and often having a greater impact than you even know. And still, the work is ongoing; as Martin Luther King Jr. reminds us, "The arc of the moral universe is long, but it bends toward justice" (SeeMeOnline, n.d.).

Centering Student Stories 4

Before anything else, teachers must consider the perspectives of their students to situate them right at the center of their own learning. That means educators, as excited and knowledgeable as they are about the content they teach, need to protect space for student voices as they plan and carry out their lessons. Teachers in connected classrooms are not mere dispensers of knowledge, spouting out wisdom and hoping their students catch it. They don't want their students to, as some educators say, *sit and get* (that is, sit in their chairs, hear information, and regurgitate it for the sole purpose of a test grade).

Instead, these teachers want students to have ownership over their learning and to get excited about topics, ask questions, find meaning in their work, apply one concept to another area, and even challenge concepts and curriculum. What a mountainous series of tasks! How do you both effectively communicate learning objectives and foster critical thinking? The answer is (you guessed it) through connection. And making these connections requires storytelling—although not the type of storytelling you might be thinking of (as you'll discover as you read on).

This chapter features narratives from five practitioners who have found their way to the online classroom. Jill Clingan, Lou Jobst, Megan Lilien,

Essential Question

How can educators cultivate connection through story sharing in online and blended classrooms?

Chapter Learning Objectives

- Revisit your educator origin story and connect it to your current hopes and goals.
- Build opportunities for empathy with students.
- Incorporate music and poetry into content-based learning and student reflection.
- Support diversity, equity, and inclusion through class conversations and activities.

Key Terms

center. To bring into focus, to honor, or to cast as important. People can center identities, experiences, ideas, voices, and individuals. Centering is an important practice in inclusion and equity work.

classroom culture. The environment where student learning takes place. A positive classroom culture fosters honest perspective sharing and respect.

empathy. The learned practice of actively listening to someone's story and striving to emotionally connect with them.

equity. The practice of evaluating and understanding context and individual needs to determine support and resource distribution. (This is both in contrast and in cooperation with *equality approaches*, where all individuals have the same supports and resources regardless of context and individual needs.)

margins. Metaphorically, people create margins through the circles they draw around groups to define them. Identities and experiences inside the margins are included and centered by dominant cultures, whereas identities and experiences outside the circles are often excluded, unknown, feared, or made invisible by dominant cultures (related term: *marginalized*).

story-based curriculum. Lessons that emphasize the beginning-middle-end (or continuation) of a topic for student exploration in this pattern: "What can we learn from the past, how does this affect our community now, and what responsibility and roles do we have moving ahead?"

Nina Sprouse, and Greg Soden didn't start their teaching careers in online and blended classrooms, yet they have learned more about connection, story, and relationships in those spaces than they could have imagined. Teaching is a learning journey. Journeys offer opportunities to start anew while staying true to the lesson learned, shedding what was not useful before and adventurously weaving in new ideas and approaches.

As you read the educator narratives and strategies in this chapter, consider the perspectives, family knowledge, cultural identities, and lived experiences that your students bring to the classroom. How can you leverage your students' prior knowledge and strengths to connect and also to deepen your class community? In this chapter, you'll consider making space for student voices, thinking intentionally about interaction, and asking important questions about who you represent in your curriculum and how. To reference an educational conference that our school community led, and that Jill references in her narrative (page 109), these stories all point to the transformative power of connection through story sharing.

Connection Built Through Stories

Educators host groups of students in their classrooms for only short periods of time, always keeping in mind that the time they spend together is meant to prepare students for the next course in a content area, the next grade, the next education level, and their communities and lives ahead. What happens when students walk away from class for the last time? They still have more to learn. They still have challenges to overcome. They still have growing to do. Through the power of story and connection, empathy moves educators beyond a single successful year with students and into the lifelong learning journey they hope that young people have.

Most teachers want students to go beyond memorizing facts to pass the test at the end of a chapter; instead, they want students to wrestle with big ideas and connect to stories across course themes. Lifelong, impactful learning is all about the story—what students learn from it, what it means for them now, and how they interact with it. Table 4.1 (page 108) shares several examples of what this learning looks like across content areas in the blended school system.

All content areas can utilize a story-based design. Through stories, students learn to connect and communicate with others. As students think about the power of stories and look at course content, educators hope to engage them not through the lens of "Will this be on the test?" but with the perspective of "What can I learn about myself and the world through this story?"

Stories open up space for students' voices to take residence in their classroom. Educators must take responsibility for protecting and keeping open the space stories work to create. How teachers and students come to a place of trust and acknowledgment, and a place that allows them to examine other stories and share their own, points again to the learned skill of empathy. Educators may not have an anxiety disorder that demands they turn off their camera in the middle of class to take deep breaths, but they certainly have experienced worry and stress. Teachers don't always know whether a student has lost a parent or sibling to violence or disease, but they have experienced loss in many heartbreaking forms over the years. Teachers might not know what it's like to struggle in their content area so much that doing well in (or even passing) the course seems out of reach, but they have faced other challenges they had to stare down and overcome. Like their students, sometimes teachers succeed, and sometimes they don't, and teachers and students understand this about each other as well.

Table 4.1: Story-Based Course Design

Subject	Focus	How to Share Stories in the Online or Blended Classroom
What subjects can practice story-based curriculum?	How do teachers integrate stories in their curriculum?	How do students engage with and share stories through projects and assignments?
Literature	Throughout the course, students focus on the power of the story. Stories connect people, reflect people's shared experience, reveal themes that impact people, and help people access truth.	Students: • Hear stories • Explore authors who affirm the need for storytelling • Share personal stories on focused prompts through writing and discussion • Author original essays, vignettes, short stories, and poems
World Religions	In this course, students learn to ask good questions across religious and cultural lines. They explore from a place of curiosity and goodwill as they develop as global community members and leaders.	Students: • Hear from course authors and guests about how stories pass on cultural traditions • Listen to stories from different perspectives through readings and podcasts • Share their own stories through class activities and writing prompts • Produce podcasts on reflective prompts about world religions
Economics	Across both micro- and macroeconomics, the class explores how people attempt to satisfy unlimited wants and needs with limited resources. This is true for individuals, for institutions, and for nations. This course introduces the knowledge, skills, and resources to make the best choices possible.	Students: • Answer reflection questions designed to tie the theory of economics to real-life, everyday practices • Analyze authentic and personal situations from the context of the class • Create budgets based on their daily routines and design projects about their choices, values, and goals

Middle School Science	Here, students learn more about the earth from its inception to humans' current global impact. Students recognize the responsibility they have as characters in this continuing story.	Students: • Read scenarios and watch videos designed to share the story of the earth • Research the earth from the perspectives of different communities and geographic locations • Create a public health story in which they research a disease, its community impacts, and individual and community efforts toward a cure, and then present this story through a slideshow presentation with images
Social Studies	Students and teachers read real-life stories together as they examine their country's social justice stories, its historical narratives, and the workings of individuals and communities. Students learn from the past and examine their current institutions, communities, and contexts.	Students: • Experience content through stories from multiple perspectives • Share their own stories through reflection prompts, discussion, and class activities • Deliver speeches, create slideshows, and engage in group projects to analyze history and tie their life experiences to current events

Connections made in the teacher narratives in this chapter include:

- How can teachers build empathy with students they may never see in person?
- How can teachers encourage story sharing?
- What role does encouragement play in empathetic communication?

These questions all point teachers to the impact of sharing their stories and experiences to create connection.

Jill Clingan:
Empathy in Blended Learning Environments

Jill Clingan has taught in online, blended, and in-person contexts for high school and college. Anyone who meets Jill comments on her encouraging and warm nature, and she is known in her school as its heart. Jill's work with international students and partners carries this empathy forward, as she shares in her narrative.

Early in the semester, I received an email from one of my composition and literature students that said, "I hope we have good moments together." I smiled and replied, "I hope we have good moments together too." As a teacher in online education, I do not usually get to see my students face-to-face. Lucas, the student who sent me this email, lives over five thousand miles away in South America. Lucas is one of many students who are eager to connect with their teachers here in the United States, just as I am eager to connect with him and his fellow peers.

The challenge many educators are experiencing as they find themselves immersed in online teaching is how to bridge the gap as they seek to connect with students in critically meaningful ways. I believe that the key to bridging this gap is the cultivation of empathy. Börje Holmberg, a Swedish educator and writer, studied empathy and distance education for decades and found that "feelings of empathy and belonging within a distance education format influenced the learning favorably and promoted students' motivation to learn" (Fuller, 2012, p. 38).

I spoke about empathy with school administrators at a virtual conference whose theme was the transformative power of connection. Before my speech, I asked some educator colleagues how they would define *empathy*. I then compiled their responses into a community poem that I read at the end of my presentation. Here is an excerpt of our poem, "What Is Empathy?"

> Empathy is . . .
>
> Listening hard and becoming vulnerable to what we hear
> Acting on the belief that we belong together
> Wearing someone else's skin
> Being the human I would want as a teacher
> Honoring someone else right where they are and being able to enter that space with them
> Seeing through the eyes and heart of the other
>
> Empathy is . . .
>
> The transformative power of connection

These creative ways of defining empathy stretch the boundaries of a textbook-style definition and help educators consider new ways of thinking about empathy. How can educators listen hard, act on the belief that everyone belongs together, and see through the eyes and hearts of students?

Both for online educators who see their students face-to-face via video and for those who primarily interact through correspondence and feedback, it is essential to extend a great deal of empathy to students. Researchers who studied empathy and student performance with feedback from mathematics tutors found "significant correlations between students who received more empathic messages and those who were more confident, more patient, exhibited higher levels of interest, and valued math knowledge more" (Karumbaiah et al., 2017, p. 96). Conversely, "students who received more success/failure [rather than empathic] messages tended to make more mistakes, to be less learning oriented, and stated that they were more confused" (Karumbaiah et al., 2017, p. 96). Teachers need to respond with empathy for both actual student learning and interest in learning.

The online environment in which I work is unique in that, while classroom teachers in Brazil instruct students, a group of teachers here in the United States grade the students' work. This format could be challenging because those grading work in the United States do not get to know their students in the intimate way that the classroom teachers do. Still, these students are eager to connect, and teachers have the challenge and the opportunity to practice empathy in the way that they grade their assignments.

I once emailed a struggling student not to discuss academics but because her teacher happened to mention that she was a brilliant musician. I passed along the compliment her classroom teacher had given her and asked her, if she was comfortable, to send me a recording of her musical work. Such small connections can make a tremendous impact on students' desire and motivation to learn as well as bolster their ability to connect with others.

Empathy is what makes us human. It is what connects us to our students in a way that helps them feel heard, seen, and understood. When I talk with other adults about their high school years, more often than not, they emphatically state that they would not like to go back and relive those years. High school is a difficult time, and when our students are adults, they may also state that they would not like to go back and relive high school. However, may we be the empathic, impactful teachers about whom our students might later say, "I would not want to go back and relive my high school years, but there was this one teacher..." (Jill Clingan, personal communication, October 7, 2020)

Strategies for Cultivating Empathy in Your Classroom

While working on this project, Jill Clingan interviewed several practitioners about how they incorporate empathy in the blended classroom. The following are strategies, insights, and reflections from her interviews.

Begin With Empathy

Each new school year is a beginning that requires new decisions, planning, and action. Jill suggests that the best classroom beginnings start with empathy. Why begin with empathy? Research professor Brené Brown (2012) explains:

> Empathy is a strange and powerful thing. There is no script. There is no right way or wrong way to do it. It's simply listening, holding space, withholding judgment, emotionally connecting, and communicating that incredibly healing message, "You're not alone." (p. 70)

Practicing empathy begins with small, repeated efforts toward connection. In physical classrooms, it looks like the teacher casually greeting students as they enter the classroom; noticing students' glances, head tilts, or slumping shoulders; holding short conversations between activities or in passing by desks; and attending sports events, concerts, and fundraisers. In online spaces, it looks like giving students a friendly greeting as they log in, noticing which students are speaking up and which are quiet, posing thought-provoking questions, playing intentional games, building in breaks for movement, and including lots of variety in discussion strategies. These moments are invitations to storytelling and calls to listen to students. Empathetic connection centers student voices, perspectives, and insights in the online classroom.

Encourage the Arts, Play, and Academics

Jill spoke with three educators who stress the importance of encouraging the arts and play along with academics. These teachers—Scott, Robert, and Catherine—all currently teach at K–12 schools in South America.

Scott told Jill, "I see school and the classroom as far more than just academic learning" (S. Harrison, personal communication, October 4, 2020). He and other teachers mentioned how important it is to spend class time on things that do not involve academic learning. Scott creates groups on Google Hangouts where "the students talk about everything from serious exam questions to stuff about Star Wars!"

Robert plays his guitar, talks about recipes he is making, and has even shared poetry he has written (which, he admits, his students have met with some playful criticism). He challenges his students to try something new each week and report back to him, and students have shown him baked goods they have made, talked about books they have read, and even played the guitar for him (R. Young, personal communication, October 5, 2020).

Catherine gets students to turn on their webcams during class by challenging them "to wear a silly hat, silly glasses, or a Hawaiian necklace [a lei] just for it to be fun," and has students create music playlists that she plays during their online work time (C. Oda, personal communication, October 5, 2020).

Consider What Students Need Most

Jill spoke with two teachers who teach more than five thousand miles apart about considering student needs and infusing empathy in interactions. These teachers, Alison and Jackie, remind other educators that being a teenager can be tough and that a kind interaction can really make a difference.

Alison told Jill, "I can remember only too well how it felt to be a teenage student. It was a big confusing mess with endless deadlines and screaming teachers. I promised myself and my students that I would never be that teacher, and so far, I think I have been true to this promise" (A. de Paulo Barbosa, personal communication, October 5, 2020). Alison practices empathy by striving to be the teacher she would have wanted as a young person.

Jackie is an online instructor who lives in the United States and works with students from around the world. She shared with Jill that she works hard to always ask herself where students are coming from in their comments and assignments. Sometimes when reading the assignment of someone who shares particularly personal or painful information, she will disregard all but the most basic academic feedback and will instead simply say, "I'm sorry you are experiencing this, and I hope you have someone to talk to about it," or "It sounds like you had a rough time for a while and now are on the road to a good place." As she notes, "You can't ignore it and just roll right over it" (J. Schroeder, personal communication, October 5, 2020). The young people in your class are people first and students second. As you review student work or meet with students, you can use one of Jackie's favorite strategies and ask yourself, "What does this student need right now, and how can I help in that area?"

Embrace Mistakes

Danny notes, "I can connect because I try to see things from [students'] perspective and give them respect. . . . I make jokes, laugh at myself and show them

I am not perfect, [that I] make mistakes, but try to learn from them" (D. Renaud, personal communication, October 6, 2020).

CONNECTED TEACHING COMMITMENT
Practice Empathy

Practicing empathy requires making space for students in the classroom not only as scholars but also as important and interesting young people. It requires seeing students as story, identity, and experience rich. It requires being open to new perspectives. When teachers commit to practicing empathy in their classrooms, they center relationships. Educators build professional relationships where they know their students well enough to notice subtle shifts in mood, excitement, and attention. Teachers prioritize connecting by meeting students at the door, pulling together a group in a virtual classroom, sending a connecting email, or making a positive or concerned call home. These behaviors send students the message that teachers care, teachers see them, and students can count on teachers to be there for them. Practicing empathy in the classroom also asks teachers to model humility, recognizing that there are some lived experiences they will never fully understand, yet they will keep striving to listen actively and learn more deeply.

Lou Jobst: Teaching as a Love Song

Lou Jobst and Jill Clingan often refer to each other as kindred spirits. Like Jill, Lou has the heart of a poet, and his words are compassionate and encouraging. Lou has taught for over forty years in elementary school, high school, and college contexts, in person and online. As you'll read in his narrative, he uses music and poetry to connect with his students.

Who would have thought a song sung by my friend Tim at a college bazaar would have a lasting effect on my teaching? It was a Saturday night at Tim's college show. My wife, Mickey, and I were enjoying a great evening when he began Elton John's "Love Song" (Duncan, 1970). A few years later, we chose to play that song as Mickey walked down the aisle at our wedding. It was perfect. At that point, I decided to make the song a cornerstone of every class I taught and workshop I offered. I use this song to create an atmosphere of care and concern in my classrooms and offer connection as the year begins. On the first day of class, as I introduce myself and sing the song, I always tell my students I want them to relax and allow the song to wash over them, knowing they are now a part of the thread connecting all my students over the years. It is a community of more than forty years of learning. Sharing this song invites students into my family, a precious part of my life. Decades later, many students are still a part of the fabric of my life.

My great literary love is poetry, and often, I ask students to find poems and songs relevant to our content. In the second half of our online American lit course, I ask students to find a predominant theme in each act of *The Crucible* and explain their choice. At the same time, I ask them to choose a musical work that reflects that theme. The range of choices is truly amazing, ranging from heavy metal to classical.

This assignment is one of my favorites because it affords me the opportunity to see a bit more clearly into my students' personalities. One student linked the second half of the play to Bartók's *Bluebeard's Castle*. Her synthesis of theme and musical expertise was stunning and insightful, and most of all, human. Another student presented an essay on breaking free and connected literary texts to his parents' sacrifice in selling their home in Florida and moving to Indiana just so he could work with a master cellist. This was his "breaking free." After reading his compelling work, I went to YouTube and found him playing one of his favorite pieces in a symphonic ensemble in Indiana. These conversations gave us the opportunity to grow to know each other as human beings.

Often, at the end of a course (both in person and online), I write a four-line verse in which I try to capture a sense of the student and the essence of my relationship with them. In person, I give the student a card with the verse and sing it to them; online, I offer the lines in the comments box. This is just one more level of human connection.

In teaching composition in person, I worked in conference times for at least half of each class. Online teaching affords me the chance to use asynchronous methods for conferencing. I encourage students to email me often with specific concerns in their assignments. For example, a student in Paris emailed me daily with questions, seeking direction. We shared a real dialogue. Once, a student from Nepal introduced herself with the hope she and I would be in close contact concerning her work. Finally, as I evaluate student work in the online learning management system, I constantly give specific feedback about coherence, focus, voice, and mechanics.

Building relationships and authentic encouragement is so crucial. Years ago, I stopped my department chair in the hallway and introduced her to a young, talented student. I said, "Laurie, I want you to meet Olivia. She's really got it. She's going to be a writer." That moment took about two minutes. Years later, Olivia contacted me to say that she had two scripts accepted for production as a film. She also writes children's books. She still remembers the moment in the hall. Two minutes. I mightily attempt to create these types of

> moments online. Every time I see that special glimmer of talent, no matter how small or huge, I point out students' effort, their talent, and their potential. (Lou Jobst, personal communication, October 7, 2020)

Strategies for Encouraging Connection Through Music and Poetry

I (Kathryn) have had the good fortune to teach with Lou in a few different contexts both online and in person. Across these spaces, I've seen firsthand how Lou connects with students through poetry and song. Now, if I am in a virtual meeting or class with Lou, I commonly ask him, "Do you have your guitar with you—you know, just in case?" In the following sections, Stephanie and I share some strategies we've learned from our arts integration work in general, and from Lou Jobst in particular.

Offer Poems or Song Lyrics to Students

People love to hear that someone is thinking of them. Lou often finds just the right poem, verse, or song to connect with a specific student. He picks this out individually. Sometimes, he includes it with his assignment feedback, and other times, he sends it on its own as a "thinking of you" message.

While he draws from a wide repertoire of classic and contemporary sources, two of his most beloved poems to share with students are "Digging" by Seamus Heaney (1998) and "September, the First Day of School" by Howard Nemerov (1977).

I (Kathryn) have a couple of standards that I use too. One is a corny joke told best with a strong Italian accent: "What did one volcano say to the other? I lava you!" In some classes where I've shared the joke several times, a quick sketch of a volcano in the margin of a student's paper has become a powerful connecting moment. Also, I've used Nikki Giovanni's (1972) "Winter Poem" to connect with students from kindergarten to graduate school.

What are some standard poems, songs, or jokes that you use to connect with students? The next time you are listening to the radio or flipping through a book of verse and you come across just the right line, stanza, or song that makes you think of a student, pass it along with a note to say, "I was thinking of you."

Use Theme Songs to Capture Major Moments

Music can sometimes help students (and adults) articulate emotions better than words alone. As you work with students on developing an emotional vocabulary—that is, the language to speak about the nuances of feelings—music can be a great tool for expression. You can use these four strategies to incorporate more music in your classroom.

1. Instead of having students write the standard journal entry, ask students to choose a song that best sums up their mood.
2. Ask students to choose a theme song for a specific project, month, or year.
3. Create a work-time playlist by having students each submit their favorite songs for studying.
4. Choose a song to be "our song," and play it when students enter the room or need a lift.

Vent Through Rhymes

When students struggle with a concept, feel weary, or seem frustrated, venting can sometimes help. Letting off some steam can be just the thing to take a big breath and start again. Suggest that students express their feelings in a playful rhyme pattern or haiku, such as the following haiku written by Stephanie:

> This assignment may
> prove to make my brain explode
> I need a short break.

Megan Lilien and Nina Sprouse: Gender Inclusivity in the Blended Classroom

Megan Lilien is a longtime science educator with a background in biology and chemistry. She serves as the health and science division chair for Mizzou Academy. Megan also coaches girls' lacrosse. In 2021, Megan became the state of Missouri's science education Technology Innovator, as awarded by the Science Teachers of Missouri. Her work to expand access to girls and young women was cited in this recognition.

Nina Sprouse serves as the middle and high school social studies division chair for Mizzou Academy. She has over twenty-five years of teaching experience in both in-person and online environments. She also has a professional background in information technology, where she often experienced being the only woman in this professional setting.

Women have been instrumental across all great advancements in society. However, the school curriculum we (Megan and Nina) have encountered in both social studies and science seldom centers or celebrates women's stories. Curriculum work might mention powerful women such as Sacagawea and Rosalind Franklin; however, students usually study them in the context of how they helped Lewis and Clark and Watson and Crick, respectively.

> The curriculum frames these women's contributions as though they are only supporting characters, not protagonists.
>
> This lack of representation has a direct impact on girls' developing sense of academic concepts, or how prepared and able they are to succeed in the classroom (Ertl, Luttenberger, & Paechter, 2017). Educational programs have made great strides in supporting women (UNESCO, 2020). Research shows that across all subjects and grade levels around the globe, young women earn higher grades than young men (Voyer & Voyer, 2014). Additionally, bachelor's degrees awarded to women outnumber the degrees awarded to men (Kay & Shipman, 2014; Voyer & Voyer, 2014). Yet, these successes do not continue past the world of academia. Despite these proficiency metrics, women account for only 27 percent of all STEM-related degrees in the United States, hold fewer senior management positions than men, and earn less than men in similar positions (Needle, 2021).
>
> Significant gender gaps exist for access, learning achievement, and continuation in education in many settings, most often at the expense of girls. Virtual classrooms offer a unique opportunity to close these gaps through increased representation and connection. Centering women's stories, teaching students to be critical thinkers when it comes to representation, and modeling inclusive practices benefit all students. (Megan Lilien & Nina Sprouse, personal communication, January 22, 2021)

Strategies for Supporting Gender Inclusivity in the Blended Classroom

While gender inequality is a multifaceted issue, Megan, Nina, and many educators we worked with during our research on connected classrooms have found intentional ways to increase gender inclusion and representation in the blended classroom. Nina and Megan shared the following three strategies they use to engage in this work in their blended classrooms.

Increase Representation

Women and gender-expansive students may struggle to see themselves or their identities in course texts written by men and from men's perspectives. Review course material for bias, assessing how many texts you have by women, including Indigenous women and women of color, and how your curriculum represents women's stories and accomplishments. Increase representation to tell more balanced and complete stories. This also applies to the images included in your curriculum and the examples used in assignments and exams. Use names and images to represent all genders and cultural groups in examples and objective assessment questions.

Rethink Class Participation

Participation points often show bias toward boys and young men (Aguillon et al., 2020). Instead of awarding grades solely based on participation, Megan and Nina advocate for reimaging ways that students can show their understanding and knowledge of course material. For example, they have both committed to offering many different ways to participate in class, including through writing, one-on-one conversations, and small-group dialogues.

Teachers and experts are also participants in the class community. Therefore, in considering whose voices and stories to center in the classroom, you should also bring in guest experts and leaders who represent the gender and cultural diversity in your class. Megan and Nina intentionally invite women leaders and guest experts.

Create Experiential Programs

Despite better academic performance, young women often show less confidence and interest in leadership and STEM roles compared to their young-men counterparts (Kay & Shipman, 2014). Create experiential programs and assignments to help build confidence. Examples include job-shadowing experiences with women in the field of interest, internships, and mentoring programs. Coding and robotics clubs provide experiential opportunities. Virtual clubs offer the added benefits of flexibility and connection with girls from around the world.

Greg Soden: How International Travel Inspires Culturally Responsive Teaching

Greg Soden is an instructor in world religions and English language arts at Mizzou Academy. He is the producer and host of The Classical Ideas Podcast *(Soden, 2017–present), on which he aims to empower students with the core knowledge of major world religions and improve citizenship and agency in a diverse society.*

As a first-year teacher living in Mexico, I was an immigrant and a racial minority (though still a privileged one, due to my ability to come and go as I pleased), something I had never experienced. After Mexico, I taught in the United Kingdom. Suddenly, I was in the most globally and religiously diverse school I had ever worked in. On any given day, I had students from the United Kingdom, Poland, Pakistan, India, Jamaica, Guyana, Turkey, and more in my classroom. I was culturally out of my depth and wasn't experienced enough to teach the group of students I did, so I decided to study immigration and native experiences at the University of Saskatchewan to remedy that. This confluence of experiences traveling and learning others' stories led to my pursuits in teaching about religion in a way that helped me connect with students.

I aimed to equip students with the lifelong ability to practice deeper inquiry into the religious traditions that steer the course of people's life philosophies across the globe. I once taught a course called "Classical Ideas and World Religions." I translated this course into an online context while keeping the goal of deeper connection in mind. The major goal of this course was to study religions from a place of seeking to understand. Modules in the course followed a pattern of exploring history, literature, and a selection of current events throughout each religion to demonstrate the modernity and contemporary nature of how religions exist around people today. The course assessed students via an array of student-produced podcasts, personalized journal entries in response to ancient religious texts, current cultural studies, and locally based projects, all of which I attempted to make as meaningful and authentic for students as possible.

It mattered tremendously to me—a white, male, able-bodied teacher—that a wide range of voices across religious, ethnic, racial, age, and professional communities be visible and present in the course content. I gathered a wide range of guest interviews from lay practitioners, scholars, clergy members, and journalists who spanned an immense range of backgrounds and experiences within religion. Throughout the course, I included more than one hundred audio clips of my conversations from *The Classical Ideas Podcast* (Soden, 2017–present), including firsthand accounts of religious practice and scholarship with people from multiple continents.

Students immediately began to demonstrate a global awareness in the course. One student, Chase, opened his first audio podcast assignment in the course with a personalized pondering and definition of *religious literacy*. In his opening statement, Chase answered the question, "What is *religious literacy* exactly?" with "I believe it is the ability to understand or comprehend religion, which I think is more important the more the world is connected." Chase was hypothesizing how he could enhance his own cultural literacy skills in the religious aspect of our social fabric to make better connections. In a single statement, Chase captured the global connectedness for the course I hoped students would realize.

> Creating a globally minded and culturally responsive online course required a wide range of personal and professional international experiences on my part as the teacher and course writer. My experiences living, teaching, and learning in international and diverse communities at least partially prepared me for this curriculum-writing and teaching experience. From there, I have had the opportunity to never stop asking questions and the privilege to help students realize the beauty in asking questions for themselves. (Greg Soden, personal communication, October 13, 2020)

Strategies for Making Global Connections

Greg Soden's narrative and the strategies he shared in conversation remind people that they are each on a journey. They are all works in progress. Reflecting on your journey, learning, challenges, and adventures matters. Connecting that learning across the global landscape opens up the potential for new kinds of pedagogies and understanding. In the following sections, we share three strategies from Greg's work on making global connections.

Reflect on What Led You to This Point

Greg's journey to becoming a world religions teacher in a blended school started right out of high school, but he couldn't have known that. Reflecting on how one choice led to another helped him see the big picture of his life. Then, he was able to use those choices to shape his career path. Use the following questions as guidelines for self-reflection.

- What led you to the point where you are right now?
- What choices brought you closer to your goals?
- What specific lessons can you draw from those choices to influence the way you connect with students?

Travel (Near or Far)

All travel is formative. Greg's narrative explores how many different geographic locations impacted his teacher journey. While financial barriers may prevent you from packing your bags and hopping on a plane to engage in an international journey, you can learn beyond your comfort zone in many ways. You might have an international learning opportunity, as in Greg's case, or you might just as likely study a new language, attend a house of worship of an unfamiliar faith, play a pickup basketball game at a park near where students live, or attend a new cultural event. In each of these situations, be open to learning, and seek ways to practice reciprocity, and afterward, continue reflecting on how these experiences mark an educator's narrative.

Apply Personal Lessons to Student Lessons

Over time, Greg realized that the study of world religions helped create a context to house the important values he held around cultural literacy. As he spent more time pursuing knowledge and experiences in that area, he was able to find a focus for his passions. Use the following prompts for self-reflection about values.

- What are your core values?
- What impact do you hope to make in your classroom, community, and world?
- Think about the people you can talk with, the places you can explore, and the resources you can consult to strengthen your experiences and teaching around these values. Write about them.

Key Classroom Takeaway: Story Sharing Makes Space for Empathy and Connection

The narratives in this chapter share a commitment to intentionally connect with, learn from, and honor students right where they are. In educational work, teachers advocate for people-centered approaches. People-centered approaches recognize differences and acknowledge everyone shares the human experience. A middle-aged mother and educator shares humanity with a fifteen-year-old poet and member of the marching band. Seeing each other as people requires vulnerability to share one's own (and graciousness in noticing others') complexities, multiple identities, and cultures.

Personality, gender, race, socioeconomic status, nationality, peer group, and a constellation of identities and circumstances contribute to the lived experience. Teachers can't talk *around* these things and hope that the class will flourish in spite of them. These topics are a framework for what you have known to be true and a lens for examining new information. They are links in a chain between your experience and someone else's experience, and they are a map for how to move ahead to where you want to be next. Teachers and students need to talk *through* their experiences together.

Knowing that classroom spaces, like all group spaces, are arenas for navigating belonging, how do teachers honor and affirm all the perspectives and experiences in their classrooms? Effective change comes from clearly seeing where the margins and center have been drawn and then intentionally choosing to draw new circles (hooks, 2015). Teaching students to notice centering, to practice inclusion, to affirm and welcome marginalized voices, and to celebrate new possibilities is powerful. Everyone has been in the center at times and in the margins at other times, and they've learned and grown through each experience. In all classrooms, whether in person, blended, or online, educators want to teach students to practice radical inclusion and to recognize wisdom across groups. The reproducible at the end of this chapter (page 124) will help you find your own definition for empathy and help you design what radical inclusion looks like in your classroom.

Summary

Personal stories create and strengthen connection. Sharing stories takes courage and vulnerability. Centering moments happen both organically and intentionally and on large scales and in small moments. As Lou Jobst shares, "Every time I see that special glimmer of talent, no matter how small or huge, I point out students' effort, their talent, and their potential." Vulnerability, courage, empathy, and storytelling in the online classroom (as in all classrooms) carry lifelong, life-changing rewards.

In this chapter, you heard from Jill Clingan, who is passionate about how cultivating empathy creates a bridge between teachers and students as they navigate online spaces. Lou Jobst shared how he notices who students are and uses music to honor their personalities and encourage them to express themselves in new ways. Megan Lilien and Nina Sprouse share an astute observation about the role gender plays in the classroom and how educators ensure an equitable experience for students of all genders. Greg Soden's invaluable experience traveling the globe highlighted that self-awareness of your identity in the world becomes easier to locate when you have become the stranger; simply put, taking yourself out of your comfort zone to learn about other cultures can be a formative act of humility and empathy.

This chapter transitioned the book into part II, "Ensuring Equity and Inclusion in the Online Classroom." So far, you've seen how teaching starts with relationship building, which you cultivate through time and intentional moments of connection, and which deeply matters to both academic success and social-emotional health. In chapter 5, you'll see how the class community is often a cultural and linguistic tapestry of strengths and experiences.

Chapter 4: Apply It to Your Practice

Working individually or in learning teams, reflect on these questions, and implement the commitments to your practice (for more information on engaging with these questions, please see the section titled Space for Reflective Practice on page 9 in the introduction). As always, strive to move your reflection to action.

React to the Chapter

What are your key takeaways from this chapter? What was surprising to read? What did you connect with?

Define Empathy

Jill Clingan asked other educators to define empathy and show how they develop it with their students. Discuss empathy with faculty and staff in your school community. How do they put it into words? Why is it important? How do they show empathy in their daily circles while online or in person?

Employ Empathetic Strategies

Review the strategies for building connection through empathy, the arts, and a positive classroom culture highlighted in this chapter. Which ones do you think you and your community already employ, and which ones would be good focus strategies for the next quarter or semester?

Amplify Student Stories

As a class activity, ask students to respond to this prompt: "Something that might surprise you to learn about me is. . . ." Some of the answers will make you laugh, and some will break your heart. After engaging in this activity, take your data and reactions back to your team. What did you learn? How will you use these lessons to expand equity, justice, and representation in your school community? Answer this last question with as many specifics and action words as possible. Then, discuss the specific steps you plan to take tomorrow, next week, and next semester to amplify student stories in your teaching practice.

Use Music and Poetry

Practitioners featured in this chapter used poetry and music to explain the power of connection with students. If you were to share a song or poem with students on the first day of school, what would it be and why? How about the last day of school? Invite students into this conversation about the power of poetry and connection. What theme songs might they choose to represent a concept they are working on this school year or in their class community?

Honoring Multilingual and Multicultural Learners

5

Creating an inclusive classroom community requires educators to highlight and honor students' home language and culture. The educator stories shared in this chapter all point to a commitment to make purposeful space for all the cultures and home languages represented in your classroom. This chapter's narratives tell stories of both teacher and student migration. The contributors explore language acquisition, support practices for English learners, and share strategies to honor home languages. These educators also talk of how they have taken the lessons they've learned on their own journeys and applied those to the online contexts where they now teach and write curriculum. As Lisa DeCastro puts it in her narrative, "By the time I left my [first] classroom, I believed in less teacher talk and more student talk. I wanted students to be the ones . . . feeling confident as learners in a community who take risks and make mistakes because that is evidence of learning. I also learned how to really listen and not always have the answers" (L. DeCastro, personal communication, October 7, 2020).

In previous chapters, you read about how cultivating inclusive spaces means that each student is well known, valued, and seen in the classroom. In this chapter, we extend that commitment to language. Doing so requires continued learning on

Essential Question

How can educators honor the multilingual strengths and perspectives students bring to their online and blended classrooms?

Chapter Learning Objectives

- Examine best practices to support and affirm multilingual learners.
- Intentionally create opportunities for language and cultural learning with students.
- Build bridges between personal language-learning journeys and students' experiences.
- Practice implementing people-centered and universal design approaches.

Key Terms

bilingual or multilingual. Terms that refer to students who speak two or more languages. This terminology positively centers the strengths of students who know many languages. These terms focus on the assets students bring to the classroom as opposed to focusing on the area in which they are still growing or only centering English.

culturally and linguistically diverse (CLD). An umbrella term for students from nondominant cultural or linguistic backgrounds. While this term has utility in equity conversations around access, it can also oversimplify diverse groups.

English as a foreign language (EFL). A term that refers to learning English as a world language, typically in a country where English is not the official language and by students for whom English is not a home or native language. We prefer *world language* over *foreign language*, as the term *foreign* is often used to otherize people.

English as a second language (ESL). Many readers may remember this term from their own education, as it had considerable staying power. This term has now been replaced mostly by *English learner* or *English language learner* (see the following term). The term centers English, does not reference a person, and is often inaccurate, as many multilingual students are learning English as a third, fourth, or even sixth language.

English learner or English language learner (EL or ELL). These two terms are the terms currently used by schools. Although they are often used interchangeably, *English learner* is now the term preferred by many states and the U.S. Department of Education.

home language or native language. Terms that both refer to the primary language or languages spoken at a student's home. In many bilingual homes, students may learn multiple languages as their home languages. These languages are also sometimes called *first languages*, *L1s*, or *family languages*. It's important to remember family systems are diverse. For example, in the case of adoption, a student's L1 may not be their home language.

living language. A language that groups of people actively use and speak.

newcomer. The U.S. Department of Education defines this term as any foreign-born student and their family who have recently arrived in the United States (National Center for English Language Acquisition, 2017). Not all newcomers arrive with families; some arrive on their own. In some schools, particularly secondary schools, there are special newcomer programs for students who arrive in the United States with either limited English or limited formal schooling.

refugee. The United Nations Refugee Agency defines a refugee as someone who has been forced to flee their country because of persecution, war, or violence; they often cannot return home or are afraid to do so (USA for the United Nations High Commissioner for Refugees, n.d.).

the part of the student's teacher and peers. As this chapter considers the power of home and culture in people's lives and classroom, imagine these strategies' possibilities in any teaching space, whether in the same room with students or separated by miles and a computer screen. Read on for stories of how fellow educators have used these tips to help their in-person, online, and blended communities thrive by honoring their multicultural students.

Teaching in a Multilingual and Multicultural World

In this multilingual and multicultural world, languages, like cultures, change over time. The twenty-third edition of the *Ethnologue* (Simons, 2020) reports that there are over 7,100 distinct living languages in the world. Of the 7.2 billion people on earth, nearly two-thirds identify one of twelve languages as their native language. These languages include (in order of number of speakers) Chinese (all dialects), Hindi-Urdu, English, Arabic, Spanish, Russian, Bengali, Portuguese, German, Japanese, French, and Italian. English continues to be the most studied world language (with 1.5 billion learners) and the most common official language for countries (Noack & Gamio, 2015).

Public schools can play an important role in honoring the wisdom, heritage, and culture that come from preserving multilingual traditions. However, often public institutions, including schools in the United States, have instead "forced acculturation and assimilation" (YIVO Institute for Jewish Research, 2014, p. 2). The contributors in this chapter advocate for a different approach, one that celebrates and honors the incredible cultural and linguistic diversity found in many public schools.

This chapter introduces key terminology and perspectives for teaching and learning with multilingual students. These are especially key in the blended classroom, where continued development of new technologies, global adoption of the internet, and the evolving digital economy (Palvia et al., 2018) may lead to even greater linguistic diversity in school programs.

Kathryn Fishman-Weaver: ¿Cómo Se Dice *Home* en Su Aula?

In addition to being a coauthor of this book, Kathryn Fishman-Weaver is an educator, researcher, and international lecturer. Her research explores the power of hope, heart, and high expectations in the classroom. Her interest in these topics started long before she traveled to South America and Asia to work with students and teachers. It started in a sunny classroom in East Oakland, California.

My first teaching position was at a public school in a Spanish-speaking community. Many of the most important lessons I've learned in education came with that first group of students and their families. This narrative features some reflections on how language learning has impacted my teaching practice.

At the start of my first year, I had eight students in my class. Across their homes, these first graders spoke five different languages. In the classroom, Spanish was a more common first or second language than English. Spanish was also the primary home language of this school's population.

I am grateful to have begun my teaching career with this particular class. These students and their families shaped who I am as an educator in countless ways. This group of young people also showed me my own language learning is essential to teaching. Studying world languages, even casually, became one way I connected with my students and their families. I grew with them, and by the end of my third year, I no longer needed a translator for short family conferences in Spanish.

From that first classroom, I moved to teaching in a large public high school. Since I couldn't become conversationally fluent in Arabic, Swahili, Vietnamese, Korean, Hindi, Chinese, and the other languages present in the hallways, I committed to learning how to greet each of my students in their home language. In these brief moments at the classroom door, I wanted my students to feel seen, welcome, and safe.

In 2016, I joined an online school with a large population of students from Brazil and immediately started studying Portuguese. My continued language studies are an important vehicle to better understand the culture of my Brazilian students. Whether I'm greeting joyful and rambunctious first-grade students or energetic middle and high schoolers, connection through language matters.

I carry the patience of mothers and aunties. I carry my clumsy attempts to communicate strengths and celebrate progress in languages I am actively still learning. I carry the gifts I learned from being in community with secretaries who double as nurses and translators, and parent leaders who serve as cultural liaisons not only for newcomer families but also for new teachers who hope to do right by their students.

Strategies for Celebrating Home Language in Your Classroom

The experiences I (Kathryn) shared in this narrative shaped the ways I think about language learning and teaching. For me, language learning remains a consistent way I try to connect with students. I know some people for whom languages come easily. I am not one of these people. Every phrase, conjugation, and pronunciation takes a lot of practice. While the Romance languages have become more familiar over the years, the tonal languages continue to elude my English-speaking tongue. I remember sitting with one of my Chinese American students working on simple phrases in Mandarin. She was a patient teacher, and thank goodness, because I just wasn't getting it. More than fifteen years later, this student and I still laugh about a lesson where I tried a phrase and then exclaimed, "There! Did I do it? Did my eyebrows go question mark?" She had been working with me on intonation, encouraging me to end the short phrase by going up the register inquisitively. I obviously mixed this all up in my brain while working so hard on pronunciation. In the end, though, we had a magic moment of connection and empathy. The following are a few strategies I have used to integrate and celebrate home language in my classroom.

Greet Each Student in Their Home Language

Many teachers know the value of meeting students at the door. In the online classroom, this might mean being present and engaged as soon as students enter the video conference or leaving a personalized welcome note for your asynchronous classes. Another layer I (Kathryn) like to add to this strategy is greeting each student in their home language. Inevitably, each semester or school year, you have more greetings to learn. You can ask your students to work with you on getting the pronunciation right. You can also ask your students to help you choose the right greeting, such as, "Good morning" or "Hello." Often, students choose the phrase they think their teacher will most quickly learn. As you progress through the year, you might be able to build from these greetings and move on to "How are you?" The goal with this strategy is connection. In these greetings, you hope that your students hear, "I see you. I am learning with you. I am so glad you are here."

Normalize Multilingual Responses

Integrate and celebrate multilingualism in your classroom by affirming linguistic diversity. The English translation doesn't always have to come first. Words and phrases in students' home languages don't necessarily need to be italicized or even defined in the writing, and you should *never* cross them off in a student's work.

Guest speakers don't have to be fluent in English to present to a class. Find a translator if needed. Often, your students are a good place to start. It is a wonderful idea to ask students to work with family members, including caregivers and grandparents, on assignments. When you do, affirm that home language is always appropriate.

The ways educators respond to linguistic diversity as it happens within the fabric of their class speak volumes about how welcome and affirmed students are in this space. Multilingualism is an incredible asset, not only when it fits in nicely with a lesson but also when it arises in the small, everyday ways people interact and communicate as human beings.

Engage in Language Learning

While nothing beats immersion, you can use online programs (shared in chapter 3, page 86) to expand your language learning. Many of these use gamification methods, such as advancing levels or earning gems, and mastery-learning methods, meaning you can keep practicing the same exercise until you get it right. Also, you can listen to language-learning podcasts for listening and sometimes even speaking practice. Since 2019, I (Kathryn) have committed to doing one Duolingo lesson a day. One lesson usually takes only five minutes and helps me continue to build vocabulary. With over seven thousand languages in the world, language learning can be a lifelong practice.

Lisa DeCastro: The Art of Listening

Lisa DeCastro is a compassionate and creative elementary educator who serves as the coordinator for the elementary program in an online school. Her experiences with EL students drive her passion to support all students as they learn and grow from right where they are. In her narrative, she shares how students inspire her to keep sharing stories and aiming for new pursuits.

Inside my heart lives a five-year-old who loves listening to stories, asking questions, singing with friends, getting messy with art projects, playing house in the dramatic play area, and asking more questions. It was no surprise that my path, after a variety of different jobs, led to serving as a kindergarten teacher in a classroom full of English learners in Oakland, California.

When Diana started kindergarten class, she had never attended preschool or been around English speakers in her young life. Diana's first language was Spanish, and for the first few months of school, she quietly took everything in. In the beginning months of kindergarten, she never spoke in English—not even a "yes" or "no" when asked a question. She often arrived early to school and helped me set up the classroom for the day. In these moments, we began to form trust. During class whenever possible, I translated content to Spanish so Diana could contribute to class discussions in her first language and have her voice heard.

Some of my most cherished memories of teaching are times when the quietest students felt safe and brave enough to speak their first words in English in front of their friends and teachers. By the end of the year, Diana was one of the top readers in the class and became particularly chatty. It is my memory of Diana speaking her second language in front of the class that gives me strength whenever I have to speak in public in front of people I have never met.

Then there was Joaquin. Picture the tiniest little student wearing a navy blue knit vest over his white-collared shirt and pressed navy pants. Joaquin had the biggest smile I'd seen among five-year-olds, and it turned out his reading level was equally as bright; he was reading multiple grade levels above kindergarten. In one of my class's Monday morning meetings when students shared what they had done over the weekend, Joaquin shared that he had spent a family dinner discussing whether John McCain would be the next president. On another Monday, he said he had started to learn Esperanto with his brother. That night, I looked up Esperanto on the internet because I truly had never heard of that language before Joaquin mentioned it.

Diana and Joaquin were only two of many kindergarten students whom I had the privilege to teach and learn from in Oakland. It was important for me to learn about them as young scholars. Diana easily made many friends in the classroom while Joaquin struggled to connect with other students. Diana was the first person in her family to attend school in the United States; her parents were from Mexico. Joaquin was the youngest child in his family, bilingual in English and Spanish, and immersed in American culture. (His favorite band was Boston.) Diana and Joaquin were remarkably different academically, socially, and linguistically. Yet, with practices rooted in equity and a culturally responsive pedagogy, each found success in school. I was dedicated to fine-tuning and differentiating student work to meet the needs of my students. I started with getting to know my students with activities that didn't center on academics. As we talked, Diana, Joaquin, and I explored learning phrases in each other's home languages, celebrating strengths along the way. Eventually, this created a safe space where we could all stretch and try new things, like learning more about each other's cultures, talking in front of the class, and reading out loud in a second or third language.

I looped with this class from the start of kindergarten through the end of first grade. (*Looping* is the practice of keeping a teacher and class community constant for two or more years. It offers opportunities to build meaningful relationships among the teacher, students, and families and to track and celebrate growth over time.) In online learning, where they can be more flexible with time, space, and pace, teachers may have even more opportunities for looping than in more traditional models.

Diana grew to be one of the most proficient readers in my class. Joaquin also made significant academic progress and went on to skip third grade a few years later. I attribute both students' success to building teacher-student relationships, maintaining constant communication with their families, and honoring the students' linguistic and cultural backgrounds just where they were when I got to know the students as five- and six-year-olds.

By the time I left my first kindergarten classroom, I believed in less teacher talk and more student talk. I wanted students to be the ones taking charge of their learning, setting goals for themselves with teacher direction, and feeling confident as learners in a community who take risks and make mistakes because that is evidence of learning. I also learned how to really listen and not always have the answers.

Over a decade since Diana and Joaquin completed first grade, I continue to receive updates about their learning and well-being. Both are approaching high school graduation. The snippet of their stories that I was privileged to be a part of had a tremendous impact on me; it's an impact I can only hope was reciprocal. I look forward to hearing more about how their stories unfold as I celebrate their successes. (Lisa DeCastro, personal communication, October 7, 2020)

Strategies for Honoring Student Voice and Home Language in the Online Elementary Classroom

Lisa DeCastro now serves as the elementary coordinator for a global online school system. Much of her work in 2020 and 2021 was in curriculum development and teacher support for elementary programming in the United States and Brazil. When she reflected on her teaching career, she identified four guiding strategies for supporting elementary students, families, and teachers in the online classroom. The following sections describe these strategies.

Let the Students Take the Lead

Even early childhood and elementary learners have wisdom to share. After students understand the classroom expectations, give them choices on how and where to complete their work. By the end of their kindergarten year, Lisa's students created their own personalized work plan for each day, complete with setting academic goals. In her work with early elementary learners, Lisa found online learning advantageous in that students have more autonomy to choose and prioritize what they will conquer first. Allowing students to plan how to complete work during their online school day can empower them.

Lisa often used visual elements to connect with and represent students and their ideas. She says this works well across online and in-person contexts. Figure 5.1 (page 136) is an example of a paper chart. In the online classroom, the teacher can share a goal and ask students to give feedback by displaying a thumbs-up, holding up a green piece of paper, or typing their name in the chat.

As the year progresses, students advance to writing their own goals. This might include simple words and phrases (often with inventive spellings) or drawings of their goals. Figure 5.2 and figure 5.3 (page 137) feature examples.

As previously mentioned, when students understand the classroom expectations, teachers can also encourage choice on how and where to complete work. Lisa often gives students a list of activities and lets them choose their own order. In the physical classroom, she would sometimes list all their afternoon centers (or activity choices) on a whiteboard and ask students to choose their order. In the online classroom, you might list these choices as a drop-down menu or printable choice board. Just like older learners, early elementary students have important insights about their learning strengths and enjoy having autonomy over their learning choices. Strategies like these make a positive difference as students develop independence and self-efficacy.

Be With Students in the Moment

Listen, observe, and honor students' age and developmental levels by keeping lessons short and intentional. Early elementary learners really cannot sit still for more than fifteen minutes, especially when their teacher is on a screen. Remember to include play, dramatic play, and make-believe in lessons and during time with these students. Using puppets or stuffed animals to talk and learn about students' likes, dislikes, and personalities engages them and enhances their joy in learning. Students and teachers have never endured screen time as it exists in the

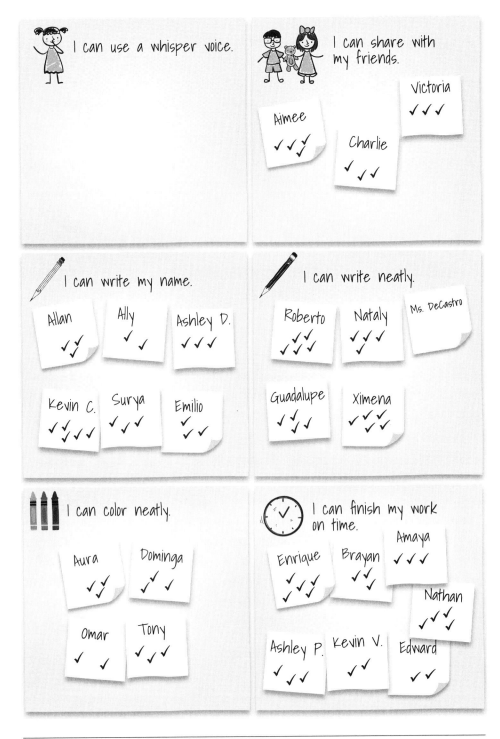

Figure 5.1: Example goal chart for a kindergarten class.

Mariana G. April 12	
Today I will work on... Reading	Today I will make... A Card for Mom

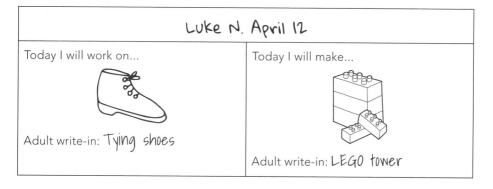

Figure 5.2: Personalized learning plan example 1, kindergarten.

Luke N. April 12	
Today I will work on... Adult write-in: Tying shoes	Today I will make... Adult write-in: LEGO tower

Figure 5.3: Personalized learning plan example 2, kindergarten.

21st century. Be aware of when students start to show fatigue and need a break. Teachers might notice that familiar glaze in students' eyes, a slumping posture, or fidgeting; they might notice that the chat has gone quiet or cameras are turning off. These are all indications that it is time to shake things up, take the lesson in a new direction, and find a way to be with students in the moment. These breaks can take many forms and can be short or long. A few strategies that Lisa uses in her online classroom include the following.

- Do an emoji check-in to see how students are feeling.
- Sing a simple or repetitive song together, especially one with hand motions. Lisa often uses "Itsy Bitsy Spider" in both English and Spanish.
- If possible, meet with small groups of students for a social occasion, like having lunch or reading a story together.

None of these techniques requires lots of English language expression, and all of them build community (and alleviate fatigue). Like all humans, even the youngest are missing play and social gathering with their peers.

Build Relationships and Communicate With Families Regularly

Getting to know families online is different from meeting and seeing them at school. Use visuals and translation tools to help further connection. At the beginning of the school year, survey families to know their preferences for communication (phone, email, text, or web meeting) and their language preference. Communicate often and let families know the best way or time for them to contact you. Regularly ask families for feedback about how they are doing with the school schedule and workload and how their children are faring. Encourage students to share their own learning during family conferences. Even the youngest learners must have practice sharing what they know or what is challenging for them. In the online classroom, teachers, families, and students are all on the same team, and they develop that sense of community over time in various types of interactions. Figure 5.4 shows a sample introductory letter. Given the student demographics at her school, Lisa typically sent these kinds of letters home in both English and Spanish.

Respect and Understand Students' Home Language

Receptive language comes before expressive language. Instruct in English as much as possible, and then give students options for how they can respond during discussions or activities. Early elementary learners may draw pictures before feeling confident to scribe letters and words. Second-language acquisition can happen differently for these younger learners. Their eyes and ears are like sponges and receptive to all kinds of information, just as Lisa witnessed with Diana; however, it may take them some time to express thoughts and ideas in their new language.

Cultivate a multilingual classroom that represents the linguistic diversity of the class as well as the linguistic diversity of the local and global communities. Greet students in their home language, and decorate the classroom walls or virtual course shells with posters, phrases, and speakers of many different languages. Create opportunities for students and their families to share their home language expertise with you and the other students. When students use their home language—whether in a greeting to a friend, in their thinking about the solution to a problem, in the margin of their notes, or in an excited response—celebrate their ability to think and work in multiple languages.

Dear Families,

My name is Lisa DeCastro. This is my tenth year teaching at our school, and I am very excited to get to know you and your child this year in our K–1 classroom! I'd like to tell you a little about myself and also learn a little more about you and your child. We will have lots of opportunities to communicate this year.

Child's name: _____

Child's preferred name or nickname: _____

Language(s) spoken at home: _____

Things your child loves or does well: _____

A goal you have for your child this year: _____

The best way to contact you:

- Email: _____
- Phone: _____
- Text: _____

Something you would like me to know about your child or family: _____

Would you like to talk about anything in this letter together?

☐ Yes! _____

☐ No thanks!

About Ms. DeCastro: Ms. DeCastro lives with her husband, Joe, and her two children, Noah and Luke. Along with their dog, Gunther, they also have a snake, two goldfish, and four praying mantes. Ms. DeCastro loves to take long walks in her neighborhood and spend time in her backyard garden.

Figure 5.4: Sample communication to families.

Kimberly Kester: The World as a Classroom

Kimberly Kester has spent over twenty years teaching multilingual students from elementary to college contexts. In 2015, she joined an online school to teach language arts to international students. At first, she wasn't sure how her in-person experience would translate to online teaching, especially with multilingual students. She soon developed the strategies for support she shares in the following narrative.

As a new college student, I wanted out of my small town in Oklahoma. Initially, I completed a degree in biology and chemistry with plans to attend veterinary school. Then in 1991, I had the opportunity to travel to Estonia. This experience set me on a completely new journey.

During those long days of perpetual darkness that are so common in the far north, I eventually mastered the strings of /u/ and /o/ sounds that make Estonian one of the most difficult languages for English speakers to learn. Estonians are supportive of novice speakers trying to learn this Finno-Ugric tongue. The Estonians in the community where I lived never tired of teaching me new words and good-naturedly laughing at my mistakes. In return for their patience, my new friends asked for practice speaking English and conversations about capitalism, freedom, and rock and roll. The most valuable lesson I learned from my Estonian friends was not about grammar or pronunciation; it was about culture. Language is inseparable from culture. The process of learning a language taught me unexpected lessons that I carried with me when I left.

I next moved to Romania, where my memories from high school correspondence courses in French helped me acquire the basics of the closest living language to Latin. I learned how to cook the Romanian sarmale, or cabbage rolls, so well that even now as I type these words, I can taste the tangy vinegar and rich bacon.

I carried my knowledge of Estonia and Romania and other European countries back to the United States, where I quickly got a job working with the children of migrant workers in North Carolina. There, I learned how to cook tamales and roll my r's as Spanish words became tangled in my dreams. I traveled to Mexico to train English language teachers and learned to salsa dance and sing bachata ballads. Now I laugh when I recognize the tune playing in a Mexican restaurant in Missouri.

These multicultural experiences were of great benefit as I moved into a role working with international students at a local university. Again, not only did I learn about Japan, Korea, Ecuador, Saudi Arabia, and many other places around the globe, but I also learned about community and culture. I asked the students as many questions as they asked me. I wanted to know more about how they learned English in their home countries. I used what I learned to influence how I taught. Arab culture is highly oral, which explained why my Saudi students often enjoyed speech and debate and loved to loudly argue with anyone whom they could corner in the hallway. I learned to cook kabsa with chicken and sit on the floor to eat with my hands and pieces of warm, fresh naan. I discovered through conversations with Japanese students that their English classes focused on grammar and writing. My Japanese students needed lots of support and encouragement in speaking class, which the Saudi students were happy to provide.

My Saudi students, in turn, were grateful for the Japanese students' tutelage in writing and grammar. My heart was happy to have what I felt was the entire world in my classroom.

I work with English learners and teachers in countries around the world. Through technology, I again get to experience how the entire world is our classroom. Giving English learners the resources they need to learn in an online environment is one key to their success; however, without culturally responsive teachers and curriculum writers, students won't achieve their learning goals or master desired skills. To be relevant and impactful, teachers' work with students must incorporate home and local culture. I strive to incorporate all I have learned about culture and international education to make students feel comfortable practicing their skills. How you feel, particularly whether you feel safe, directly impacts your capacity for learning. I want students to know I value and respect the culture, language, and experiences they bring to their class community. (Kimberly Kester, personal communication, September 11, 2020)

Strategies for Learning With Multilingual and Multicultural Students in Online Settings

Kimberly Kester has taught in many different cultures, countries, and contexts. She now serves as an expert on support strategies for multilingual learners in a global school system. The following are her top-two strategies for supporting multilingual learners.

Practice Communication and Learn About Other Cultures

Culture consists of language, food, music, fashion, rituals, the arts, and more. Celebrating culture is a pathway to connection. During lessons or throughout the day, ask students questions about their culture, experiences, and background, and encourage students to ask you questions in return. Never press students to share more than they are comfortable sharing. Many students have been through traumas and may be triggered by too many questions. Be patient, show interest, and share your own lived experiences as you all get to know each other. Pay attention to patterns of speech and writing and what those say about students' comfort levels in sharing in different ways. Throughout these perspective-shifting conversations, listen closely to what students say, and try to weave a variety of cultural experiences into lessons using their insights. Don't be surprised if it begins to feel like the entire world is right there in the classroom, as it did for Kimberly.

Learn and Plan With Other Educators

Take a fresh look at the entire school community. Families, staff, faculty, and other learning partners who have experience connecting to students through culture surround educators every day. Who in your content area can help develop lesson plans celebrating culture? What opportunities are there for professional development in this area? What great books on this topic might others recommend? Who in the community would benefit students by joining the class for a short presentation or question-and-answer session? What experiences are available to explore language, food, music, fashion, rituals, and the arts? By seeking out others in the local school community, educators can combine curiosity and experience to create powerful relationships all around. You might use the answers from the preceding questions to form a focus group on culturally inclusive practices in school. Families can be important advocates and teachers in this work.

CONNECTED TEACHING COMMITMENT
Celebrate Global Connections

Audit your curriculum for cultural and linguistic diversity. Do the books, posters, and examples in the classroom celebrate and reflect the diversity of local and global communities? Ask students to share their own examples and to bring in beloved texts, songs, and sayings. While lesson planning, check for representation, and if certain identities are missing or underrepresented, create more connecting points for the students. In addition to letting students see their own identities reflected and celebrated in the curriculum, connected global classrooms open windows for students to learn about cultures and identities beyond their own.

Katie McClintic: Culturally Inclusive Instructional Design for Online Courses

Katie McClintic is a senior instructional designer for the Pandemic Initiative for Equity and Action, University of California San Francisco. Her passion for literature and language comes through in her teaching techniques, which focus on making connections between texts, students' lives, and the world as a whole. Her goal in the classroom is to demonstrate respect for all cultures and backgrounds in order to facilitate equal learning opportunities for everyone. In her narrative, you'll see the benefit of seeking out learning and professional development opportunities in your area to improve what and how you teach students.

When I served as a cross-cultural adviser in an intensive English language program at the University of Kansas, I had the joy of facilitating orientations for new international students at the beginning of each semester. I remember one orientation happened on a snowy January day. There were only a few students in the classroom for the orientation, one of whom was a forlorn-looking student from a central African country, who I'll call Davion. As a cross-cultural adviser, I helped students navigate the U.S. education system, adjust to academic expectations in the United States, and move through the stages of cultural adjustment. Thus, I had become accustomed to seeing new students experience culture shock to varying degrees when they first arrived in Kansas. By the look on his face and his body language, I could tell Davion was definitely experiencing a strong case of it. I asked him how he was feeling about taking classes at the university and moving to the Midwest. His response is something I often still think about: "I am happy to be here, but where are all the people? In my country, there are always people in the streets and in front of their houses, but here, the streets are empty. Where is everyone?"

It was an easy question to answer on the surface. I explained cold, snowy Kansas winters made most people stay in their houses, where it was warm. But upon thinking more deeply about the question, I realized moving to a place where people value privacy and isolation within their own spaces rather than connection and community could have contributed to Davion's shock.

Now as an instructional designer, I often come back to Davion's dilemma, which is an allegory for transitioning to online learning. Face-to-face classrooms develop their own culture in which the learning becomes a collective endeavor. Thus, when students transition to learning in an online space, they, too, experience a sort of culture shock. Learning online can make students feel isolated. These students, like Davion, may ask themselves, "Where are all the people?" In other words, students may be wondering, "Where is the community and classroom culture I am used to from my face-to-face learning?"

Online learning opened new avenues for educational experiences unbound by traditional temporal and spatial constraints. However, this brave new world of learning can also create some unique challenges. The challenges are harder for students who may need extra support in online cultural spaces involving the negotiation of identity, social presence, power distance,

> educational expectations, temporal space, and more. This presents a dual difficulty to students from more collectivist cultures who are used to group belongingness and cooperative learning, which are difficult to replicate in some online learning environments. While technology-mediated instruction has been around for some time, though, at first, many educators viewed it as an option rather than a necessity. Now, knowing how to create quality online learning experiences to engage all learners and foster a sense of belonging is more important than ever. Rather than mourn the loss of what could have been, educators can see online learning as an amazing opportunity for what could be as they bring in a new era of learning. (Katie McClintic, personal communication, October 13, 2020)

Strategies for Building Culturally Responsive, Self-Paced E-Learning

Katie McClintic moved from her work as a cross-cultural adviser to a position in instructional design for a global online school system. In the following sections, she offers her top strategies for building culturally responsive, self-paced learning approaches. These include streamlining content and eliminating distractions according to the Universal Design for Learning framework, including diverse voices within the lesson content, providing a global perspective, and creating meaningful assignments to solve real-world problems (CAST, n.d.).

Follow the Universal Design for Learning Framework

The Universal Design for Learning guidelines offer a set of concrete suggestions, applicable to any discipline or domain, to ensure all learners can access and participate in meaningful, challenging learning opportunities (CAST, n.d.). This framework encourages using multiple modes of engagement, representation, and expression for learners. A first step in applying UDL is to use simple, clear syntax and structure when designing lesson plans. Also, be intentional about using specific cultural references and idiomatic language; teach these references and language usages in context to celebrate culture, but avoid relying on them as part of everyday language. Table 5.1 shows examples of how to use UDL to support multilingual learners.

Table 5.1: UDL Language Suggestions

	Avoid This	**Try This Instead**
Use simple, clear syntax.	Say things like, "William Shakespeare was a prolific writer, obviously, who wrote many plays that he's known for, but what I want to focus on in this unit are a few of his many published sonnets—154, to be exact, which was a lot even for the time period when poetry was an especially popular art form."	Say things like, "Our William Shakespeare unit will focus on selections from his 154 sonnets."
Avoid or clearly define idioms.	Say things like, "Students should *touch base with* their teachers regularly to make sure they are *on the right track* with their assignments."	Say things like, "Students should contact their teachers regularly to make sure they are following assignment requirements."
Define new or difficult content words with footnotes or glossaries. When speaking, pause to check for understanding.	Give students directions like, "Avoid ambiguous writing in your book analysis."	Give students directions like, "Avoid ambiguous* writing in your book analysis," but provide definitions. *Insert a footnote. *Refer to the glossary.
Use images to support content.	Give students descriptions like, "There are four main types of writing: (1) expository, (2) descriptive, (3) persuasive, and (4) narrative. Expository writing is writing that explains; it is informative, factual, detailed, and unbiased. Descriptive writing is writing that describes…"	Create a visual list of the four types of writing, and include the following information. 1. Explain (expository): Informative, factual, detailed, unbiased 2. Describe (descriptive): Nonfiction, sensory, detailed, imaginative 3. Convince (persuasive): Opinionated, supported, emotional, influential 4. Tell the story (narrative): Fiction or nonfiction, story like, descriptive, creative

continued ▶

	Avoid This	Try This Instead
Present content in a variety of ways.	All class lecture and textbook reading, all the time.	Design lesson plans that use a variety of delivery methods and point students to resources, such as videos, interactives, infographics, manipulatives, and collaboration.
Offer students a variety of ways to participate and complete assignments.	All written responses, all the time.	Give students options when it fits course objectives. Essays, paragraphs, and journals represent one important type of assessment technique. Slideshow presentations, podcasts, speeches, demonstrations, interviews, and visual projects display learning in different important ways.

Vocabulary is another area to consider carefully. Include vocabulary support for not only domain-specific terms but also high-level academic vocabulary that could impede understanding for non-native English speakers. Finally, use a friendly tone, rather than an overly formal, nonconversational tone. From the lesson design to the support, to the activities, to the very tone they use when speaking, educators want students to hear how much they value students and welcome them in class. The reproducible worksheet at the end of this chapter (page 150) includes a practical guide to auditing a course for UDL.

Include Diverse Voices Within the Course Content

Greg Soden (whom you met in chapter 4, page 119) and Katie McClintic worked together to develop an online world religions class. Katie says that during the curriculum design process, "another way to include culturally inclusive design strategies is by including diverse voices in the content. For example, in our world religions course, we (literally!) included voices from educators, scholars, and religious practitioners for each religion in the course." Greg Soden has been a prolific podcaster since 2017, so he gave the class access to a wealth of interviews with different people who practice a particular religion. This representation matters because not only are students hearing first-person perspectives but they also hear the practitioners' voices, which provide a rich display of diverse accents and variations of the English language. Podcasts, audio stories, interviews, and class visitors and speakers all support diversity and perspective sharing in your classroom.

Create Community-Based Learning Opportunities

Communities are the best classrooms. Katie's experience teaching multilingual learners informed her work to develop meaningful assignments grounded in real-world application. This also aligns with the UDL principle of engagement by optimizing relevance, value, and authenticity. When working with writers on course design, Katie encourages opportunities where students practice skills or connect content to their communities, such as by interviewing a community leader, organizing a service project, photographing a special place in the community, organizing an art project, telling a community story, or helping with an event. These experiences extend the course beyond the confines of the learning management system (Wiggins & McTighe, 2005).

Key Classroom Takeaway: Celebrate Linguistic Diversity

English learners are the fastest-growing student population in the United States (National Council of Teachers of English, 2008). English learners also represent an incredibly heterogeneous population. In 2000, 8.1 percent of students in U.S. public schools were English learners. By 2017, this number had increased to over 10 percent (or five million students; National Center for Education Statistics, 2018). The nine most represented home languages in U.S. public schools, and the numbers of EL student speakers of these home languages in 2017, are as follows (National Center for Education Statistics, 2018).

1. **Spanish:** 3.7 million
2. **Arabic:** 136,500
3. **Chinese:** 106,500
4. **English:** 94,900
5. **Vietnamese:** 77,800
6. **Somali:** 41,300
7. **Russian:** 36,800
8. **Portuguese:** 33,300
9. **Haitian:** 32,700

Since 2011, schools have seen Swahili, Nepali, and Karen increase by more than 400 percent as the home languages of EL students in the United States (National Center for Education Statistics, 2018). These data point to languages and cultures educators need to learn more about.

Table 5.2 (page 148) shares a framework you can use to evaluate the language your school community employs. This framework helps support an ongoing perspective shift in centering and celebrating multilingual learners in your classroom. You can remember it by starting with the *who* and then focusing on *identities* and *strengths* with *specificity*.

Table 5.2: People-Centered Language Framework

Ask yourself...	Because...
Who are we centering?	This question is particularly illuminating, as dominant language, cultural, and power groups are centered in the terminology you use in schools. It is for this reason you often seek new perspectives and terms.
What term does the person identify with?	People matter and can speak for themselves. Across experiences and identities, value the way individuals choose to identify. If a person shares their preference, believe them. This trumps almost all other criteria.
Is our language strengths based?	How individuals talk about groups of people often reveals biases (conscious and unconscious) that lead to behaviors (humanizing or damaging). In evaluating terms, specifically seek out asset-based frameworks. For example, notice how *multilingual* suggests a different (strengths-based) approach than the term *limited English proficient*.
Can we be more specific?	Specificity matters. For example, *Argentinian* is more specific than *Latino* or *Latinx*, and *Yemeni* is more specific than *Arab*. If you have a more specific term, it is better to choose that over a general term. That said, umbrella terms do have some utility in doing equity work and understanding large and systematic trends. For example, it can be helpful to know that culturally and linguistically diverse groups are collectively underrepresented in gifted education (Ford, Grantham, & Whiting, 2008). Zeroing in to then understand what this means for specific groups, such as recent newcomers from Vietnam, helps inform specific action plans for change.

Summary

How can educators safeguard community, build classroom culture, and continue to be vigilant about student support? What does this mean in a world that is increasingly multilingual, multicultural, and technology mediated? As Katie McClintic shared in her narrative, transitioning to online learning can offer its own kind of culture shock. Learning online can cause feelings of isolation for students, who, like Davion, may ask themselves, "Where are all the people?" Educators must navigate what it means to do right by their students in these blended spaces, which present their own challenges and possibilities.

In this chapter, you heard from Kathryn Fishman-Weaver, who shared that what could have been a language barrier became a connection point and a call to deepen her personal study of world languages. Lisa DeCastro explained how using small moments throughout the day to learn languages from her students made the students more willing and eager to practice language in front of others. Kimberly Kester shared how languages are integral to culture and how inviting her students to share rituals, traditions, and recipes strengthened their class community. Finally, Katie McClintic explained how intentionally using universal design theory as she develops online lessons helps support and challenge learners from all cultures.

The narratives and discussion in this chapter are a starting place for honoring your students' multicultural strengths. The commitment to centering student voices, experiences, and languages creates more vibrant, relevant, and inclusive classrooms. In chapter 6, you will learn how you can build on this work to support the gifted and talented students in your classroom. Please find the space for reflective practice for chapter 5 on the following page.

Chapter 5: Apply It to Your Practice

Working individually or in learning teams, reflect on these questions, and implement the commitments to your practice (for more information on engaging with these questions, please see the section titled Space for Reflective Practice on page 9 in the introduction). As always, strive to move from reflection to action.

React to the Chapter

What are your key takeaways from this chapter? What was surprising to read? What did you connect with?

Review Positionality

How has language, culture, or international travel impacted your lived experiences and perspective on teaching and learning? Write a blog post, journal entry, or vignette capturing the impact of these experiences.

Define Home

Why does home matter to classroom practice? How can educators both cultivate and honor home in their online or blended classroom, particularly when students are multilingual and multicultural learners? What are the challenges and possibilities of creating a sense of home in the online space? Talk with fellow educators about how they foster a sense of home in their classrooms.

Learn About Culture for Culturally Responsive Teaching

Are there cultural groups in your school or classroom you know little about? These could be linguistic, ethnic, identity, or religious groups. Choose a group to start with, and commit to learning more. Read scholarly works. Watch documentaries. Reach out to leaders in the community. Invite guests into your classroom to share their cultural traditions. Remember, your students and their families are valuable experts.

Become a World Language Learner

Spend the next thirty days studying a language spoken by one or more students in your school. You can use one of many different language-learning programs, such as Rosetta Stone, Babbel, or Duolingo. What does this experience teach you about learning a language, having empathy, and connecting with multilingual students? Add the layer of committing to learn how to greet each of your students in their home language. (Note: You can make this a practice with fellow grade-level educators, your department, or your collaborative team to increase accountability and add a little friendly competition.)

Audit a Course for UDL

Choose a course you teach, and analyze it for the following.

- How accessible is this course for your English learners? How accessible is it for your neurodiverse students?

- What opportunities do you see to add multimodal learning and performance opportunities?

- Which cultures are well represented in this course, and which are missing?

Sometimes, it is hard to see your own work clearly or critically. Asking an outside expert to review your work or audit it for accessibility can reveal issues you might have missed.

Leveraging Opportunities for Gifted and Talented Students

6

Honoring students' strengths, genius, and talent domains can lead to new educational possibilities. As educators rethink space, place, and pacing in education, online and blended approaches can open the capacity for talent-based, passion-focused learning that celebrates students' talent domains. This chapter focuses on the potential online and blended classrooms have to support gifted and talented students.

When first considering this work, you must look deeply at who has access to advanced and accelerated learning opportunities. Too many high-ability students do not have access to gifted and advanced programs. It is for this reason that we (Kathryn and Stephanie) have situated this chapter in part II, which focuses on inclusion and equity.

Implicit and explicit biases in tracking, referral, and identification processes contribute to an underrepresentation of African American, Latinx, low-income, and twice-exceptional learners (Ford & Grantham, 2003; Renzulli, 2011). In 2018, Donna Y. Ford, Kenneth T. Dickson, Joy Lawson Davis, Michelle Trotman Scott, and Tarek C. Grantham authored what they titled "A Culturally Responsive Equity-Based Bill of Rights for Gifted Students of Color." This bill of rights responds directly to Ford's (2013) body of research on the underrepresentation of gifted students

Essential Question

How can educators rethink space, place, and pace to help students soar in online and blended classrooms?

Chapter Learning Objectives

- Consider the unique physical, emotional, and intellectual advantages of self-paced, online, or blended learning.

- Identify opportunities to differentiate, challenge, reach, and support gifted and talented learners.

- Design wholehearted approaches for teaching.

- Recognize coaching as a strategy to build connection.

- Honor strengths and individual context in individual student-support plans.

Key Terms

acceleration. Moving through curriculum at a quicker pace than grade-level peers.

flow. The act of being so absorbed in a task that an individual loses track of time. Flow contributes to creativity, productivity, and happiness (Csikszentmihalyi, 1990).

gifted. Students who "have the capability to perform . . . at higher levels compared to others of the same age, experience, and environment in one or more domains. They require modification(s) to their educational experience(s) to learn and realize their potential" (National Association for Gifted Children, 2019, p. 1). Gifted students come from all backgrounds and identities and may have learning needs beyond giftedness, including social-emotional needs and disabilities.

neurodiversity. An asset-based term for necessary variation in the human population that includes developmental, intellectual, and cognitive differences.

talent development. A movement in gifted education to focus on developing talent within varied domains and different types of abilities and paths. The aim of this work is for educators and families to "identify more talented children and ensure that they have the opportunities they need to develop their potential to the fullest degree possible" (Olszewski-Kubilius, Subotnik, & Worrell, 2019).

thrice exceptional (3E). A term to describe the complex intersections of culturally and linguistically diverse (CLD) students who also present with two diagnoses—(1) giftedness and (2) learning or developmental disabilities (Collins, 2021).

twice exceptional (2E). A term that refers to individuals with two diagnoses, one as gifted and a second in developmental or learning disabilities.

of color as well as the limited access students from marginalized backgrounds have to gifted and advanced programs. The bill of rights for gifted students of color is:

> grounded in equity and cultural responsiveness. . . . Gifted students of color have rights that must be heard, honored, and addressed. They have gifts and talents that must be recognized, affirmed, and developed as districts endeavor to recruit and retain them in gifted education. (Ford et al., 2018, p. 125)

Three Barriers to Learning for Gifted Students

In this section, we highlight three key barriers that contribute to the chronic underrepresentation of gifted students from historically marginalized backgrounds—gifted students of color, gifted students from low-income backgrounds, gifted multilingual learners, and twice-exceptional students (gifted learners who also have disabilities). These barriers form a gatekeeper system that is flawed by implicit bias, inadequate identification instruments, and limited professional learning related to identifying and supporting culturally and linguistically diverse gifted learners. The barriers are not isolated; they work together to create systematic inequalities in gifted programs.

Implicit Bias and Gatekeepers

A 2020 report in *Gifted Child Today* cites the system asks teachers to serve as "gatekeepers" to the identification process (Novak, Lewis, & Weber, 2020). Teachers operating as gatekeepers contribute to underrepresentation of culturally and linguistically diverse students in gifted education (Novak et al., 2020). General education teachers often have limited training on the needs and nature of gifted learners. They have even less training on recognizing gifted students from CLD backgrounds. The lack of teacher preparation in these areas contributes to pervasive inequalities in teacher nomination for gifted programs (Ayala, 2015).

Eliminating teacher referral altogether and universally screening all students for gifted programs at established times in the district calendar has promise in addressing this barrier. Numerous studies support that this practice contributes to a dramatic increase in diversity in gifted education programs (Card & Giuliano, 2016; Morgan, 2020). But universal screening alone isn't a comprehensive solution. First, it requires a considerable economic investment by districts (Card & Giuliano, 2016; Lakin, 2016). Second, it requires educators to use identification instruments properly. Third, it still requires an ongoing commitment to support and retain gifted students from historically underrepresented backgrounds (Ford et al., 2018).

Identification Instruments

Most states and districts use a version of a general intelligence test as part (or all) of their identification process. Although there is some variation, for too long, an IQ equal to or greater than 130 (ninety-eighth percentile) has been considered a standard metric for identifying giftedness. IQ tests can provide only limited information and are biased in whom they identify. The National Association for Gifted Children (n.d.) recommends against using this (or any) single instrument to determine giftedness, as "relying on IQ or performance results alone may overlook certain gifted populations." Instead, educators should use multiple methods and measures to identify gifted and talented youth, such as qualitative and quantitative assessments, including portfolios of student work and special projects. Then, foster those talents through supportive and challenging educational opportunities.

Professional Learning and Development Related to CLD Gifted Students

As discussed, teachers seldom have comprehensive training on identifying and supporting CLD gifted students. Therefore, Donna Y. Ford and Tarek C. Grantham (2012) have laid out a framework for culturally relevant professional development in this area. Key commitments from their framework include research on the characteristics of culturally diverse gifted learners; strategies for recruitment and retainment; training on discrimination, prejudice, and bias; and professional learning on racial identity, such as reading multicultural literature and inviting culturally diverse experts and trainers (Ford & Grantham, 2012).

If used equitably, the online and blended classroom has the potential to expand access to new possibilities, coursework, and connections. In this chapter, you will meet students and educators who are thinking deeply about what gifted education means and how schools can expand access to gifted services and advanced programs. Because teaching and learning can happen anywhere, the settings for the following narratives are diverse. You'll visit a school bus, a classroom, online spaces, and academic competitions. As you read these stories, consider what representation and access look like in your own gifted and advanced programs.

Talent Development

Research on talent development suggests achievement and giftedness are malleable. Many factors, including social-emotional conditions, environment, and opportunity, impact students' achievement (Subotnik, Worrell, & Olszewski-Kubilius, 2016). This means teachers have a tremendous responsibility and potential to identify and foster the talents of students. In 2015, the National Association for Gifted Children assembled a task force to better understand and disseminate information about talent development within the context of gifted education. Guiding questions for this work included these: "Who are these students we call gifted? In what ways are they different from peers with similar experience levels? Which of their needs might be addressed effectively through a [talent development] model?" (National Association for Gifted Children, 2015, p. 3).

- **Who are these students we call gifted?** Gifted students come from all cultural and identity backgrounds across racial, ethnic, linguistic, socioeconomic, and exceptionality groups. However, not all students are equitably identified. Further underrepresentation of students from historically marginalized backgrounds is widespread (National Association for Gifted Children, 2015). "Reversing the underrepresentation of culturally and linguistically diverse students (CLD) in gifted education will require that educators have a thorough understanding of the reasons that CLD students have traditionally been excluded from participation in gifted programs," and it will require that educators develop clear action plans to address these inequities (National Association for Gifted Children, 2011, p. 1).

- **In what ways are gifted students different from their peers?** Gifted students' needs are both specific to giftedness—intensity, asynchrony (uneven development), and anxiety (which can manifest both socially and academically)—and highly contextualized to their individual strengths, challenges, and lived experiences.

- **Which of their needs can a talent development model address?** A 2019 post by leading scholars in gifted education asserts that "the field of gifted education is moving towards a greater focus on developing talent within varied domains" (Olszewski-Kubilius et al., 2019). Talent development can play a pivotal role in developing potential. Paula Olszewski-Kubilius, Rena Subotnik, and Frank Worrell (2019) continue:

> We would argue that knowing the early signs of talent in a field and understanding what is necessary for its development will enable educators and parents to identify more talented children and ensure that they have the opportunities they need to develop their potential to the fullest degree possible.

Provided this work extends across student populations, seeking out and developing talents is a promising practice in the field.

Giftedness

Although there are many definitions of giftedness, most agree gifted students have different processing and behaviors than their age-level peers. Clinical child psychologist Deirdre V. Lovecky (2011) identifies five traits often inherent to gifted children: (1) divergent thinking ability, (2) excitability, (3) sensitivity, (4) perceptiveness, and (5) entelechy (also known as *self-determination*). In terms of processing, repeated studies show gifted individuals have a more activated right prefrontal cortex, enhanced cerebral bilateralism, and different neural processing often characterized by both more complex (meaning more parts of the brain work together during complex tasks) and more efficient (meaning less brain activity is required for similar tasks) processes (Fishman-Weaver, 2020).

Despite these similarities, gifted youth also have important differences both among peers and within their talent domains. Asynchronous (or uneven) development is common among gifted youth. For example, a fifth-grade student may read college-level texts, have the handwriting of a first grader, do abstract mathematics in her head, make simple calculation errors on paper, and collapse to the floor in a fit of despair over spilled juice. This uneven development, where the student is highly advanced in some areas (sometimes multiple grades beyond same-age peers) and still developing in others (sometimes grades behind same-age peers), can make forming friendships and finding fitting work more challenging. Gifted students need educators who honor their strengths, support them in their challenges, and help connect them with multiple peer groups to foster belonging (Guilbault & Kane, 2016).

Differentiation

Differentiation refers to adjustments in pacing and instruction to work with diverse learners who bring many skill sets, talents, and challenges to the classroom. These adjustments are important in all classrooms and vital in gifted education. Figure 6.1 is a chart of questions you might use in working with students at varying stages of a project, assignment, or unit.

Beginning	Middle	End
What are your first impressions?	How are things going?	What are the final results?
What challenges do you anticipate?	Where do you need help?	What are you proudest of?
What strengths will this play to?	What questions do you have?	What would you do differently next time?

Figure 6.1: Reflective questions for the beginning, middle, and end of a project or unit.

Visit **go.SolutionTree.com/technology** *to download the reproducible version of this figure.*

Read on for stories of how fellow educators have used these tips to help their in-person, online, and blended communities thrive.

CONNECTED TEACHING COMMITMENT
Commit to Equity

Offer advanced, accelerated, and gifted services with equity in mind. Intentionally build equity into teaching and giftedness identification processes to better identify and support students from marginalized or underrepresented backgrounds in advanced programs. These strategies include universal screening for gifted services, nonverbal and multiple identification measures for gifted education, open-access programming, strengths-based family conferences, and equity audits of gifted and advanced programs. High expectations, differentiation, appropriate services, and opportunities for challenge and engagement must be universally accessible to all students in local school communities.

Marilyn Toalson: Coaching Gifted Learners

Marilyn Toalson is a veteran educator first introduced in chapter 1 (page 18). In this narrative, she shares about the importance of coaching in the classroom.

Forty-four middle school gifted students are lined up waiting to board the bus for home. There is happy chatter, as the classmates and friends have had a long day competing in their Missouri Future Problem-Solving Competition. Their arms are full of props, costume parts, scripts, and pillows. They enter the bus one by one, anticipating the two-hour drive home.

Everyone sits in their teams. The buzz among the students drifts to a quieter hum as the bus begins to move. The coach waits for near quiet and then stands at the front of the bus. She smiles and congratulates the students as winners because they have all made it to the state finals. She reminds the students of all the hard work they have put forth in the research, writing, and team skit. She talks about how much she has learned and how much they have learned. The students listen as they anticipate what comes next.

The coach holds up the evaluation packets for each team's work. She reminds the students not to open the sealed envelopes until all teams have theirs. When the last evaluation packet finds the correct team, they anxiously open the judges' notes. The students already know how they placed in the competition and if they are progressing to the next level, but they do not know what the judges said about them individually and as a team.

It is quiet for a few seconds as each student reads their individual and team evaluations. They focus on their positive comments first. There are fist bumps, high fives, and whoops among the groups. Written compliments from the judges send positive cheers throughout the bus. It gets quiet again, and the teams continue to review the comments from the judges, particularly the ones they skimmed over at first because they scream, *Negative!* Immediately, the tone changes among many of the young learners. One team of learners is outraged at the negative comments, and they start arguments with the absent judges.

> "They said my idea was not creative, and I was the most creative."
>
> "This incompetent evaluator says our best solution was 'not futuristic.' What does that even mean? It is so futuristic!"
>
> "This has to be the same evaluator: our underlying problem is 'not supported by science.'"
>
> "This is such a bad judge; he doesn't even understand the process."

The coach sits down with this team and listens to their frustrations. At the same time, she notices the team next to them is absorbed in reading comments too, but they are much calmer. The coach looks over the shoulder of one student and reads the score sheet.

> "Even though your best solution is good, you will want to add more future elements to the solution if you advance to the international competition. The underlying problem was right on target, but as you prepare for future competitions, work on finding the perfect verb."

As the coach watches both teams, it is obvious the second team agrees with the evaluation because of the way the judge communicated the remarks in positive, helpful wording.

This was an aha moment for me, the future problem-solving coach. As a teacher of gifted learners for thirty years, I recall many bus rides like this, but the preceding one was a pedagogical epiphany. It has stayed with me in my current role teaching high school students online. Another student story emphasizes the influence of positive language. The setting is a Regional Congress Speech Competition, hosted remotely.

It is a Friday evening. High school students are putting on suit jackets but skipping shoes altogether. They each are holding a computer tablet as they log on, standing next to the kitchen counter podium in their home. They are ready to present their case for the Regional Congress Speech Competition. There are notes up on the screen. Bottles of water are close by. Younger siblings are banished to the basement or closed rooms in each home. Parents are trying to spy from down the hall with an eye on their high school competitor.

The coach pops up on the screen of each participant from his high school. He has a few motivating words to the team, and all the team members receive the times they will join digitally for their round. For a few minutes, chatter and excitement run through the team members as they share greetings and show off their socks. Then the computers go quiet in anticipation of the first round.

The first round for Joe is over. He saunters to a comfortable chair in his living room office and looks for the results on his tablet. His coach appears on the monitor, and they read over the feedback together. The coach begins with, "What do you think?"

Joe agrees with the first judge. "She is probably right. She enjoyed my joke, but in the middle of my opening was not a good time to tell it. She liked the way I began with my opponent's statement right at the beginning of the rebuttal. I will do that in the next round."

The coach asks about the second judge. Joe replies, "He was a novice judge; he did not like my opening, and it was a good opening. Nothing he said helps."

The competition itself is not the moment to unpack this. During the competition, students need abundant meaningful, positive feedback throughout the process. The coach gives just that, offering encouragement and a few reminders before having to join a digital meeting for another round. He then suggests Joe bring all the comments from each round to class the next time they meet so they can go through them in their online class. The post-reflection is a critical growth opportunity. Responding to "occasions of perceived unfairness in judging" can create "good opportunities for teaching valuable lessons to students" (Ozturk & Debelak, 2008, p. 51). The coach jots down a note to work through all the judges' comments with Joe next week.

My *aha* moment and Joe's intricate work with his team reveal learning continues from beginning a project all the way through digesting feedback and considering how best to use it to improve. Young people need the kinds of challenges and accomplishments that expect, demand, and nurture their best effort. As Mehmet A. Ozturk and Charles Debelak (2008) suggest, there are affective benefits to authentic learning opportunities, including academic competitions. "The process in which children strive to realize their intellectual or talent potential is an important part of gathering self-confidence and self-awareness" (Ozturk & Debelak, 2008, p. 50). These opportunities allow students to stretch, take risks, and respond to constructive criticism. The latter is an ongoing lesson for all human beings and a teachable moment for coaches everywhere. (Marilyn Toalson, personal communication, January 3, 2021)

Strategies for Bringing Coaching and Connection to the Online and Blended Classroom

The scenarios Marilyn shared celebrate students as they become autonomous learners. These stories show good teaching is everywhere. Whether in person, remote, hybrid, or online, teachers of gifted learners will find ways to help students learn at a very high level. They know evaluation is key to gifted learners' intellectual growth as they nurture self-evaluation skills. Marilyn told us she is "excited to see how technology becomes a part of the evaluation and education process. Our future classrooms look different from those that came before." The following are two strategies she uses to practice coaching and connection in her online classrooms.

Coach With Heart

Like Marilyn, many of the contributors we (Kathryn and Stephanie) learned with have experiences coaching both sports and academics. I (Kathryn) asked three of these educators and coaches for their best advice for new coaches. Here are their top strategies for coaching youth.

- **Practice positive corrections:** Just as Marilyn shared in her stories, the way teachers deliver feedback matters. Megan Lilien, a longtime lacrosse coach and science educator, says, "Make your expectations clear and always use a positive approach. Lots of corrections are needed to teach a sport. The method you use to deliver these corrections matters." See chapter 3 (page 90) for more information on giving effective feedback.

- **Teach active listening:** Jeff Kopolow, a triple-diamond speech and debate coach, says, "Teach your students not just to hear their opponents but to listen for understanding. Only then will you be able to adequately respond. This applies to reading a play in football, to following the ball in baseball, and to winning a debate tournament." For more information on active listening, see chapter 1 (page 20).

- **Focus on values first:** Matt Miltenberg has coached cross-country and track for years. While he has helped his athletes improve their times, get stronger, and win meets, he says teaching character is more important than winning. "Figure out what you truly believe in and value. Name those two to four foundational values and talk with your team about how these values will guide your culture. In the end, it will be that culture more than anything else that determines how your team navigates challenges and finds success." Matt is working with a new team at a new school, and he's drawn his runners together around the values of tradition, character, and team.

Marilyn echoes a concept we encountered throughout our research on connected classrooms. She writes that "coaching and giving quality feedback in the online space is an exercise in empathy." The reproducible at the end of this chapter (page 171) includes prompts to help you identify what it means to coach with heart in your classroom.

Use Opportunities for Synchronous Feedback

Even while teaching online, seek opportunities to give live feedback. This feedback can take many forms, including the following.

- Use messaging and chat windows, which can provide real-time feedback and conversations.
- Have drop-in office hours via video conferencing where students can share projects, ask questions, and stop by to connect.
- When synchronous meetings are not possible, send short videos; these can help humanize interactions.

CONNECTED TEACHING COMMITMENT
Build in Affective Supports

The old adage, "Teachers teach kids first and content second," is present throughout the narratives in this chapter. As with all students, supporting gifted and high-ability learners extends beyond academics. Affective development is in the *feeling* domain, which is distinct but related to the cognitive or *thinking* domain. Build in affective supports by attending to students' identities, feelings, and behaviors in the classroom, and by directly teaching strategies related to self-efficacy, emotional regulation, healthy relationships, and self-care. Often in teaching students that there are skills and strategies to use when school (or life) gets challenging, educators can teach one of the greatest affective lessons of all: "You are not alone."

Brian Stuhlman: Orchestrating Connection for Gifted and Talented Learners

Brian Stuhlman has spent over twenty years teaching English language arts, performing and liberal arts, and gifted education. He has taught in public, private, rural, urban, and international schools. Currently, he serves as the middle school coordinator for Mizzou Academy, where he coordinates both online and blended middle school programming.

All educators strive to help students reach their potential and shine. Those who work with gifted and talented students are well aware this population needs support and guidance commensurate with their unique needs, skills, and talents. Specialized educational programming—including in-person, online, and blended courses and enrichments—can offer gifted, talented, and high-achieving students opportunities for equitable and enriching education.

When faced with how to serve this student group whose needs include a dynamically shifting intersection of pedagogical methods, I like to think of a modern symphony. How can I craft and execute a harmonious program with diverse instruments, musicians, tempos, and styles? Throughout my career, I have served as a conductor for gifted and talented students. I have encountered a panoply of students with diverse gifts, talents, and interests. It has been my job and delight to meet each student in their right orchestra section. The following examples recount key melodies I've gotten to hear and the talented musicians who played them.

In the brass section of my gifted orchestra was Matthew. He was brassy and fun. I coded Matthew's permanent file in two distinct categories: (1) a delight to have in class and (2) a disruption and distraction. When he was in my class, Matthew took great delight in finishing some of my lessons for me, not necessarily because I asked him to but because he knew he could. He purposefully pushed the limits of irreverence and orneriness with his art. He loved to be the center of attention, but he was also his classmates' most ardent cheerleader. He processed information quickly, making him accomplished in debate and skilled in making connections. In a classroom with a teacher who held tightly to a set schedule at a tight pace, people sometimes perceived Matthew's self-confidence as negative, or a challenge to authority. Yet, in those moments when teachers could harness the volume of his character, I witnessed intense learning, and stately, brilliant music.

Providing a very different sound was the much more mellow Mandy. While Matthew was a brassy, verbal processor, Mandy was a quieter woodwind. Her processing was reflective and personal. Mandy was an integral part of every team. She was in it to learn and to grow; she did not crave the spotlight and was usually more comfortable in the background. I had the great fortune of working with Mandy over the course of three weeks at a statewide program for exceptionally gifted youth. She participated; in fact, she excelled, but she was particularly quiet to the point that I didn't always know if she was really understanding or enjoying the content of the course. On the last day of the class, I discovered through some of her reflective writing the depth of her understanding. She had followed every word and activity with a quiet intensity. Like so many gifted students, Mandy was an *ambivert*, able to shine during extroverted situations, while more comfortable in personal quiet. Mandy developed proficiency in the tools and skills of effective learning based on listening, reading, and quiet processing, but she didn't need to actively work with others to be academically successful.

In this metaphorical orchestra, Harper was the first-chair violinist. He led by example and with excellence. He worked well in any ensemble, but he also shined in solos. Harper was advanced by almost every metric. He was a strong student who excelled in his classes. He could solve high-level mathematics problems in his immaculate notebook, and then compose writing that excelled in both poetic beauty and structure. He was insatiable in his learning and had a strong social circle. I had the pleasure of challenging ninth grader Harper in a game of *Trivial Pursuit*. I posed a near-impossible question about an event from President Harding's administration. Harper not only understood the question but also recalled Harding's years in office, quoted the major policies and scandals, and inferred the answer out of thin air. While he was well liked, many of his teachers didn't know how to keep up with him, much less challenge him. Unfortunately, teacher education programs rarely include training on strategies for supporting the unique needs of gifted learners.

Multipotentiality is not uncommon in gifted education, but Michaela's ability to realize that potential across so many unrelated topics and passions certainly set her apart.

When I first encountered Michaela, she was excited for a future in education. Then something shifted during her first year in college, and she began pursuing a career in medicine with aspirations of being a heart surgeon. Just before medical school, her road forked again and took her down the path of ministry. Following the beat of her own drum, Michaela became a pastor. She is a pastor first and foremost. However, she's also an accomplished teacher with a harmonious ability to address higher-level topics of ecology, economics, medicine, and spirituality.

Gifted programs are failing to identify many students, particularly students from marginalized backgrounds. Some of these missing musicians may receive labels like *energetic*, *challenging*, or even *a handful*. Some are twice exceptional, meaning they both are gifted and present with disabilities. Some are so out of tune with the way schools work or other rules of social interaction they may present as occasionally disrespectful, irreverent, or defiant of the expected way things should be done.

You didn't have to spend much time with Li to see he was extremely bright in a number of subjects but also was socially different. At times, he was a difficult student to like being around. However, both his peers and I could always tell he was just trying to fit in. On the other side of that spectrum was Jayden. Jayden didn't present with many of the more typical

> characteristics of gifted and talented behavior. He didn't get good grades and considered dropping out of school altogether. Yet, he could do anything with machines. He had an otherworldly notion of how things worked, and he loved to take things apart and put them back together. He understood machines in every sense. He was spatially gifted, which, unfortunately, schools have too few courses and assessments to foster.
>
> There is an adage that says, "No one can whistle a symphony. It takes a whole orchestra to play it." In the great jukebox of life, gifted and talented students represent a far-reaching range of characteristics and genres that make working with this population invigorating and challenging at the same time. In my interactions with gifted and talented students, I aim to conduct learning experiences with energy, gusto, flexibility, and variety. The online environment is uniquely suited for this flexibility. The opportunities for acceleration, differentiation, and personalized pacing can support the unique needs of gifted learners. In my work, I've seen students like Matthew, Mandy, Harper, Michaela, Li, and Jayden have the potential to leverage their strengths and grow through their challenges. (Brian Stuhlman, personal communication, January 10, 2021)

Strategies for Engaging Learners Beyond Content Areas

In chapter 4 (page 117), you met Nina Sprouse, a career educator who is passionate about gender inclusivity and gifted education. Nina shares, "For the past twenty-five years, I have worked with gifted and talented students in both in-person and online contexts. Too often, educators overlook gifted and talented learners in curriculum projects, and I believe this may be even more pronounced in online contexts. However, if we center our lesson planning and curriculum development on creating and creativity, the possibilities for interdisciplinary connections and student learning are vast" (N. Sprouse, personal communication, January 22, 2021).

We (Kathryn and Stephanie) met with Brian and Nina to talk about strategies educators can use to give students creative and accelerated opportunities, particularly in the blended and online classroom. The following are three strategies they offered, which you can use in your metaphorical orchestra.

Integrate STEAM Across Content Areas

Gifted and talented students need space to create and be creative. Computer science and coding concepts give students engaging ways to create interactives, animations, games, music, and art. Scratch, a free learning tool developed by the MIT Media Lab, can help support a computer science unit in class. The software builds on mathematical concepts, deepens fluency with digital technology, and promotes 21st century learning skills while providing a safe space to create a personalized expression of self. These multidisciplinary subjects and projects require students to draw on and develop skills across many different talent domains.

Leverage the Power of Creative Problem Solving

Solving complex, creative, and real-world challenges is a hallmark of an engaged gifted classroom. The following ideas have worked well in and can apply to various content areas.

- **Science:** One semester, students in a gifted education program conducted research at partner labs at the neighboring university and then authored a scientific journal on their experiences and results.
- **Communication:** Another semester, the students partnered with a local NPR member station to produce original personal narrative "This I Believe" essays.
- **Service and leadership:** Students organized art shows on social issues, wrote grants to subsidize enrichment programs for low-income youth in their communities, and organized a Valentine's Day party at a nearby nursing home to help combat loneliness among the elderly.

Prioritize Affective Learning

Affective education can occur throughout a class or lesson. Start the class or day with personal check-ins; host drop-in times, such as before or after school or during lunch, for students to play games, laugh, and share their worries and celebrations; provide opportunities for service projects; pay attention to belonging and friend groups; and hold open conversations about these dynamics. Bring in guest experts who can openly share about concepts such as *impostor syndrome* (the belief that your accomplishments have happened to you by sheer coincidence or trickery and people will eventually find out you are a fraud because you have not truly earned your accomplishments) and *perfectionism* (the compulsive and often debilitating belief that everything you produce or do must be flawless). It is often affirming and helpful to hear from successful adults who have had similar experiences and challenges. These types of lessons are essential to student well-being, development, and success.

Key Classroom Takeaway: Employ Wholehearted Teaching for Neurodiverse Classrooms

Australian sociologist and disability rights activist Judy Singer and American journalist Harvey Blume are credited with first using the term *neurodiversity*. They intended to highlight difference over disability. The term gained traction and is now used across business, education, counseling, and medicine (Armstrong, 2015).

Neurodiversity refers to the necessary and complex cognitive diversity across the human species. In our (Kathryn and Stephanie's) work, we have met talented students who were able to accelerate years beyond their age-level peers through our online coursework. The students we worked with offered strong solutions to class problems and connected with mentors through an online computer science panel we held at the end of the semester. We have also met student leaders who used the connections possible through messaging and email to organize impressive campaigns for social issues. A student leader in our honor society contacted the school counselor to share she had started a WhatsApp group with sixty students at our school to launch a mental health campaign, which is now sponsored by a major mental health organization in the United States. When educators employ wholehearted approaches celebrating neurodiversity, the possibilities are vast.

From 2009 to 2015, I (Kathryn) conducted a longitudinal study with groups of gifted students. This study resulted in a framework called *wholehearted teaching*. Wholehearted teaching disrupts standard definitions of what it means to be a teacher or student and suggests teaching and learning are both ubiquitous and fluid. Students' lived experiences, communities, and peer groups are critical and didactic forces. "Wholehearted teaching is the practice of helping young people (1) recognize these interactions and (2) recalibrate when needed back to courage, connection, and self-care" (Fishman-Weaver, 2018b, p. 127).

When Marilyn sits next to a student on the bus to talk through competition results, when Brian builds relationships with students by honoring their strengths, and when Nina gives students opportunities to use creativity as a vehicle to differentiate learning, they are each practicing wholehearted teaching—a pedagogy based on courage, connection, and self-care (Fishman-Weaver, 2018b).

Wholehearted teaching emphasizes community and relationships. Practicing courage and cultivating wholehearted classrooms are not solo activities. My research consistently found that students feel stronger when they are connected to stable communities, including classes, teams, families, religious groups, and peer groups (Fishman-Weaver, 2018b). This study offered two frameworks that pointed to connected classrooms. The first looked at peer groups and communities, the social landscape of school. I suggested that connection is the sum of belonging, relatedness, and closeness (Fishman-Weaver, 2018b). The second looked at behavior patterns and suggested that connection is also the sum of critical thinking, active listening, and communication (Fishman-Weaver, 2018b). Thriving classrooms, whether online, blended, or in person, require commitments to connection.

During our research, Stephanie and I met with an Advanced Placement computer science teacher in our school. In our student-support conversation about a young woman who was taking his advanced computer science course years ahead of her peers, he shared some important takeaways on the cultural, cognitive, and linguistic diversity in our classrooms. As a programming teacher, he is dedicated to recruiting and retaining diverse students in his computer science classes. He believes people need many different experiences and kinds of thinkers to solve complex problems and create new solutions. Recruitment is not just the right thing to do for equity; it is the only way to advance the field.

The world needs all kinds of brains, and so does your classroom.

Summary

In this chapter, you looked at how access to gifted and advanced programs can point educators to pertinent equity and inclusion work needed across all school settings. While we focused on gifted and talented learners, these stories offer many important takeaways for educators across content areas and populations. For example, Brian Stuhlman compared gifted students to a symphony, each student with a unique role to fill. An educator's job is to be a noticer; each of your students brings their talents, strengths, struggles, and cultural identities to your community. You then have important decisions to make about how to honor, celebrate, and support growth.

As we close these chapters, we want to take a moment to recap the journey of this book. Throughout, Kathryn and I (Stephanie) have championed the power of connection across all teaching contexts. We believe that relationship building and community building are not ancillary to the work of teaching and learning; they are the foundational elements of effective education.

Taking a community approach, you read about seeking out resources in your school and local community and considered how partnering with others through asset mapping can strengthen your teaching practice (Simmons, 2017). You then considered strategies to support students with different needs—the importance of noticing and analyzing strengths and challenges as you build various levels of support. Next, you looked at the everyday life of a teacher, including what you do at the beginning, middle, and end of a class. You read about how you can give efficient and meaningful feedback on assignments and how each daily moment is an opportunity for conversation. You've also looked at ways to make sure students are at the center of both their own learning and your class community. You looked at the power of everyday conversations, intentional curriculum, community-based projects, and family and cultural celebrations as avenues to strengthen community and honor the rich experiences your students bring to class.

We have covered a lot of ground in this book, geographically, philosophically, and pedagogically. As we close these chapters, we hope we are leaving you with many useful strategies and inspiring ideas. We also expect we are leaving you with some big and important questions, including, What are the most important lessons we have learned in blended education, and what do we need to learn next? Read on to know how Stephanie and I (Kathryn) answer this very question. We will also share key takeaways from our research.

Chapter 6: Apply It to Your Practice

Working individually or in learning teams, reflect on these questions, and implement the commitments to your practice (for more information on engaging with these questions, please see the section titled Space for Reflective Practice on page 9 in the introduction). As always, strive to move your reflection to action.

React to the Chapter

What are your key takeaways from this chapter? What was surprising to read? What did you connect with?

Center Strengths, Recognize Barriers

Review demographic data for your gifted and advanced programs.

- What do you notice about access and equity?

- Who are you representing?

- Who is underrepresented?

Next, focus on your culturally and linguistically diverse students, including twice-exceptional learners.

- List some barriers your twice- or thrice-exceptional learners are experiencing in school.

- Discuss how you can reduce or remediate those barriers.

- Consider the specific opportunities and identification measures your school community uses to ensure gifted and advanced programming is equitable.

Finally, brainstorm classroom-based solutions as well as broader school- and district-based initiatives.

- What can you do from your immediate sphere of influence to expand equity, celebrate strengths, and create greater opportunities?

- What ideas from this brainstorm do you want to bring to school and district leaders to expand equity, celebrate strengths, and create greater opportunities?

Identify Online Opportunities

Consider and discuss how you can use online and blended learning to support high-ability and advanced learners. For instance, what courses and opportunities are available for acceleration, advancement, or enrichment? Brainstorm how you can lower access barriers and provide support to ensure that all students who are interested in or ready for advanced coursework can take these courses. (These barriers may include access to technology, financial resources, and support networks.)

Coach With Heart

In this chapter, Marilyn Toalson, Matt Miltenberg, Jeff Kopolow, and Megan Lilien identified three key strategies for coaching with heart: (1) practicing positive corrections, (2) teaching active listening, and (3) focusing on values first. What coaching strategies can you use to promote student ownership of growth? How can you give feedback in a way that is well received and promotes learning? Ask students to help you identify the beloved academic and athletic coaches in your school. Observe these educators during practice, and take note of ways you can translate their coaching strategies to the classroom. While you are at practice (whether that is debate, basketball, or scholar bowl), be sure to congratulate and encourage any of your students you see in this new setting. Getting out of the classroom to connect with young people is a powerful relationship builder.

CONCLUSION

When we started this book project, Stephanie and I (Kathryn) believed we had some stories and strategies to share about our experiences teaching and leading in blended and online classrooms. In sharing and writing these stories, we found they sometimes went in directions we hadn't anticipated. Through the narratives, conversations, and wisdom of this project's contributors, we learned how much we still have to learn. As is often the case in both writing and research, as we got deeper into the project, we discovered surprising patterns of convergence. In this shared space, the key themes for this book emerged. These include the importance of culture, connection, relationships, and feedback. As we close out this book, we each want to share a few key takeaways from the project.

Essential Question

What are the most important lessons to learn next in education?

Kathryn's Takeaways

While I could never summarize all that I learned in working with Stephanie and our participants on this project, I have four key takeaways I'd like to highlight here.

Teaching Is Always About People First and Technology (or Other Tools) Second

Many of our contributors have multiple decades of experience in schools, and three (Marilyn Toalson, Lou Jobst, and Jeff Kopolow) have over forty years of experience each. Learning from these veteran and career educators how technology has changed (or not changed) their approach to teaching is an important takeaway. This book centers the importance of teaching from the heart, of using whatever tools are available to bridge distance in the classroom and create greater proximity and connection. The second half of this book details how digital approaches can help expand access, equity, and inclusivity, particularly in connecting with multilingual and neurodiverse learners. Although technology gives new tools, it doesn't create a connection. People do, just as they always have. Karen Scales, an online language arts teacher who participated in our connected classroom research, told us the following:

> There are some strategies that translate so beautifully from the online space to our in-person classrooms and back. If you can incorporate some of the technology we have in discussion boarding and use that to build relationships and give individualized feedback, imagine how that can work in conjunction with taps on the shoulder and all our in-person strategies.

As we share throughout this text, relationships and community are the heart of great teaching, and educators build these relationships through interaction, care, and intentionality.

Teaching Is the Art of Writing a Collective History

The histories teachers are writing today are global and connected. Our contributors proved to us if you work in schools long enough, you will teach through major events in history. They referenced civil rights movements, war, significant scientific advancements, terrorist attacks, assassinations, and recessions. When Stephanie and I started this book, the global community was navigating the COVID-19 pandemic, and our country was wrestling with a racial reckoning we hope brings about systemic change and strengthens collective commitments to anti-racist work. My memory of these periods in history will be forever shaped by my experiences teaching and learning through them. Our veteran participants taught me the same is true for our students. The community you live in when major events happen shapes your experiences of those historical moments. For teachers and students, the class community is often a key sounding board. Several contributors to this project referenced how their classes responded to and processed significant local or global events together. Teachers and their class communities will have the opportunity to navigate unfolding current events and to ask important questions such as, "Why did this happen? What can we learn from this? How can we support each other and those directly affected? And what should we do next?" These are history-writing questions. In working with schools, educators continue to find classes and students who are writing diverse and connected histories charged with hope.

Voice and Visibility Matter

A core teaching philosophy of mine is that students have important stories, solutions, and ideas to share and the world is better for listening deeply to them. I often think about this in my work in terms of visibility, agency, and student leadership, and I strive to cultivate countless opportunities where students feel seen, heard, and known. As I reflect on this project and what it means for me as a school leader, I remember our focus-group dialogue and the reflections Karen Scales and Diane Johnson shared about visibility.

Diane told us that in the online setting, you have to "embrace anonymity and then scaffold up to visibility." Karen shared a story about an online English student who reached out to her to say how much he appreciated feeling less spotlighted in the online space. This was a significant moment for me, the educator, who loves nothing more than to shine proverbial spotlights on her students as she passes them the microphone. I knew I would need to lean in and learn more.

Karen went on to say this student appreciated being able to send in work and let the work speak for itself, to write discussions without having his peers looking at him, and to think deeply about his response to a question or assignment rather than respond on the spot. These two educators encouraged me to ask new questions about what it looks like to feel seen, heard, and known in the online space.

What new possibilities do online and blended classrooms give educators to make sure students feel safe, known, and able to soar? To continue the preceding metaphor, when do teachers need to soften the spotlight, and how can they create different entry points to invite more students to share their voices and experiences? We carried these essential questions throughout our research. In learning with this project's contributors, we got to explore these questions and more across geography, experience, and content. I am grateful to all who participated in this project. I want to thank them for being patient with us through this process and generous in sharing their stories, questions, and strategies not only with me and Stephanie but also with all of you, our readers. May we use this wisdom to cultivate people-centered and connected classrooms.

Teaching Is Celebrating Together

In 2018, I wrote an article for the local newspaper about an in-person graduation ceremony we held for several online students. In that article, I celebrate our graduating class while focusing on a few special moments with a student I'll call June (like Aliyah from chapter 2, page 63, June was an adult learner). The following is an excerpt from that article (Fishman-Weaver, 2018a):

> She is 30 years old. Earlier, when she received her diploma on stage, she asked if she could give me a hug.
>
> Over the past 13 years, she's started, paused and restarted her high school education. And now she has completed her degree.
>
> [She] had flown here by herself and after the ceremony wants to take some pictures on campus. A colleague and I ask if she would like some company.
>
> The storm clouds have cleared, and we spend the next hour taking pictures and hearing more about [her] story. She is beaming, pausing every so often to text pictures to her husband and mother.
>
> "You know," she tells us when we say goodbye, "I choked up when the closing performer sang, 'All your life, you were only waiting for this moment to arise'" [McCartney, 1968].
>
> My colleague and I look at each other and smile. "Us, too."

As Lou Jobst shared in his story (page 114), there is music in online education, more than I would have ever predicted. One day, I was pouring some coffee when my phone dinged. I checked, and there was a video message from one of our students in Brazil. She had just finished her high school coursework. Like so many, this student went through difficulty to get to that graduation stage, including challenges like financial and health strains for her family. I hit play. Without any context or introduction, this bright young woman broke into song. Her voice was so clear, proud, and joyful that I almost knocked over my coffee cup looking for a tissue.

These powerful moments of connection and celebration so often catch teachers by surprise: the student who comes in for a hug at graduation, the video message that starts in song, the thank-you note sent over email, or that essay they pass around the faculty because everyone "just needs to read this." As a school leader for a global blended school system, I find that these moments of connection affirm the potential for reimagined classroom spaces. These celebrations, and the millions more they represent, are all rooted in relationships. Our research on connected classrooms has taught me that educational leadership must be intent on collapsing distance, resolved in expanding connection, and committed to celebrating every student who joins a school.

Stephanie's Takeaways

As I reflect on the time we've spent writing this book, like Kathryn, I am grateful for the educators who have so genuinely shared their experiences with us. I'm reminded of the famous Chief Inspector Gamache in Louise Penny's (2012) novel series, who believes four sayings lead to wisdom: (1) "I don't know," (2) "I need help," (3) "I'm sorry," and (4) "I was wrong" (pp. 253–254). Education is messy, complex, and humbling. I have needed help many times along the way, and the voices in this book have encouraged me to think more deeply and strive more ardently for meaningful connection through the stories of students and others with us on this path.

Online Education Offers Unique Opportunities

Many teachers I talk with say something along the lines of, "Oh, I could never teach online. I wouldn't be able to get to know anyone!" I get it. This is a valid response—one I, too, had previously. For a while, online education seemed a second choice, a backup of sorts when something went awry in accessing an in-person context. However, as teachers *and* students who love online and blended contexts will all too enthusiastically tell you, our experiences have shown us online education is not a second choice; it's the best choice for our reality. Of course, online and blended teaching looks different from in-person teaching, but the key point is *different* is not *less than* or *better than*.

Online and blended contexts are just two of many avenues students might take to build their education. Some students genuinely thrive in the online environment and there far surpass what they could accomplish in face-to-face classrooms. Some of our students are professionals who are fostering a passion. We've had actors, Olympic athletes, dirt-bike racers, horseback riders, and circus performers who chose the online path so they could pursue their goals and earn a diploma at the same time. Many of our students have severe anxiety disorders that can paralyze their ability to communicate and perform in person; online education gives them the chance to explore at their own pace and not just survive but thrive. They often mention, as you heard from Karen Scales, this context gives them a chance to focus on their work rather than their challenges. Some students are high achievers who like to work at an accelerated pace. Still others live in rural or remote areas, and online programs give them access to courses they might not have. Other students have physical challenges, travel often, or simply don't flourish in the traditional brick-and-mortar environment. One graduate shared he loved the online path because he could finish his high school requirements while starting online college classes and be that much closer to his dream of practicing medicine.

Online teaching similarly allows teachers to develop curriculum, work closely with students, and serve various needs in a refreshing and exciting way. As you've heard from the practitioners in this book, this kind of teaching is real. As you explore online and blended contexts, remember they don't have to be runners-up to another model of teaching. They are simply other choices offering unique benefits. We love online teaching, and we love where we are going from here as we learn more about the possibilities of connection and best practices in this area.

Assessments and Feedback Belong in the Conversation

In 2003, I chose to move from in-person education to online teaching. It was a big decision, and I was nervous. Like Jason Williamson (see the appendix, page 185), I was a "be there" kind of teacher and had a hard time imagining how I could connect with students I would never see in person, let alone spend every day with. If you had asked me my least favorite part of in-person teaching, I would have said, "All that grading!" When I moved to the online context, I thought, "What am I thinking? Now all I'll do is grade!"

I've noticed most new adventures in my life follow the *three-year rule*. Anytime I start something new I want to maintain long term, something magical about the three-year mark makes it stick. This is certainly true in my teaching career. As an emerging teacher, I felt like a little flower blooming, first bowing its head down, then tilting it up just a bit, and then finally turning its face forward. It took me awhile to appreciate the sunlight and to recognize I was in the middle of a big, blended flower garden. The first year, I got to know who I was as a teacher and built a curriculum that best fit my style and my students' needs. The second year was about noticing and reflecting on what was going well and what needed work. And the third year saw things rolling a little more smoothly as practices and processes fell into place. The progression of these years moved from self-focused ("How am *I* doing?") to student focused ("How are *they* doing?"), and I moved forward from there.

When I began teaching online, I noticed the rule of three pop up again. In year one, I did wrestle with what teaching looked like when my students and I had so much distance between us. I did not immediately warm up to "all that grading." It felt forced and a little cold. To me, the real beauty of teaching came in the discussions and the activities, the day-to-day conversations, and the bustle of classroom life. I hadn't yet learned a student's work *is* a conversation, and my ability to talk with students through what they shared was just as important as any other discussion we shared. But applying what I had learned about connection in my in-person experience helped me move toward connection in online teaching, and sure enough, by year three, I found a strong rhythm with students.

Putting into practice the encouragement of story sharing through notes, noticing what a student mentions and following up on it, and asking questions will break the ice over time and help the conversations flow in a classroom context. The four-step feedback process discussed in chapter 3 (page 89) will help you blend this relationship building with meaningful comments to help students grow as communicators. Together, these strategies will take you from "just grading" to meaningful conversations through student work.

Self Expression Is Necessary for Learning

Gretchen Rubin (2015), one of my favorite authors on forming habits and generally soaking up the joy in life, compiled a list of the twelve most important principles to live by. At the top of her list is "Be Gretchen" (Rubin, 2015, p. 31). Know yourself, and do, say, and try things true to who you are. I say teachers claim Rubin's nugget of wisdom for themselves. While writing this book, I have felt so lucky to have talked with so many educators I admire. Reading through their narratives reminds me of that big, blended flower garden. We are all so different. Adrian is super enthusiastic and a fan of using props and music. Karen is organized and compassionate. Marilyn is a storyteller, and Jill is empathetic. Jeff is wise and a bit mischievous, and Jason connects through asking lots of questions. Diane is a researcher who collects information and then weaves it into her lessons. Kimberly is detail oriented, and Greg is energetic and active. Lou is soft spoken and thoughtful. Quiet. Loud. Funny. Straightforward. Messy. Organized. Empathetic. What ties us all together? We all care about students and want to connect with them.

As you further explore the beauty and challenges of teaching in online and blended contexts, can I give you permission to be yourself? Let your personality show through the screen and out of your feedback and notes. Celebrate big when things go well. Reflect often and keep tweaking. You don't need to have it all together. It's OK to make mistakes, and it's perfectly understandable if you fumble with the technology. If you have to change your lesson midstream because it's not vibing with your class, good for you! If you think to yourself, "Whoa, I have a lot to learn! I don't always know what I'm doing," welcome to our happy club.

We've learned some great lessons so far, and like all caring educators, we are open to the miles of lessons we still get to learn. Keep reflecting, stay true to what lights you up, and put connection at the heart of all you do, whether in person or online.

We Close With Heart

In our dedication, Stephanie and I (Kathryn) wrote that this book is a gift for new teachers. We wrote it from our hearts with deep admiration and respect for all the new educators who are embarking on this noble path. However, as we close this text, I am realizing that this research has expanded our understanding of what it means to be a new teacher. The educators who worked with us on this project collectively have centuries of teaching stories. Yet, we found that in so many ways, we are all new teachers. Some of you reading this may be new for the first time, and others may be finding that you are like a new teacher again. For those of you who, like us, bring many experiences with you to this new landscape, remember those experiences matter. Much of what we know about teaching and learning is constant—students, relationships, and connection are still the magic elements that make learning possible. However, the context has changed, and you must change with it. As classrooms become more technology mediated, global, and connected, these changes invite you to boldly step into new kinds of classrooms and instructional spaces. This work, like all teaching work, requires courage.

CONNECTED TEACHING COMMITMENT
Teach With Courage

Teaching is heart work because it requires courage. Courage requires you to dare, connect, and venture. When educators launch a new school year, a new lesson, or a new class, they never know exactly how it will go. Commit to prioritizing learning and community. Pour yourself into planning and preparation, and then give yourself the grace and flexibility to change course as needed. When a student shows up at the classroom door, you don't know what that young person might need. Commit to meeting them where they are, listening actively, and connecting. Practice intentional strategies to show students you are present (whether physically in person or at a distance) and you care. Do this even when you feel tired, frustrated, or unsure of the outcome, and when a strategy or lesson plan fails. Educators model grace, flexibility, and the courage to try again.

Just as educators teach with courage, they should also teach *for* courage. In the classroom, let students know they are safe to dare and venture new ideas. As students study literature, history, science, or current events, encourage students to practice perspective taking and critical thinking, including admitting the limits of their current understanding. Across the arts, writing, and mathematics, create space for students to problem solve, practice creativity, and try a new approach, even when their solution doesn't yet work. As students navigate the complexities of both peer and adult relationships, help them cultivate grace and authenticity. Teaching for courage in these ways requires educators to practice honesty, modeling, and a deep commitment to validating all experiences and feelings in the classroom.

We hope this research on connected classrooms has stirred in you a resolve to teach with courage and radical hope (Fishman-Weaver, 2017). It certainly has for us (Kathryn and Stephanie). From Hanoi to São Paulo to Oakland, we are grateful for all the stories gifted to us throughout this journey and for the many more that they represent. Thank you to you, our readers, so many of whom are educators. You are doing transformative work in the lives of young people. We look forward to the possibilities of new classroom spaces, the connections you will make, the projects your students will lead, and the ways we all can continue to improve and iterate this noble field of education.

APPENDIX
Focus Group Transcript

What follows is an edited transcript from a focus group we held with five midcareer professionals who span the continuum of preschool through graduate school. We have coded the data for strategies, have pulled the strategies to the surface, and are pleased to present them in this appendix.

We organized a small focus group of educators who worked across elementary, middle, and high school and teacher education. We intentionally recruited educators we admired and formed a diverse group across race, gender, and geography. We wanted to create a context where everyone knew at least one other participant and where everyone had the opportunity to meet a participant they hadn't before. In this way, we hoped to share our own ideas while also building on each other's observations through authentic conversations.

On June 9, 2021, the five educators joined us for a focus-group conversation we recorded on our digital meeting platform. After more than an hour of dialogue, we found everyone still had more to share, so we continued the conversation on Google Drive. The transcripts from these conversations shape the narrative of this appendix. Some sections have been edited for length and clarity.

Question 1: How Do You Create Connection in the Blended Classroom?

Stephanie Walter: We wanted to frame this around your work, particularly in online and blended spaces. A lot of teachers have questions about how to create connections when you're not in the day-to-day details with students and what that looks like online. I'd love to hear some of your stories about either a moment of connection, a meaningful experience, or a student who inspired you.

Keep Books in the Hands of Students
Diane Johnson, middle school teacher

I'm a lover of literature, and I try to foster that in kids. I got very excited and probably a little over the top. At the beginning of the school year, we did not have electronic copies of the books available, and I had three students ask how they could get the books. For various reasons, they couldn't go to the public library, and they weren't sure how to download a copy, so I thought, "OK, I'm gonna try this once." And I checked out the books for them in our building and then drove them to their houses. A great connection happened for us, through the literature, because they wanted books I had read or was familiar with and I was able to bring the books to them.

Being able to connect with students about books with questions like, "Are you enjoying it? Do you like it?" was a bright spot in our virtual semester. I ended up making multiple trips and delivering books, which was fine because the payoff was honestly my first meaningful connection in the online setting. Having a not directly content-based experience made the kids more willing to talk to me; we definitely built from there all year. (Diane Johnson, personal communication, June 9, 2021)

Build Connection Into Your Assignments
Megan Lilien, science educator

When I write [online] curriculum, I always try to have at least one assignment that's a little bit different from the norm. It's not a report or a written paragraph for a paper, but it is something that brings in other talents (like creating an infographic or a presentation of some sort, or something [students] have to bring in from their personal life). That just opens the door to so many things you didn't expect. When a student talks about a hobby of theirs you find intriguing, you can say, "Oh, you're a professional horseback rider. Tell me more!" or "This is a really cool picture. Is this you?" We do a fitness brochure, so instead of just writing up a fitness plan, we add in elements outside of the typical writing and math so we can bring in some of those personal things. That sparks those connections between the student and those of us giving feedback. (Megan Lilien, personal communication, June 9, 2021)

Practice Your Students' Home Languages
Adrian Clifton, international English language arts teacher

I have the privilege of introducing the English language to kindergartners and first graders and their families. Many of them, like I said, don't speak English, so the thing connecting me with them is language. What further connects me is learning their language and being able to greet their mother or sister: "Oi! Tudo bem?" ("Hi! How are you?")

It's a challenge [to learn Portuguese], but I'm doing so slowly and surely, and my students are lighting up. We can talk a little bit more. I'm learning about their families, their toys, their sisters, the trips they're on. Taking the extra step to learn their first language has been a way for us to connect and understand each other a lot better this semester. (Adrian Clifton, personal communication, June 9, 2021)

Leave a Little Note (It Can Make a Big Difference)
Jason Williamson, high school teacher and teacher education instructor

Teaching online has been a struggle for me because I'm a very in-person teacher. I love *being there*. But with my university going totally digital, and then teaching a class where we rely on a lot of conversations this fall, six feet of distance was just not going to work.

Through teaching online, I rediscovered the importance of feedback, how we give feedback, and how we connect through feedback. I'm thinking of one student in the fall who wrote in an assignment that they have ADHD and failed seven of their classes. I reached out to the student in my feedback to say, "We need to talk, and the sooner the better." Then, I just left it unresolved for a while. The student was still not doing well a while later, so I reached out again and said, "Remember that note?" and they connected back to me. We started meeting about once every two weeks.

[They] finished the class. Yes, there were hiccups and bumps, but we got it all done. That reminded me how important those quick little notes are. Quick little feedback sessions take thirty seconds of my life. I'm not sure that it would have happened if I hadn't said, "Let's talk."

We can still create personal connections; we just have to do them differently now. In person, I would have sat down next to this student in class for a long conversation. I just have to find different ways of doing that [in an online setting]. (Jason Williamson, personal communication, June 9, 2021)

Question 2: What Strategies Do You Use to Foster Meaningful Conversations That Leverage the Power of Your Students' Lived Experiences in Online and Hybrid Spaces?

Find Ways to Connect Through Feedback
Karen Scales, online English language arts teacher

Especially in those early lessons, notice at least one personal thing about a student you can connect with, and comment on it, even if it's just, "Oh, this description of baking cookies made me hungry." You want students to know you're actually reading what they're saying and you think they matter.

Take a moment to introduce yourself and call the student by their name. The first thing I say is, "My name is Mrs. Scales, and you'll see some other teachers grading your reports. But this is who I am, and this is how you find me." It's important to recognize you're not just reading for grammar, but to connect with something they have said. In my courses, we ask students to be pretty vulnerable, and we ask them to connect with some pretty heavy stuff. Literature selections in high school can be dark places, and we frequently ask students to go to those places. It's hard for them to go there if you haven't created a safe space and built personal connections. You want students to know there's a human being on the other side of this computer screen who cares about [them] and is rooting for [them]. (Karen Scales, personal communication, June 9, 2021)

Practice Vulnerability
Adrian Clifton, international English language arts teacher

Well, now I'm thinking of my middle schoolers. Something happens between first grade, where they don't care what anyone thinks (they'll pick their nose right in front of the class), and middle school, where they don't want to talk and they're so self-conscious of what everybody thinks.

It was very tricky at first to break the ice. I know there are a lot of stories inside these students and a lot of experiences, and so I use vulnerability. For middle school students, I become vulnerable first and share about myself, my life, and even personal struggles in an appropriate way—even my own ADHD and learning difficulties. I am open about common things middle schoolers deal with. I put it on myself: "I was bullied once, so let me tell you about that." Then, we start to melt over time, and then they become more comfortable with connecting with me. And then we begin to connect with each other, and then we start to have more dialogue through the semester.

Model Thoughtful Assertiveness
Megan Lilien, science educator

Model how you'd like others to talk to you. We have all gotten emails with no punctuation, no hello, no greeting, and are just asking for something. When I receive these, I model how to have those connected conversations. I write a greeting. I call the student by their name. I use a warm sign-off. Modeling thoughtfulness can go a long way.

However, there's another side to this I want to share. This often comes from my young women students whose emails start with, "I'm sorry to bother you." When I'm coaching in person, we have some pretty direct conversations about needless apologizing. I ask my athletes, "Why are you apologizing to all your teammates? You didn't do anything wrong." We talk about why students apologize and assume they are a nuisance and what they can do instead.

In the online space, that's a little harder to do, but when I see it, I send a note back saying something like, "You never need to apologize for asking for help. My job is to answer your questions." I try to find a positive way to try to teach my students those little life lessons and make those connections and help them be thoughtful and strong.

Recognize Students as Teachers
Karen Scales, online English language arts teacher

My students love to teach me something. It can be anything. For example, I am always asking students to teach me text speak. I did not know what *be right back* (*BRB*) meant until this.

If I notice something in their writing that I don't know much about, I write a note saying, "I would love to hear more about that." In our classes are musicians, scientists, and athletes.

I've found when I say, "I don't know about this," or "I have never heard that expression before," or "I would love to know more about that," and then give students a quick opportunity to teach me or our whole class something, it can have an extraordinary impact on their confidence later in class.

Organize Small Groups to Foster Community
Jason Williamson, high school teacher and teacher education instructor

I'm thinking about building relationships with students but having them also build relationships and connect to each other in the classroom. When we moved to our class online, we had to find ways to create groups again and eventually chose to do it through breakout rooms on our digital meeting platform.

Students loved their group. They were excited to talk to people and see their group members. The peer groups were a place where they would turn on their cameras, talk, and ask questions honestly. These groups made a huge difference in fostering community.

Use the Power of Direct Message
Diane Johnson, middle school teacher

Let me share one thing I messed up to start with and, once I corrected it, went so much better. This has to do with building a safe space, particularly with online students. I had to learn to embrace anonymity and then scaffold up to visibility for a lot of kids.

One quick and easy engagement tool I used was to let students respond anonymously to an open-ended question. We used direct messages in our video conference, and students could send their responses right to me. Those conversations are always crucial, but after teaching in a year that included a pandemic and the Black Lives Matter protests and everything happening in the world, those conversations with kids felt even more important.

Using the direct chat feature in our online meeting platform, students could respond to me and then scaffold up to sharing with a bigger group. So, I would have students send me a chat, and the majority of them would chat me, whereas most were reluctant to unmute and speak up in the space. And then I would chat them back and say, "Oh, this is really great. May I share this with the class anonymously?" And the student would write me back, and usually, they said yes. And then as we all got more comfortable, I could include their names. We really built from those first direct messages. This practice improved my classroom culture significantly.

Question 3: How Do You Engage Learners Who Are Not Immediately Responsive?

Use Humor
Adrian Clifton, international English language arts teacher

I engage middle school students who are not immediately responsive through gentle humor: "Vitor, the dog emoji you are using for your profile picture is *muito legal* ('very cool'). Do you know what would be even cooler? Hearing from you! Can you share your response to question 3?" I also call out my students directly to participate: "Carol, what do you think?" or "João, how do you feel about that?"

I let my learners know at least a week in advance if I will expect them to present their assignment or example to the class. This gives them time to prepare, especially if English is their second language. I ask questions about their weekend or morning school day during class time. This makes us comfortable talking in an online group setting and often laughing with each other.

Communicate Positively and Proactively
Karen Scales, online English language arts teacher

In an entirely online space, I try to use feedback to start conversations. For example, if I notice a student consistently struggles with topic sentences and isn't improving following instruction, rather than continuing to give one-sided feedback pointing out a weakness or even modeling a sample revision, I try to ask direct questions to invite (or sometimes require) direct answers: "You've been doing a great job in your opening sentences of identifying what a paragraph is going to be about, but I often can't tell right away how you feel about that topic or the argument about it you most want to make. Can you tell me in one sentence what your main idea is for this paragraph? Reply here, or send it to my inbox, and we can talk through some strategies for strengthening your topic sentences!"

For students who consistently don't engage or reply to my prompts, I try to connect through a variety of means: assignment feedback, email, Canvas inbox, phone number (text or call), guardian or partner educator on file. Once I've made contact, I ask them their *preferred* method for communication (that often breaks through a wall), and I make sure they know where and how to find feedback and how to reach me with questions. I try first to learn a little bit about them and what's going on in their lives or with their schoolwork more broadly before we get into anything specific with regard to their work in my class. I want to understand *why* they're not being responsive, which informs the strategies we might then use to help solve whatever problem the student may be having.

Question 4: If You Could Give One Tip About Connection or Community Building to a New Teacher, What Would You Share?

Connect With Students in Their Spaces
Adrian Clifton, international English language arts teacher

I'm so excited about supporting new teachers. I have taught everything from spaces in poverty to now in this private school I am teaching here in Brazil. My best advice for you is to visit where your students live.

I was surrounded by police brutality, poverty, and some difficult things as a child. I wish I had a teacher who said, "I visited your neighborhood. I ate in that restaurant on the corner, and I went to the ice cream shop." It would have been amazing.

Show pride in your students' spaces. Go to the restaurants, the street market, the parks, and candy stores. Get to know where your students live, their spaces, their families, and their lives.

You're not going to connect deeply with every student, and there are going to be some you worry about all the time. That can become overwhelming and lead to burnout and feelings of failure. There are strategies you can use to help anchor you to your purpose. Focus on celebrating the successes, and end each day asking yourself the following.

- Who did you learn more about?
- Who did you connect with?
- What did you learn about your students and their lives?

Make Positive Calls Home
Megan Lilien, science educator

Calls home are often for struggling students or negative things. Every time I had to make one of those calls, I would try to then end on a call home for something good. Teachers are sometimes required to do this, and we just never do it enough. Positive phone calls build relationships. They help you remember the successes and your students' strengths. That is my simplest tip for making connections.

Celebrate the Good
Karen Scales, online English language arts teacher

For new teachers, I would remind them to do the same for students. So often, we as teachers are deducting points, making corrections, and telling students where they can improve. Notice when students do something good as often as possible. Tell them you're noticing whether they're earning an A or they just made an improvement, or especially if you're making corrections. If there's something you can celebrate or end a lesson on a positive note, do so. Remember this especially for the students who are struggling. These celebrations matter so much more than you know.

Get to Know the Students You Don't Know
Diane Johnson, middle school teacher

Get up to speed and educate yourself on the demographic you are teaching. Take the time on the front end to find out who they are because you can't see someone if you don't know who they are. You can't get to know someone if you don't get out of your comfort zone.

Find out what kind of music your students are listening to and what kind of movies they're watching, because media can be an instant connecting point. Ask students about something real in their lives at the time, and something fun and nonthreatening. These conversations are the best segue to building relationships, which then translates to increasing achievement.

Question 5: Any Final Words of Encouragement You'd Like to Share When It Comes to Connecting in Online Spaces?

Practice Genuine Enthusiasm
Diane Johnson, middle school teacher

First, take the time to really get to know your students. Share pictures, funny stories, favorite videos from the internet, whatever it takes. Encourage them to do the same. While this might feel like "wasted" time, it is not. To the contrary, this may be the most valuable time investment you can make.

Second, students pick up on a lack of enthusiasm. If the teacher feels disconnected, they will too. This is real teaching in virtual settings too; it just looks different. We are building a different skill set for ourselves, and embracing those changes is an important key for teachers to foster a warm, welcoming online classroom. Teachers and students absolutely can connect virtually!

Adrian Clifton, international English language arts teacher

I want to piggyback on what Diane said about *enthusiasm*. Yes! Enthusiasm is vitally important in an online setting. Please do not overthink it. Make a "fool" of yourself if you have to. Dress up in costume. Create themes: sunglasses day, PJ day, et cetera. Incorporate curveballs and surprises. Book special guests, even if they are your own pets. I personally like to bring in guests from the surrounding community, particularly people [students] would not normally have access to, like artists, activists, business owners. Make learning even more enthusiastic.

Online Teaching Is Real Teaching
Karen Scales, online English language arts teacher

To echo one more point Diane brought up, online teaching is real teaching. There remains a stigma and a misconception, I think, that online learning (no matter how beneficial it might be for other objectives) inherently requires a sacrifice of personal connection. I have found sometimes the opposite is true.

In a classroom of over thirty students at a time (for an hour of teaching time per class if we're lucky), how much personal, individual attention can we really give each student? Online spaces can enhance and enrich a one-on-one dynamic if we embrace it. Remind students and yourself: the screen is just the vehicle, not the driver. Human connection in all spaces is what we make it. Students today are way ahead of us on this. *Online* is an appendage for most of them, so if there's a disconnect in the platform, it's probably on our end as teachers. If we can find our own voices in the online space and be intentional about the effort to connect authentically and to meet students where they are, students will respond to the effort in the same way they do in any other classroom. Show them there is a real human person on the other side of the screen who is rooting for them, and more often than not, relationships will grow from there.

GLOSSARY

504 plan. Section 504 of the Rehabilitation Act of 1973 is a disability civil rights law in the United States. Students may qualify for services under section 504 if they "have a physical or mental impairment that substantially limits one or more major life activities" (Office for Civil Rights, 2020). If a student qualifies for services, schools may write a 504 plan, which is an articulated plan for accommodations or supports to ensure the student can access the full range of school activities. Some examples of these supports include extended time on tests, health breaks with the school nurse, audio resources, larger print, and a quiet place to take exams. *Read more in chapter 2 (page 43).*

acceleration. Moving through curriculum at a quicker pace than grade-level peers. *Read more in chapter 6 (page 153).*

asynchronous learning. *Asynchronous* refers to components happening at different times. In the case of online learning, this refers to approaches that allow for students to work on their own time and at their own pace. For this reason, courses utilizing all asynchronous methods are sometimes referred to as *self-paced* courses. *Read more in the introduction (page 1).*

bilingual or multilingual. Terms that refer to students who speak two or more languages. This terminology positively centers the strengths of students who know many languages. These terms focus on the assets students bring to the classroom as opposed to focusing on the area in which they are still growing or only centering English. *Read more in chapter 5 (page 127).*

blended learning. Used to refer to learning solutions in which educators use a combination of online and in-person methods for instruction. This digital approach is expanding globally (Hilliard, 2015). This method is also known as *hybrid learning*. *Read more in the introduction (page 1).*

center. To bring into focus, to honor, or to cast as important. People can center identities, experiences, ideas, voices, and individuals. Centering is an important practice in inclusion and equity work. *Read more in chapter 4 (page 105).*

classroom culture. The environment where student learning takes place. A positive classroom culture fosters honest perspective sharing and respect. *Read more in chapter 4 (page 105).*

community-based learning. Intentionally connecting the classroom or content and the community in mutually beneficial ways that honor the inherent wisdom and richness of community-based spaces and organizations. (Service-learning or learning-through-service approaches sometimes fall under this umbrella.) *Read more in chapter 1 (page 15).*

comprehensive school counseling. A systematic and holistic approach to student support including guidance curriculum, individual planning, responsive services, and system support (Gysbers & Henderson, 2012). *Read more in chapter 2 (page 43).*

culturally and linguistically diverse (CLD). An umbrella term for students from nondominant cultural or linguistic backgrounds. While this term has utility in equity conversations around access, it can also oversimplify diverse groups. *Read more in chapter 5 (page 127).*

culturally responsive pedagogies. Teaching and learning practices that create opportunities for learners to (1) act with agency and leadership and (2) think beyond their own culture in competent and affirming ways. This framework comes from the seminal works of Gloria Ladson-Billings (1995) and Geneva Gay (2002), which continue to inform relevant teaching practices around equity, diversity, and high expectations. *Read more in chapter 1 (page 15).*

culturally sustaining pedagogies. A belief that effective classroom practices must honor, affirm, and sustain the identities and cultural richness students bring to the classroom. This work comes from Django Paris (2012), who built on and affirmed the ideas buttressing culturally responsive pedagogies (Ladson-Billings, 1995) and extended them to specifically call out a commitment to asset-based approaches. *Read more in chapter 1 (page 15).*

empathy. The learned practice of actively listening to someone's story and striving to emotionally connect with them. *Read more in chapter 4 (page 105).*

English as a foreign language (EFL). A term that refers to learning English as a world language, typically in a country where English is not the official language and by students for whom English is not a home or native language. We prefer *world language* over *foreign language*, as the term *foreign* is often used to otherize people. *Read more in chapter 5 (page 127).*

English as a second language (ESL). Many readers may remember this term from their own education, as it had considerable staying power. This term has now been replaced mostly by *English learner* or *English language learner* (see the following term). The term centers English, does not reference a person, and is often inaccurate, as many multilingual students are learning English as a third, fourth, or even sixth language. *Read more in chapter 5 (page 127).*

English learner or English language learner (EL or ELL). These two terms are the terms currently used by schools. Although they are often used interchangeably, *English learner* is now the term preferred by many states and the U.S. Department of Education. *Read more in chapter 5 (page 127).*

enrichment. Opportunities to extend or expand the content or curriculum. *Read more in chapter 1 (page 15).*

equity. The practice of evaluating and understanding context and individual needs to determine support and resource distribution. (This is both in contrast and in cooperation with *equality approaches*, where all individuals have the same supports and resources regardless of context and individual needs.) *Read more in chapter 4 (page 105).*

feedbacking. The complete process of assessing a student's work through considering the goals of the assignment, designing rubric- or goal-centered comments, and balancing individual points scoring with a holistic assessment. *Read more in chapter 3 (page 75).*

flipped classrooms. A blended approach where students learn content at home via online methods and then practice these concepts during in-person classes. *Read more in the introduction (page 1).*

flow. The act of being so absorbed in a task that an individual loses track of time. Flow contributes to creativity, productivity, and happiness (Csikszentmihalyi, 1990). *Read more in chapter 6 (page 153).*

the four-step feedback process. A step-by-step process designed to offer warm, full, rubric-centered feedback to students. *Read more in chapter 3 (page 75).*

gifted. Students who "have the capability to perform…at higher levels compared to others of the same age, experience, and environment in one or more domains. They require modification(s) to their educational experience(s) to learn and realize their potential" (National Association for Gifted Children, 2019, p. 1). Gifted students come from all backgrounds and identities and may have learning needs beyond giftedness, including social-emotional needs and disabilities. *Read more in chapter 6 (page 153).*

growth mindset. Carol Dweck's (2006) theory that talent development is malleable (as opposed to fixed). Educators who work to cultivate growth mindset in their classrooms emphasize process over product and teach that hard work and persistence are teachable and important skills in achieving goals. Dweck's research asserts that "it is our [educators'] responsibility to create a context in which a growth mindset can flourish" (Gross-Loh, 2016). *Read more in chapter 2 (page 43).*

holistic comments. General comments that give an assessment of the overall assignment. They are written in a clear space on the assignment and use the sandwich technique to give advice. *Read more in chapter 3 (page 75).*

holistic grading. An assessment style that takes into consideration whether students are in or out of control on a prompt, their general work on an overall piece, and their growth over time. *Read more in chapter 3 (page 75).*

home language or native language. Terms that both refer to the primary language or languages spoken at a student's home. In many bilingual homes, students may learn multiple languages as their home languages. These languages are also sometimes called *first languages*, *L1s*, or *family languages*. It's important to remember family systems are diverse. For example, in the case of adoption, a student's L1 may not be their home language. *Read more in chapter 5 (page 127).*

individualized education program (IEP). In special education, a legally binding document outlining a qualifying student's goals, services, accommodations, and needs. The public school a student attends must carry out this plan. Qualifying for an IEP requires an identification and evaluation of a student's disability. Note: Some educators have transferred the idea of individualized education programs to other student populations beyond special education. *Read more in chapter 2 (page 43).*

Individuals With Disabilities Education Act (IDEA). A federal law in the United States that guarantees every student access to a free and appropriate public education in the least restrictive environment possible. *Read more in chapter 2 (page 43).*

learning management system. A software application to deliver, manage, and support student progress and curriculum. *Read more in chapter 1 (page 15).*

living language. A language that groups of people actively use and speak. *Read more in chapter 5 (page 127).*

margins. Metaphorically, people create margins through the circles they draw around groups to define them. Identities and experiences inside the margins are included and centered by dominant cultures, whereas identities and experiences outside the circles are often excluded, unknown, feared, or made invisible by dominant cultures (related term: *marginalized*). *Read more in chapter 4 (page 105).*

multitiered system of supports (MTSS). Models that are often illustrated by a pyramid with a broad Tier 1 layer as the foundation (supports all students receive) and a smaller pointed Tier 3 layer at the top (intensified supports needed only by a small percentage of the school population). *Read more in chapter 2 (page 43).*

neurodiversity. An asset-based term for necessary variation in the human population that includes developmental, intellectual, and cognitive differences. *Read more in chapter 6 (page 153).*

newcomer. The U.S. Department of Education defines this term as any foreign-born student and their family who have recently arrived in the United States (National Center for English Language Acquisition, 2017). Not all newcomers arrive with families; some arrive on their own. In some schools, particularly secondary schools, there are special newcomer programs for students who arrive in the United States with either limited English or limited formal schooling. *Read more in chapter 5 (page 127).*

online learning. Used to refer to learning solutions in which all or nearly all the instruction and learning happen online in an either synchronous or asynchronous manner. Definitions of online learning are varied and have evolved over time alongside the expansion of technology and teaching approaches (Singh & Thurman, 2019). Online learning is also sometimes referred to as *e-learning*. *Read more in the introduction (page 1).*

point comments. Constructive and positive comments that directly relate to certain parts of student work and tie to the goals of the assignment. They are written to the side of student work and are brief, friendly, and specific. *Read more in chapter 3 (page 75).*

radical hope. The practice of embracing possibility in the face of challenges. Radical hope asks people to assume positive intent from others and to be open to new and unfamiliar solutions. *Read more in chapter 2 (page 43).*

refugee. The United Nations Refugee Agency defines a refugee as someone who has been forced to flee their country because of persecution, war, or violence; they often cannot return home or are afraid to do so (USA for the United Nations High Commissioner for Refugees, n.d.). *Read more in chapter 5 (page 127).*

rubric-centered grading. An assessment style that connects teacher comments on student work to specific rubric strands (or goals and objectives). *Read more in chapter 3 (page 75).*

rubric comments. Comments that give general advice for what is especially well done and what could be improved in an assignment. They are written in the rubric strands with an encouraging tone. *Read more in chapter 3 (page 75).*

the sandwich technique. A set of comments that emphasize what is well done while also pointing forward to growth. This is structured as a positive comment followed by a suggestion for improvement, and ending with another positive comment. *Read more in chapter 3 (page 75).*

school community. The social groups that directly affect students and schools through resources, cultures, and strengths. These include within-school groups such as classroom peers, faculty and staff, and the school population. They also include beyond-school groups such as families, neighborhoods, and cities. Throughout this book, we take a broad view that school is a community project with a myriad of influences and stakeholders. *Read more in chapter 1 (page 15).*

story-based curriculum. Lessons that emphasize the beginning-middle-end (or continuation) of a topic for student exploration in this pattern: "What can we learn from the past, how does this affect our community now, and what responsibility and roles do we have moving ahead?" *Read more in chapter 4 (page 105).*

synchronous learning. *Synchronous* refers to things happening at the same time. In the case of online learning, this refers to approaches that require students to work at the same time as their peers. For this reason, courses utilizing mostly synchronous methods are sometimes referred to as *scheduled* courses. *Read more in the introduction (page 1).*

talent development. A movement in gifted education to focus on developing talent within varied domains and different types of abilities and paths. The aim of this work is for educators and families to "identify more talented children and ensure that they have the opportunities they need to develop their potential to the fullest degree possible" (Olszewski-Kubilius et al., 2019). *Read more in chapter 6 (page 153).*

technology-mediated instruction. An umbrella term for a wide variety of methods that use digital technology for teaching and learning. *Read more in the introduction (page 1).*

thrice exceptional (3E). A term to describe the complex intersections of culturally and linguistically diverse (CLD) students who also present with two diagnoses—(1) giftedness and (2) learning or developmental disabilities (Collins, 2021). *Read more in chapter 6 (page 153).*

twice exceptional (2E). A term that refers to individuals with two diagnoses, one as gifted and a second in developmental or learning disabilities. *Read more in chapter 6 (page 153).*

REFERENCES AND RESOURCES

Abadzi, H. (1985). Ability grouping effects on academic achievement and self-esteem: Who performs in the long run as expected. *Journal of Educational Research, 79*(1), 36–40.

Aguillon, S. M., Siegmund, G.-F., Petipas, R. H., Drake, A. G., Cotner, S., & Ballen, C. J. (2020). Gender differences in student participation in an active-learning classroom. *CBE—Life Sciences Education, 19*(2).

American Hospital Association. (2019, February 26). *Why telehealth is critical to health care transformation.* Accessed at www.aha.org/aha-center-health-innovation-market-scan/2019-02-26-why-telehealth-critical-health-care on November 5, 2021.

Armstrong, T. (2015). The myth of the normal brain: Embracing neurodiversity. *AMA Journal of Ethics, 17*(4), 348–352. Accessed at https://journalofethics.ama-assn.org/article/myth-normal-brain-embracing-neurodiversity/2015-04 on February 1, 2022.

Ayala, A. A. (2015, February 24). *Diversity and gifted children: Are we doing enough?* [Blog post]. Accessed at https://educationaladvancement.org/blog-diversity-gifted-children-enough on March 18, 2022.

Bennett, M. J. (2017). *Developmental model of intercultural sensitivity.* Accessed at www.researchgate.net/profile/Milton-Bennett2/publication/318430742_Developmental_Model_of_Intercultural_Sensitivity/links/5c49d6c6299bf12be3e05f91/Developmental-Model-of-Intercultural-Sensitivity.pdf on February 1, 2022.

Bishop, R. S. (1990). Mirrors, windows, and sliding glass doors. *Perspectives, 6*(3), ix–xi.

Brackett, M., Levy, S., & Hoffmann, J. (2020, May 21). *How to foster a positive school climate in a virtual world.* Accessed at www.edsurge.com/news/2020-05-21-how-to-foster-a-positive-school-climate-in-a-virtual-world on November 4, 2021.

Brown, A. (2013). Waiting for Superwoman: White female teachers and the construction of the "neoliberal savior" in a New York City public school. *Journal for Critical Education Policy Studies, 11*(2), 123–164.

Brown, B. (2012). *Daring greatly: How the courage to be vulnerable transforms the way we live, love, parent, and lead.* New York: Gotham Books.

Brown, B. (2018, October 15). *Clear is kind. Unclear is unkind.* Accessed at https://brenebrown.com/articles/2018/10/15/clear-is-kind-unclear-is-unkind on November 4, 2021.

Buffum, A., Mattos, M., & Malone, J. (2018). *Taking action: A handbook for RTI at Work.* Bloomington, IN: Solution Tree Press.

Card, D., & Giuliano, L. (2016). Universal screening increases the representation of low-income and minority students in gifted education. *Proceedings of the National Academy of Sciences of the United States of America, 113*(48), 13678–13683.

CAST. (n.d.). *About Universal Design for Learning.* Accessed at www.cast.org/impact/universal-design-for-learning-udl?utm_source=udlguidelines on November 10, 2020.

CDC Foundation. (n.d.). *What is public health?* Accessed at www.cdcfoundation.org/what-public-health on November 5, 2021.

Charmaz, K. (2014). *Constructing grounded theory* (2nd ed.). Thousand Oaks, CA: SAGE.

Collins, K. H. (2021, May). *Servicing 2e and 3e learners using Collins' culturally responsive multi-tiered system of supports.* Accessed at www.sengifted.org/post/3e-learners on November 4, 2021.

Csikszentmihalyi, M. (1990). *Flow: The psychology of optimal experience.* New York: Harper Perennial.

Cummins, J., Bismilla, V., Chow, P., Giampapa, F., Cohen, S., Leoni, L., et al. (2005). Affirming identity in multilingual classrooms. *Educational Leadership, 63*(1), 38–43.

Dereshiwsky, M. (2013). *Continual engagement: Fostering online discussion.* River Falls, WI: LERN Books.

Draves, W. A. (2007). *Advanced teaching online.* River Falls, WI: LERN Books.

Duckworth, A. L., & Gross, J. J. (2014). Self-control and grit: Related but separable determinants of success. *Current Directions in Psychological Science, 23*(5), 319–325.

Duckworth, A. L., Milkman, K. L., & Laibson, D. (2019). Beyond willpower: Strategies for reducing failures of self-control. *Psychological Science in the Public Interest, 19*(3), 102–129.

Duckworth, A. L., & Yeager, D. S. (2015). Measurement matters: Assessing personal qualities other than cognitive ability for educational purposes. *Educational Researcher, 44*(4), 237–251.

Duncan, L. (1970). Love song [Recorded by E. John]. On *Tumbleweed connection.* London: DJM.

Dunst, B., Benedek, M., Jauk, E., Bergner, S., Koschutnig, K., Sommer, M., et al. (2014). Neural efficiency as a function of task demands. *Intelligence, 42*(100), 22–30.

Dweck, C. (2006). *Mindset: The new psychology of success.* New York: Ballantine Books.

Dweck, C. (2014, November). *The power of believing that you can improve* [Video transcript]. TED Conferences. Accessed at https://www.ted.com/talks/carol_dweck_the_power_of_believing_that_you_can_improve/transcript?language=en on November 4, 2021.

Ertl, B., Luttenberger, S., & Paechter, M. (2017). The impact of gender stereotypes on the self-concept of female students in STEM subjects with an under-representation of females. *Frontiers in Psychology, 8,* Article 703.

Fishman-Weaver, K. (2017). A call to praxis: Using gendered organizational theory to center radical hope in schools. *Journal of Organizational Theory in Education, 2*(1), 1–14.

Fishman-Weaver, K. (2018a, July 23). Guest commentary: Reflections from the principal of an online high school. *Columbia Missourian.* Accessed at www.columbiamissourian.com/opinion/guest_commentaries/guest-commentary-reflections-from-the-principal-of-an-online-high-school/article_3c05c82c-8e06-11e8-b723-2f0ed73f65db.html on November 5, 2021.

Fishman-Weaver, K. (2018b). *Wholehearted teaching of gifted young women: Cultivating courage, connection, and self-care in schools.* Waco, TX: Prufrock Press.

Fishman-Weaver, K. (2019). *When your child learns differently: A family approach for navigating special education services with love and high expectations.* New York: Routledge.

Fishman-Weaver, K. (2020). *Brain-based learning with gifted students, grades 3–6: Lessons from neuroscience on cultivating curiosity, metacognition, empathy, and brain plasticity.* Waco, TX: Prufrock Press.

Fishman-Weaver, K., & Walter, S. (2021, March 30). *5 tips to center student wellness during school reentry.* Accessed at www.edutopia.org/article/5-tips-center-student-wellness-during-school-reentry on November 5, 2021.

Ford, D. Y. (2013). *Recruiting and retaining culturally different students in gifted education.* New York: Routledge.

Ford, D. Y., Dickson, K. T., Davis, J. L., Scott, M. T., & Grantham, T. C. (2018). A culturally responsive equity-based bill of rights for gifted students of color. *Gifted Child Today, 41*(3), 125–129.

Ford, D. Y., & Grantham, T. C. (2003). Providing access for culturally diverse gifted students: From deficit to dynamic thinking. *Theory Into Practice, 42*(3), 217–225.

Ford, D. Y., & Grantham, T. C. (2012). Using the NAGC gifted programming standards to create programs and services for culturally and linguistically different gifted students. In S. K. Johnsen (Ed.), *NAGC pre-K–grade 12 gifted education programming standards: A guide to planning and implementing high-quality services* (pp. 45–70). Waco, TX: Prufrock Press.

Ford, D. Y., Grantham, T. C., & Whiting, G. W. (2008). Culturally and linguistically diverse students in gifted education: Recruitment and retention issues. *Exceptional Children, 74*(3), 289–306.

Fuller, R. G. (2012). Building empathy in online courses: Effective practical approaches. *International Journal of Information and Communication Technology Education, 8*(4), 38–48.

Gay, G. (2002). Preparing for culturally responsive teaching. *Journal of Teacher Education, 53*(2), 106–116.

Giovanni, N. (1972). *My house: Poems.* New York: Morrow.

GLSEN. (n.d.). *Pronoun guide.* Accessed at www.glsen.org/activity/pronouns-guide-glsen on February 1, 2022.

Gross-Loh, C. (2016, December 16). How praise became a consolation prize. *The Atlantic.* Accessed at www.theatlantic.com/education/archive/2016/12/how-praise-became-a-consolation-prize/510845 on February 2, 2022.

Guilbault, K., & Kane, M. (2016). *Asynchronous development*. Washington, DC: National Association for Gifted Children. Accessed at www.nagc.org/sites/default/files/Publication%20PHP/NAGC%20TIP%20Sheet-Asynchronous%20Development-FINAL%20REVISED-OCTOBER%202017(1).pdf on February 1, 2022.

Gysbers, N. C., & Henderson, P. (2012). *Developing and managing your school guidance and counseling program* (5th ed.). Alexandria, VA: American Counseling Association.

Heaney, S. (1998). Digging. In *Opened ground: Selected poems, 1966–1996* (p. 3). New York: Farrar, Straus and Giroux.

Heath, D. (2020). *Upstream: The quest to solve problems before they happen*. New York: Avid Reader Press.

Hierck, T. (2017). *Seven keys to a positive learning environment in your classroom*. Bloomington, IN: Solution Tree Press.

Hilliard, A. T. (2015). Global blended learning practices for teaching and learning, leadership and professional development. *Journal of International Education Research*, *11*(3), 179–188.

Holmes, C. (2020). *Be there. Worked with two students tonight via Zoom: a 7th grader, and an 11th grader, both attending school virtually* [Status update]. Facebook. Accessed at www.facebook.com/chris.holmes.946/posts/10221922617507357 on November 5, 2021.

hooks, b. (2015). *Feminist theory: From margin to center* (3rd ed.). New York: Routledge.

Individuals With Disabilities Education Act. (n.d.). *About IDEA*. Accessed at https://sites.ed.gov/idea/about-idea on January 25, 2022.

Individuals With Disabilities Education Act. (2017). *Sec. 300.8 Child with a disability*. Accessed at https://sites.ed.gov/idea/regs/b/a/300.8 on March 18, 2022.

Karumbaiah, S., Lizarralde, R., Allessio, D., Woolf, B., Arroyo, I., & Wixon, N. (2017, June). *Addressing student behavior and affect with empathy and growth mindset* [Conference presentation]. Tenth International Conference on Educational Data Mining, Wuhan, China. Accessed at https://files.eric.ed.gov/fulltext/ED596572.pdf on November 5, 2021.

Kay, K., & Shipman, C. (2014, May). The confidence gap. *The Atlantic*. Accessed at www.theatlantic.com/magazine/archive/2014/05/the-confidence-gap/359815 on February 2, 2022.

King, L. (2018). *The impact of multilingualism on global education and language learning*. Cambridge, England: Cambridge Assessment English. Accessed at www.cambridgeenglish.org/Images/539682-perspectives-impact-on-multilingualism.pdf on February 1, 2022.

Ladson-Billings, G. (1995). Toward a theory of culturally relevant pedagogy. *American Educational Research Journal*, *32*(3), 465–491.

Lakin, J. M. (2016). Universal screening and the representation of historically underrepresented minority students in gifted education: Minding the gaps in Card and Giuliano's research. *Journal of Advanced Academics*, *27*(2), 139–149.

Lopez, S. J. (2013). *Making hope happen: Create the future you want for yourself and others*. New York: Atria Paperback.

Love, B. L. (2019, February 12). "Grit is in our DNA": Why teaching grit is inherently anti-Black. *Education Week*. Accessed at www.edweek.org/leadership/opinion-grit-is-in-our-dna-why-teaching-grit-is-inherently-anti-black/2019/02 on February 2, 2022.

Lovecky, D. V. (2011, September 14). *Exploring social and emotional aspects of giftedness in children*. Accessed at https://sengifted.org/exploring-social-and-emotional-aspects-of-giftedness-in-children on November 5, 2021.

Malfatti, G. (Ed.). (2020). *People-centered approaches toward the internationalization of higher education*. Hershey, PA: IGI Global.

McCartney, P. (1968). Blackbird [Recorded by the Beatles]. On *The Beatles*. London: Apple.

McKinlay, J. B. (1979). A case for refocusing upstream: The political economy of illness. In E. G. Jaco (Ed.), *Patients, physicians, and illness: A sourcebook in behavioral science and health* (3rd ed., pp. 9–25). New York: Free Press.

Morgan, H. (2020). The gap in gifted education: Can universal screening narrow it? *Education, 140*(4), 207–214.

Nadler, R. (2020). Understanding "Zoom fatigue": Theorizing spatial dynamics as third skins in computer-mediated communication. *Computers and Composition, 58*, 102613.

National Association for Gifted Children. (n.d.). *Identification*. Accessed at www.nagc.org/resources-publications/gifted-education-practices/identification on November 5, 2021.

National Association for Gifted Children. (2011). *Identifying and serving culturally and linguistically diverse gifted students* [Position statement]. Accessed at www.nagc.org/sites/default/files/Position%20Statement/Identifying%20and%20Serving%20Culturally%20and%20Linguistically.pdf on February 1, 2022.

National Association for Gifted Children. (2015). *Talent development task force report to the board of directors* [Report]. Accessed at www.nagc.org/sites/default/files/Governance/Talent DevelopmentTFReport_11%2003%2015_FINAL.pdf on March 18, 2022.

National Association for Gifted Children. (2019). *A definition of giftedness that guides best practice* [Position statement]. Accessed at www.nagc.org/sites/default/files/Position%20Statement/Definition%20of%20Giftedness%20%282019%29.pdf on November 5, 2021.

National Center for Education Statistics. (2018). *English language learners in public schools*. Accessed at https://nces.ed.gov/programs/coe/indicator/cgf on November 5, 2021.

National Center for English Language Acquisition. (2017). *Newcomer tool kit*. Washington, DC: U.S. Department of Education. Accessed at www2.ed.gov/about/offices/list/oela/newcomers-toolkit/ncomertoolkit.pdf on October 25, 2020.

National Council of Teachers of English. (2008). *English language learners: A policy research brief produced by the National Council of Teachers of English*. Urbana, IL: Author. Accessed at https://cdn.ncte.org/nctefiles/resources/positions/chron0308policybrief.pdf on November 5, 2021.

Needle, D. (2021, July 2). *Women in tech statistics: The latest research and trends*. Accessed at www.techtarget.com/whatis/feature/Women-in-tech-statistics-The-latest-research-and-trends on February 1, 2022.

Nemerov, H. (1977). September, the first day of school. In *The collected poems of Howard Nemerov* (p. 426). Chicago: University of Chicago Press.

Noack, R., & Gamio, L. (2015, April 23). The world's languages, in 7 maps and charts. *The Washington Post.* Accessed at www.washingtonpost.com/news/worldviews/wp/2015/04/23/the-worlds-languages-in-7-maps-and-charts on February 1, 2022.

Novak, A. M., Lewis, K. D., & Weber, C. L. (2020). Guiding principles in developing equity-driven professional learning for educators of gifted children. *Gifted Child Today, 43*(3), 169–183.

Novak, K. (2020, August 24). *Creating nurturing environments for students in remote and in-person settings* [Blog post]. Accessed at www.novakeducation.com/blog/creating-nurturing-environments-for-students-in-remote-and-in-person-settings on March 18, 2022.

Office for Civil Rights. (2020). *Protecting students with disabilities.* Accessed at www2.ed.gov/about/offices/list/ocr/504faq.html?exp on November 5, 2021.

Olson, C. L., & Kroeger, K. R. (2001). Global competency and intercultural sensitivity. *Journal of Studies in International Education, 5*(2), 116–137.

Olszewski-Kubilius, P., Subotnik, R., & Worrell, F. (2019, May 1). *Developing talent within varied domains* [Blog post]. Accessed at www.nagc.org/blog/developing-talent-within-varied-domains on November 5, 2021.

Ozturk, M. A., & Debelak, C. (2008). Affective benefits from academic competitions for middle school gifted students. *Gifted Child Today, 31*(2), 48–53.

Palvia, S., Aeron, P., Gupta, P., Mahapatra, D., Parida, R., Rosner, R., et al. (2018). Online education: Worldwide status, challenges, trends, and implications. *Journal of Global Information Technology Management, 21*(4), 233–241.

Paris, D. (2012). Culturally sustaining pedagogy: A needed change in stance, terminology, and practice. *Educational Researcher, 41*(3), 93–97.

Penny, L. (2012). *Still life.* Waterville, ME: Thorndike Press.

Point to Point Education. (2018, June 20). *Positive classroom culture strategies* [Blog post]. Accessed at www.pointtopointeducation.com/blog/positive-classroom-culture-strategies/ on November 5, 2021.

Psychology Today. (n.d.). *Empathy.* Accessed at https://www.psychologytoday.com/us/basics/empathy on November 5, 2021.

Renzulli, J. S. (2011). More changes needed to expand gifted identification and support. *Phi Delta Kappan, 92*(8), 61.

Robinson, K. (2009). *The element: How finding your passion changes everything.* New York: Penguin.

Rubin, G. (2015). *Better than before: What I learned about making and breaking habits—to sleep more, quit sugar, procrastinate less, and generally build a happier life.* New York: Broadway Books.

Saville, N. (2018). Foreward. In L. King, *The impact of multilingualism on global education and language learning* (p. 4). Cambridge, England: Cambridge Assessment English. Accessed at www.cambridgeenglish.org/Images/539682-perspectives-impact-on-multilingualism.pdf on February 1, 2022.

SeeMeOnline. (n.d.). *Remaining awake through a great revolution.* Accessed at https://seemeonline.com/history/mlk-jr-awake.htm on May 3, 2022.

Seligman, M. E. P. (2006). *Learned optimism.* New York: Vintage Books.

Simmons, D. (2016, May 26). Forging partnerships with our school communities. *Learning for Justice.* Accessed at www.learningforjustice.org/magazine/forging-partnerships-with-our-school-communities on February 1, 2022.

Simmons, D. (2017, June 7). Is social-emotional learning really going to work for students of color? *Education Week.* Accessed at www.edweek.org/education/opinion-is-social-emotional-learning-really-going-to-work-for-students-of-color/2017/06 on February 1, 2022.

Simons, G. (2020, February 21). *Welcome to the 23rd edition* [Blog post]. Accessed at www.ethnologue.com/ethnoblog/gary-simons/welcome-23rd-edition on November 5, 2021.

Singh, V., & Thurman, A. (2019). How many ways can we define online learning? A systematic literature review of definitions of online learning (1988–2018). *American Journal of Distance Education, 33*(4), 289–306.

Soden, G. (Host). (2017–present). *The classical ideas podcast* [Audio podcast]. Accessed at https://classicalideaspodcast.libsyn.com/ on November 8, 2021.

Sparks, S. D. (2019, March 12). Why teacher-student relationships matter. *Education Week.* Accessed at www.edweek.org/teaching-learning/why-teacher-student-relationships-matter/2019/03 on November 5, 2021.

Subotnik, R. F., Worrell, F. C., & Olszewski-Kubilius, P. (2016). The psychological science of talent development. In M. Neihart, S. I. Pfeiffer, & T. L. Cross (Eds.), *The social and emotional development of gifted children: What do we know?* (2nd ed., pp. 145–158). Waco, TX: Prufrock Press.

Swenson, S., Horner, R., Bradley, R., & Calkins, C. (2017, January 18). *In recognition of Hill Walker's contributions to multi-tiered system of supports (MTSS).* Accessed at https://sites.ed.gov/osers/tag/mtss/ on March 18, 2022.

The Trevor Project. (2020, July 29). *Pronouns usage among LGBTQ youth.* Accessed at www.thetrevorproject.org/research-briefs/pronouns-usage-among-lgbtq-youth on September 14, 2021.

Turner, C. S. V. (2017). Remaining at the margin and in the center. *Journal for the Study of Postsecondary and Tertiary Education, 2*, 121–126.

UNESCO. (2020). *Gender report: A new generation—25 years of efforts for gender equality in education.* Paris: Author. Accessed at https://unesdoc.unesco.org/ark:/48223/pf0000374514 on February 1, 2022.

UNICEF. (2019). *Every child learns: UNICEF education strategy 2019–2030.* New York: Author. Accessed at www.unicef.org/media/59856/file/UNICEF-education-strategy-2019-2030.pdf on November 5, 2021.

University of California San Francisco LGBT Resource Center. (n.d.). *Pronouns matter.* Accessed at https://lgbt.ucsf.edu/pronounsmatter on February 1, 2022.

USA for the United Nations High Commissioner for Refugees. (n.d.). *What is a refugee?* Accessed at www.unrefugees.org/refugee-facts/what-is-a-refugee on November 5, 2021.

Voyer, D., & Voyer, S. D. (2014). Gender differences in scholastic achievement: A meta-analysis. *Psychological Bulletin, 140*(4), 1174–1204.

Wiggins, G., & McTighe, J. (2005). *Understanding by design* (Expanded 2nd ed.). Alexandria, VA: Association for Supervision and Curriculum Development.

Willis, J. (2018, July 13). *The value of active listening.* Accessed at www.edutopia.org/article/value-active-listening on February 1, 2022.

World Health Organization. (n.d.). *Service organizations and integration.* Accessed at www.who.int/teams/integrated-health-services/clinical-services-and-systems/service-organizations-and-integration on February 1, 2022.

YIVO Institute for Jewish Research. (2014). *Basic facts about Yiddish.* Accessed at www.yivo.org/cimages/basic_facts_about_yiddish_2014.pdf?c= on November 5, 2021.

INDEX

NUMBERS
504 plans, 44, 58, 193

A
acceleration, 154, 193
active listening, 20–21, 162. *See also listening*
adult learning, 63–66
affective learning, 167
affirming identities, strategies for, 62–63
assessments
    as a conversation, 77
    feedback and, 75–76
    four-step feedback process and, 92, 94, 96
    goals and, 83
    online teaching and, 178–179
asset mapping, 23
asset-based approaches, 52–53, 54
asynchronous learning, 8, 193
authenticity, 84–85

B
bilingual or multilingual, 128, 193. *See also honoring multilingual and multicultural learners*
Bixby, A., 57–58
blended learning. *See also online learning*
    case study for, 109–111
    creating connection in, 183–185
    definition of, 8, 193
    gender inclusivity and, 117–118
    increase in, 2
    journeys to blended education, xiii–xviii
    key terms for, 8
    strategies for bringing coaching and connection to, 161–163
    strategies for building a positive classroom culture in, 32–35
    strategies for building a support system in, 51–57
books and creating connection, 183–184
Boonseng, T., 26–27

Brown, B., 112

C
CDC Foundation, xv–xvi
center/centering, 106, 193
centering student stories. *See student stories*
choice, 25
classroom culture
    definition of, 31, 106, 194
    strategies for building, 32–35
classroom setting, 19–23, 87–88
Clingan, J., 109–111
coaching, 159–163
codes of conduct, 32–34
communication
    building relationships and communicating with families, 138
    engagement and, 188–189
    practicing communication and learning about other cultures, 141
    sample communication to families, 139
community
    building/fostering, 187, 189–190
    choice, language, and, 25
    drawing from, 22–23
community-based learning, 16, 18–19, 147, 194
comprehensive school counseling, 44, 194. *See also strengths-based approaches for inclusion, support, and counseling*
conclusion
    closing with heart, 179–181
    connected teaching commitments for, 180
    essential questions for, 173
    Kathryn's takeaways, 173–176
    Stephanie's takeaways, 176–179
connection-based feedback. *See also feedback; relationships*
    about, 75–76
    case studies for, 77–78, 80–81, 85–86, 89–90
    connected teaching commitments for, 88

essential questions for, 75
feedback as a conversation, 76–77
key classroom takeaways for, 99
key terms for, 76
reproducibles for, 101–102
strategies for connecting daily with students, 79–80
strategies for connecting through feedback, 81–85
strategies for cultivating connection, 86–88
strategies for using the four-step feedback process, 90–98
summary, 99–100

connections/connecting
building connections, 189–190
connecting with intention, 4–5
connecting with your village, 51–52
connections built through stories, 107–109
strategies for bringing coaching and connection to the online and blended classroom, 161–163
strategies for connecting daily with students, 79–80
strategies for connecting language and community, 23–26
strategies for connecting through feedback, 81–85
strategies for cultivating connection, 86–88
strategies for encouraging connection through music and poetry, 116–117
strategies for making global connections, 121–122

context and building a support system, 51
critiques and connecting through feedback, 84
cultivating strengths-based approaches for inclusion, support, and counseling. *See strengths-based approaches for inclusion, support, and counseling*
culturally and linguistically diverse (CLD)
definition of, 128, 194
professional learning and development related to, 156
talent development and, 156–157
three barriers to learning for gifted students and, 154–156
"Culturally Responsive Equity-Based Bill of Rights for Gifted Students of Color, A" (Ford, Dickson, Davis, Scott, and Grantham), 153–154
culturally responsive pedagogies
case study for, 119–121, 142–144
definition of, 16, 194
strategies for building culturally responsive, self-paced e-learning, 144–147
culturally sustaining pedagogies, 16, 194
curriculum. *See also student stories; universal design for learning (UDL) framework*
and celebrating global connections, 142
and radical hope, 55–56

D

da Silva, R., 66–68
Davis, J., 153–154
de Paulo Barbosa, A., 113
Debelak, C., 161
DeCastro, L., 127, 132–134
Denney, S., 63–64
Dickson, K., 153–154
differentiation, 158
digital chat rooms, 79
direct messages, 187–188
diversity, equity, and inclusion (DEI) commitments, 103

E

emotional literacy, 79–80
emotional safety, 19, 20
empathy
case study for, 110–111
definition of, 106, 194
strategies for, 112–114
student stories and, 122–123
endings/transitions, 30, 94–96
engagement
gifted and talented learners and, 163–166
how to engage learners who are not immediately responsive, 188–189
strategies for, 166–167
English as a foreign language (EFL), 128, 194
English as a second language (ESL), 128, 195
English learner or English language learner (EL or ELL), 128, 147, 195
enrichment, 16, 26–27, 195
ensuring equity and inclusion in the online classrooms
about, 103
centering student stories. *See centering student stories*
honoring multilingual and multicultural learners. *See honoring multilingual and multicultural learners*

leveraging opportunities for gifted and talented students. *See gifted and talented students*
equity, 106, 195
expectations, 34, 69–70
experiential programs, 119
explicit bias, 155
extracurricular activities, strategies for creating community through, 28–30

F

feedback. *See also connection-based feedback*
    connecting through, 185–186
    as a conversation, 76–77
    feedbacking, 76, 195
    and inviting student responses, 98
    and online teaching, 178–179
    synchronous feedback, 162–163
Fishman-Weaver, K.
    celebrating home language, 129–130
    Kathryn's background: education is a public health profession, xv–xvii
    Kathryn's takeaways, 173–174
flexibility and stability during periods of instability, 60
flipped classroom, 8, 195
flipped instruction, 1
flow, 154, 195
Ford, D., 153–154
fostering relationships through connection-based feedback. *See connection-based feedback*
four-step feedback process. *See also feedback*
    case study for, 89–90
    definition of, 76, 195
    strategies for using, 90–98
fun
    and cultivating connection, 87
    and cultivating empathy, 112–113
    and playfulness, 30

G

gatekeepers, 155
gender inclusivity, 117–119
gifted and talented students
    about, 153–154
    case studies for, 159–161, 163–166
    connected teaching commitments for, 158, 163
    differentiation and, 158
    essential questions for, 153
    giftedness/gifted, 154, 157–158, 195
    key classroom takeaways for, 168–169
    key terms for, 154
    reproducibles for, 171–172
    strategies for bringing coaching and connection to the online and blended classroom, 161–163
    strategies for engaging learners beyond content areas, 166–167
    summary, 169–170
    talent development and, 156–157
    three barriers to learning for gifted students, 154–156
goals
    brainstorming learning goals and values, 34–35
    considering your goals, 82–83
    example goal chart, 136
    student leadership and, 135
grading style, 97–98
Grantham, T., 153–154
greeting rituals, 79, 131
grounded theory, xvii–xviii
growth mindset, 2, 44, 196

H

Harrison, S., 112
Healy, J., 85–86
holistic comments
    definition of, 76, 196
    four-step feedback process and, 91, 94
    sample holistic comments, 95–96
holistic grading, 76, 94, 196
holistic scores, 92–94
Holmberg, B., 110
Holmes, C., 77–78
home language or native language
    case study for, 129–130
    definition of, 128, 196
    practicing your students' home languages, 184–185
    strategies for celebrating, 131–132
    strategies for honoring student voice and, 134–138
honoring multilingual and multicultural learners
    about, 127, 129
    case studies for, 129–130, 132–134, 139–141, 142–144
    connected teaching commitments for, 142
    essential questions for, 127
    key classroom takeaways for, 147
    key terms for, 128

reproducibles for, 150–152
strategies for building culturally responsive, self-paced e-learning, 144–147
strategies for celebrating home language, 131–132
strategies for honoring student voice and home language, 134–138
strategies for learning with multilingual and multicultural students, 141–142
summary, 148–149
teaching in a multilingual and multicultural world, 129
humor
creating context and using humor, 24–25
engagement and, 188
playfulness and, 30

I

icebreakers, 79, 99
identification instruments, 155
identities, strategies for affirming, 62–63
implicit bias, 153, 155
imposter syndrome, 167
inclusivity/inclusion
culturally inclusive instructional design for online courses, 142–147
diversity, equity, and inclusion (DEI) commitments, 103
gender inclusivity, 117–119
increasing inclusion, 66–68
individual planning, 57–60, 137
individualized education programs (IEP), 44, 52, 58, 196
Individuals with Disabilities Education Act (IDEA), 44, 196
in-person learning, 5, 8, 87, 193
intellectual safety, 19, 20
introduction/people-centered approaches to teaching
about, 1–3
connecting with intention, 4–5
essential questions for, 1
key terms for, 8
opening with heart, 3–4
people-centered practices, 5–6
reproducibles for, 11
structure of this book, 6–10

J

Jobst, L., 114–116, 123
Johnson, D., 175

Journal of Global Information Technology Management, 8
journeys to blended education. *See also blended learning*
Kathryn's background: education is a public health profession, xv–xvii
note about methodology, xvii–xviii
Stephanie's background: education is a journey together, xiii–xv

K

Kester, K., 139–141
King, M., 103
Kopolow, J., 31–32, 162

L

language. *See also home language or native language; honoring multilingual and multicultural learners*
connecting choice, language, and community, 25
language learning, 26, 132
living language, 128, 129, 197
people-centered language framework, 148
and relating to challenges, 86
learning goals and values, 34–35. *See also goals*
learning management systems, 16, 196
leveraging opportunities for gifted and talented students. *See gifted and talented students*
Lilien, M., 117–118, 162
listening, 20–21, 132–134
lived experiences
applying personal lessons to student lessons, 122
case study for, 46–50
drawing on your own experiences, 82
leveraging, 185–188
people-centered practices and, 2
radical hope and, 56
valuing lived experiences, 65–66
wholehearted teaching and, 168
looping, 134
Love, B., 56
Lovecky, D., 157

M

margins, 106, 197
McClintic, K., 142–144, 146
Miltenberg, M., 46–50, 162
miscommunication and connecting with intention, 4–5
mistakes, 113–114

multicultural students. *See honoring multilingual and multicultural learners*
multilingual responses, 131–132
multitiered system of supports (MTSS)
    about, 45–46
    definition of, 44, 197
    lived-experiences and, 46–50
    strategies for, 51–57
music, 114–117

N

neurodiversity, 154, 168–169, 197
newcomer/newcomers, 59, 128, 197

O

Olszewski-Kubilius, P., 157
onboarding students, faculty, staff, and guests, 28
online learning. *See also blended learning*
    adaptation to online instruction, 16–18
    connecting in online spaces, 191–192
    culturally inclusive instructional design for online courses, 142–147
    definition of, 8, 197
    people-centered practices and, 2
    presence online, 77–78
    strategies for building a positive classroom culture in, 32–35
    strategies for building a support system in, 51–57
    strategies for building culturally responsive, self-paced e-learning, 144–147
    unique opportunities for, 177–178
    virtual programs, 60–61
opening and closing class, ideas for, 21–22
Ozturk, M., 161

P

participation, 29, 119
peer review, 97–98
people-centered approaches. *See also introduction/people-centered approaches to teaching*
    empathy and, 122
    people-centered language framework, 148
    people-centered practices, 5–6
    strategies for taking a people-centered approach to student support, 68–70
perfectionism, 167
personalized learning plans, 57–60, 137
physical safety, 19–20
playfulness, encouraging, 30
Plogger, A., 60–61
poetry, 114–117

point comments, 76, 90, 91, 92, 96, 197
positive corrections, 162
power of the pause, 9
problem solving, 167
professional development, 16–18, 62–63, 156
pronouns, 62–63
public health, xv–xvi

R

radical hope
    definition of, 44, 197
    practicing radical hope, 55–57
    strengths-based approaches for inclusion, support, and counseling and, 70
redefining time, 28–29
reflective practice, 9–10, 11, 121, 158
refugees, 128, 198
reimagining the online classrooms
    cultivating strengths-based approaches for inclusion, support, and counseling. *See strengths-based approaches for inclusion, support, and counseling*
    fostering relationships through connection-based feedback. *See connection-based feedback*
    reimagining school as a community project. *See school as a community project*
relationships. *See also connection-based feedback*
    building relationships, 21–22, 138
    and connecting with intention, 4–5
    and connecting with your village, 51–52
    and creating connections, 183–185
    and direct messages, 187–188
    and feedback, 185–186
    and people-centered approaches to teaching, 2
    and presence online, 77–78
    and setting the tone, 20
    and stability, 60
    strategies for connecting daily with students, 79–80
Renaud, D., 113–114
representation, 118–119, 142, 146, 153
reproducibles
    for centering student stories, 124–125
    for classroom habits of reflective practitioners, 11
    for cultivating strengths-based approaches for inclusion, support, and counseling, 72–74
    for fostering relationships through connection-based feedback, 101–102
    for honoring multilingual and multicultural learners, 150–152

for reimagining school as a community project, 38–41
Robinson, K., 36
rubrics
    and holistic scores, 92–94
    and planning from the beginning, 97
    rubric comments, 76, 91–92, 198
    rubric-centered grading, 76, 91, 94, 96, 198
    sample rubric, 93
    tying feedback to the rubric, 90–92

S

sandwich technique, 76, 94, 198
Scales, K., 174
school as a community project
    about, 15
    adaptation to online instruction, 16–18
    case studies for, 18–19, 24, 26–27, 31–32
    connected teaching commitments for, 28, 34
    essential questions for, 15
    key classroom takeaways for, 35–36
    key terms for, 16
    reproducibles for, 38–41
    strategies for building a positive classroom culture, 32–35
    strategies for connecting language and community, 23–26
    strategies for creating community through extracurricular opportunities, 28–30
    strategies for establishing virtual classrooms, 19–23
    summary, 36–37
school community
    definition of, 16, 198
    drawing from, 22–23
    learning and planning with others, 142
Schroeder, J., 113
Scott, M., 153–154
self-expression, 179
self-review, 97–98
setting the tone, 20
Simmons, D., 23, 55
Soden, G., 119–121
Sprouse, N., 117–118, 166
stability in times of instability, 60
STEAM, integrating, 166–167
Stoker, N., 80–81
story-based curriculum, 106, 107, 108–109, 198
strategies for bringing coaching and connection to the online and blended classroom, 161–163
strategies for building a positive classroom culture in blended and online settings, 32–35
strategies for building a support system in online and blended models, 51–57
strategies for building culturally responsive, self-paced e-learning, 144–147
strategies for celebrating home language in your classroom, 131–132
strategies for connecting daily with students, 79–80
strategies for connecting language and community, 23–26
strategies for connecting through feedback, 81–85
strategies for creating community through extracurricular opportunities, 28–30
strategies for cultivating empathy in your classroom, 112–114
strategies for encouraging connection through music and poetry, 116–117
strategies for engaging learners beyond content areas, 166–167
strategies for establishing virtual classrooms, 19–23
strategies for honoring student voice and home language in the online elementary classroom, 134–138
strategies for individual planning, 58–60
strategies for learning with multilingual and multicultural students in online settings, 141–142
strategies for making global connections, 121–122
strategies for supporting gender inclusivity in the blended classroom, 118–119
strategies for taking a people-centered approach to student support, 68–70
strategies for using the four-step feedback process, 90–98
strengths-based approaches for inclusion, support, and counseling
    about, 43–46
    case studies for, 57–58, 60–61, 63–64, 66–68
    connected teaching commitments for, 55
    essential questions for, 43
    key classroom takeaways for, 70
    key terms for, 44
    lived experiences and, 46–50
    reproducibles for, 72–74
    strategies for adult learning, 65–66

strategies for affirming identities, 62–63
strategies for building a support system, 51–57
strategies for individual planning, 58–60
strategies for taking a people-centered approach to student support, 68–70
summary, 70–71
student stories
  about, 105–106
  case studies for, 109–111, 114–116, 117–118, 119–121
  connected teaching commitments for, 114
  connections built through stories, 107–109
  essential questions for, 105
  key classroom takeaways for, 122–123
  key terms for, 106
  reproducibles for, 124–125
  strategies for cultivating empathy, 112–114
  strategies for encouraging connection through music and poetry, 116–117
  strategies for making global connections, 121–122
  strategies for supporting gender inclusivity, 118–119
  summary, 123
students
  getting to know, 190
  student leadership, 135
  student needs, 68–69, 113, 135, 137
  students as teachers, 187
Stuhlman, B., 163–166
Subotnik, R., 157
synchronous feedback, 162–163
synchronous learning, 8, 198

T

talent development, 154, 156–157, 198
teacher-student relationships. *See relationships*
teaching
  Kathryn's takeaways, 173–176
  online teaching is real teaching, 191–192
  Stephanie's takeaways, 176–179
  teaching from a place of respect, 65
  teaching in a multilingual and multicultural world, 129
  teaching with courage, 180
technology/technology-mediated instruction
  definition of, 8, 199
  learning goals and values and, 34–35
  people-centered practices and, 173–174
  wraparound resources and, 60

thoughtful assertiveness, 186–187
three-year rule, 178
thrice exceptional (3E), 154, 199. *See also gifted and talented students*
Tier 1 (universal support), 45, 46, 48–49
Tier 2 (targeted intervention), 45, 46, 49–50
Tier 3 (intensive intervention), 45, 46, 49–50
Toalson, M., 18–19, 159–161
tone
  amplifying your tone, 84
  setting the tone, 20
transfer students, 59
transitions/endings, 30, 94–96
travel and making global connections, 121
twice exceptional (2E), 154, 199. *See also gifted and talented students*

U

universal design for learning (UDL) framework, 144, 145–146, 147
universal screening, 155, 158
University of California San Francisco's LGBT Resource Center, 63

V

values, 34–35, 162
Vidal, D., 24
virtual programs. *See online learning*
visibility and voice, 175
visualizing your students, 23, 81–82
voice
  including diverse voices, 146
  strategies for honoring student voice and home language, 134–138
  voice and visibility matter, 175
vulnerability, 186

W

Walter, S.
  four-step feedback process, 89–90
  Stephanie's background: education is a journey together, xiii–xv
  Stephanie's takeaways, 176–179
wholehearted teaching, 168–169
Willis, J., 20–21
Worrell, F., 157
wraparound resources, 60

Z

Zola, I., 47
Zoom fatigue, 100

The Complete Guide to Blended Learning
Catlin R. Tucker
Harness technology to enhance student learning in both a classroom and online environment. Combining theory, reflection, and personal experience, this book equips educators with strategies and tools to support student and educator success in blended environments and beyond.
BKG082

Creating the Anywhere, Anytime Classroom
Casey Reason, Lisa Reason, and Crystal Guiler
Discover the steps K–12 educators must take to facilitate online learning and maximize student growth using digital tools. Each chapter includes suggestions and examples tied to pedagogical practices associated with learning online, so you can confidently engage in the best practices with your students.
BKF772

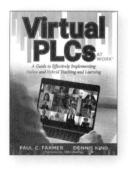

Virtual PLCs at Work®
Paul C. Farmer and Dennis King
As the educational landscape continues to evolve, ensure your PLC evolves right along with it. With this resource you'll acquire an abundance of tools and tips for maintaining your PLC in a virtual environment along with proven best practices to help your team thrive beyond the four walls of your school.
BKG028

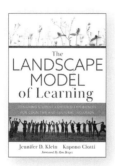

The Landscape Model of Learning
Jennifer D. Klein and Kapono Ciotti
This essential guide offers the landscape model and its three elements: understanding what students bring to the ecosystem, defining the horizon, and charting the pathway. Access practical strategies for drawing on students' experiences and strengths to create a more meaningful and inclusive educational ecosystem.
BKG043

Visit SolutionTree.com or call 800.733.6786 to order.

Wait! **Your professional development journey doesn't have to end with the last pages of this book.**

We realize improving student learning doesn't happen overnight. And your school or district shouldn't be left to puzzle out all the details of this process alone.

No matter where you are on the journey, we're committed to helping you get to the next stage.

Take advantage of everything from **custom workshops** to **keynote presentations** and **interactive web and video conferencing**. We can even help you develop an action plan tailored to fit your specific needs.

Let's get the conversation started.

Call 888.763.9045 today.

SolutionTree.com